Early
American Almanacs

1763.

The *Pennsilvania*
Town and Country-Man's
ALMANACK,
For the Year of our LORD 1763.
Being the third after *Leap-Year*.
Containing almost every Thing useful in Almanacks.

By JOHN TOBLER Esq;

Germantown printed and sold by C. *Sower*. And
to be had in *Philadelphia* of *Solomon Fussel*, at the Sign of the
Hand-Saw over against the Church in *Second-Street*, and also,
of *Jonathan Zane*.

Early American

ALMANACS:

The Colonial
WEEKDAY BIBLE

By Marion Barber Stowell

BURT FRANKLIN *Publisher* New York

Printed in the U.S.A.
Designer: Ernst Reichl

The author gratefully acknowledges the courtesy of the following institutions which have extended permission to reproduce illustrations from their collections: To the American Antiquarian Society, for illustrations appearing on pages (*frontis.*), x, xi, xii, xiii, xvi, xvii, 3, 15, 20, 33, 47, 48, 49, 54, 55, 68, 73, 81, 87, 89, 90, 94, 95, 96, 97, 98, 100, 101, 105, 115, 119, 129, 130, 131, 144, 145, 167, 177, 178, 180, 181, 188, 193, 199, 211, 212, 214, 215, 217, 220, 222, 230, 236, 239, 243, 246, 250, 253, 255, 256, 257, 274; the Dedham Historical Society, 23, 74, 75; the Eleutherian Mills Historical Library, 1, 9, 21, 24, 27, 82, 83, 138, 139, 197, 202, 225; the DeRenne Collection, University of Georgia Library, 6, 277; the North Carolina Collection, University of North Carolina Library, 19, 173, 194; the Maryland Historical Society, 108, 128; the Massachusetts Historical Society, xiv, 51; the Historical Society of Pennsylvania, 13, 57, 71, 116, 117, 187; the Rhode Island Historical Society, 16, 18, 79, 120, 127, 153, 170, 233, 283.

Library of Congress Cataloging in Publication Data
Stowell, Marion Barber.
Early American almanacs.

(Studies in literature and criticism; no. 2)
Bibliography: p.
Includes index.
1. Almanacs, American—History. I. Title.
AY31.A1S8   051   76-50583
ISBN 0-89102-063-2

Contents

Preface

Contemporary historians of early American literature have almost entirely overlooked the almanac, the only secular medium of expression through which colonial America has made a distinctive and in some respects a major literary contribution. Almost from its beginning in 1639, the colonial almanac bears the unmistakably original stamp of, first, its Harvard College compilers and, before long, its eccentric and humorous Yankee author-printers. Their talents created a medium of literary expression whose unique flavor, new to the world of letters, might be considered a precursor both of Poe's fantasy and of Twain's humor.

The unprecedented degree of collaboration between author and printer in the development of the almanac was almost matched, for oddity, by the extent to which the creation of so many of the finest almanacs ran in series produced by families—Daniel, Titan, and Felix Leeds; Nathaniel Ames, father and son; the Bradfords; the two Nathanael Lows; Isaiah Thomas, father and son, and Robert B. Thomas, their unrelated rival; and most notable of all, the four Franklins—James, Sr., Ann, Benjamin, and James, Jr. Without their conscious design—and almost in spite of themselves—these and other giants of the colonial almanac made of it, if not an art form, at least a literary form of some originality and, in some instances, considerable distinction.

The debased specimens of almanacs that continued to appear during the twentieth century result from a decline in quality that began in the early nineteenth. This debasement—primarily due to exploitative commercial advertising—no doubt discouraged any inclination on the part of twentieth-century literary scholars to investigate the antecedents of a genre whose acquaintance they had perhaps made only in its senility. Current American literary histories dismiss the almanac in a line or two. The best work on the early American almanac can be found in the few checklists and articles prepared by librarians of historical societies; in the first literary history of the United States (1878) by

Moses Coit Tyler, the first to make a reliable appraisal of its importance and quality; in two special studies by fine scholars—Samuel Briggs (1891) on the Ames almanacs and George Lyman Kittredge (1924) on the *Old Farmer's Almanac;* and in *Seeds of Liberty* (1948) by Max Savelle, who has thoroughly attested its importance as intellectual and social history.

I hope that the reader will share my pleasure in the excitement of discovering a new-old literature, the sheer fun of the almanackers' feuds with one another and with their printers (who were sometimes themselves), the pixieish unction and drollery of the Franklin family's prefaces and proverbs, the satires on lawyers, the preposterous recipes and cures, the ambivalent astrology and weather prediction, the broad jokes, the sometimes acceptable poetry, and the occasional serious essays not unworthy of Steel or Addison or Goldsmith.

In uncovering a neglected phase of our colonial past, I am indebted to the American Antiquarian Society Library for permission to examine original copies of early almanacs; and to the libraries of Florida State University, Duke University, University of Southern Mississippi, Purdue University, the University of Georgia (Miss Florrie Jackson, Microforms Division), and the University of Alabama at Tuscaloosa for access to Microprint and periodicals. The AAS Library, which has the best collection of almanacs in the United States, also furnished the photos for most of the illustrations, a tremendous task for an already hard-working and dedicated staff. Special thanks go to Mr. Marcus McCorison (Director), Miss Mary Brown, and Mrs. Georgia Bumgardner. I particularly appreciate editorial help from Dr. Mary Magginis (Florida State University); library assistance from Mrs. Gertrude Roche (Micro-Materials Librarian at Florida State University); bibliographical advice from Dr. Griffith Pugh (Florida State University); and proofreading, editing, and moral support from Dr. Carroll Miller (Louisiana State University, Baton Rouge), Mrs. Patricia Burns (Tallahassee, Florida), Dr. Mary Frances Estes (Clayton Jr. College, Georgia), Mr. John Rea (Indianapolis, Indiana), Miss Patilee Tate (Milledgeville, Georgia), and Mrs. Mary Barbara Tate (Georgia College).

Readers will perhaps share my gratitude to my husband, Dr. Hilton Stowell, neuroscientist and objective critic: it was his insistence upon (and his suggestions for) revision that made my scholarship readable.

Introduction

For all but a few American colonists, the almanac was the only secular source of useful information and literary entertainment. Throughout the seventeenth and eighteenth centuries, almanacs were the principal practical guides for farmers, tradesmen, navigators, fishermen, physicians, lawyers, educators, clergymen, and anybody else who simply wanted to know what day it was, how to get rid of rats, how to cure a corn, or how to get from Boston to New York.

The almanac was, perforce, a miscellany: it was clock, calendar, weatherman, reporter, textbook, preacher, guidebook, atlas, nagivational aid, doctor, bulletin board, agricultural advisor, and entertainer. The entire colonial family consulted its almanacs freely and regularly; these served the various family members not only as their general handy helper but even as their diary, memorandum book, and early-day *Reader's Digest*. In his own almanac for 1683, the eminent Puritan sermonizer Cotton Mather avowed that "such an *anniversary composure* comes into almost as many hands, as the *best of books* [the Bible]."

Most owners literally wore out their almanacs. Of the many thousands of almanac copies printed before 1700, only a few hundred exist today. Those that have survived to an honored place in museums and the rare book rooms of libraries bear witness of dogged attempts to preserve them, despite constant use and primitive methods of storage, transportation, and distribution.

Part of the colonial almanac's popularity was due to the lack of other reading matter: in Massachusetts, for example, eighty almanacs made up four-fifths of the secular literature published there before 1700. Of the 157 books published by the press at Cambridge, Massachusetts, between 1639 and 1670, almanacs were outnumbered only by books on religion—the most popular subject in America for more than a century. In sheer quantity, almanac publications during the seventeenth and eighteenth centuries actually outnumbered all other books combined—religious included. Very few books were being printed in America, and those imported from England and the continent were neither bought nor borrowed by the general public. Libraries—whether private, parochial, academic, or public (and all these kinds existed by the mid-eighteenth century)—had a negligible influence on the American majority, whose culture derived from the only ubiquitous printed matter: the Bible and the almanac. The circulation of some almanacs has been recorded. Ames's sold between 50,000 and 60,000 annually.[1] A business statement of the partnership of Franklin & Hall for 1766 reports 141,257 *Poor Richard* almanacs and 25,735 pocket almanacs for the years 1752 to 1765. Annually, the figures are 10,000 *Poor Richard* and 2,000 pocket almanacs, or approximately one for every hundred colonists.[2] A rather mediocre almanac, Stephen Row Bradley's *Astronomical Diary* for 1775, was issued in an edition of 2,000 copies.[3] In comparison, the second largest newspaper in 1770 (William Goddard's *Pennsylvania Chronicle*) had only 2,500 subscribers.[4]

The average New England home library consisted of a Bible, an almanac, the *New England Primer,* and perhaps a few sermons. Some such libraries may have contained Bunyan's *Pilgrim's Progress* and Michael Wigglesworth's poem, "The Day of Doom." The Bible took care of the hereafter, but the almanac took care of the *here.* The Puritan layman rarely disputed the scriptures: God's Word was usually interpreted by the theologians, the church preacher, or the church teacher. But the almanac was the layman's to do with as he pleased; he could study it, disagree with it, and scribble in it. The anonymous owner of a copy of Ezra Gleason's *Massachusetts Calendar* for 1774 was so exasperated by the new findings of "Mr. Lewenhoek" (Van Leuwenhoek) in a paragraph

JANUARY, Second Winter Month.

Days.	☉	♄	♃	♂	☿	♀
1	♑ 11 42	♍ 26	♈ 2	♑ 10	♒ 28	♐ 21
7	17 49	26	3	21	♓ 5	24
13	22 41	26	3	26	11	♑ ½
19	29 48	26	4	♒ ½	17	7
25	♒ 5 54	26	5	5	22	15

Of the SUN.

MR. WHISTON fays the Sun is 763,000 miles in diameter, and is 230,000 times bigger than the Earth, and is eighty-one millions of ftatute miles diftance from the Earth, each of which miles is 5280 Englifh feet.

Of the EARTH.

THE Earth, according to Mr. Whifton, is 7970 miles in diameter; which will make nigh 24000 miles in circumference. It revolves about its Axis in 23 hours 56 minutes: It moves in the fpace of one hour 56,000 miles, and is 365 days 6 hours and 9 minutes revolving about the Sun.

Of the Divifibility of MATTER.

THE ingenious Mr. Lewenhoek fays, that in the Milt of one Cod-Fifh there are more little animals, than there are inhabitants on the face of the earth. Several thoufands of them can ftand upon a needle's point. And Dr. Keil has fhewn, that the fmalleft vifible grain of fand would contain more of the Globules of that fluid (which ferves thefe animals for blood) than ten thoufand two hundred and fifty-fix of the higheft mountains in the world would contain grains of fand. *A David Lye,*

Of the Fixed STARS.

DR. HOOK and Mr. Flamfteed fay, that the diftance of the fixed Stars from the Sun is fo great, that a bullet fhot out of a mufket would not reach them in 5000 years. *Another*

Almanac owner's handwritten comments in Gleason's
Massachusetts Calendar for 1774.

Diary of R.W. Carter on blank leaf of Purdie & Dixon's *Virginia Almanack* for 1774.

called "Of the Divisibility of MATTER" that he added in his own hand, "A Damd Lye." On reading the following paragraph about the estimated distances "Of the Fixed STARS," he could not refrain from adding "Another." [5] Blank leaves were frequently inserted so that the owner could record important family events, the deaths of people in the neighborhood, business records, farming data about cattle and crops, and navigational records (for sea captains). Lacking a blank page, readers often made marginal notes on the calendar pages. In a Stearns' almanac (1771) we find this idiosyncratic comment, "The Mar[e] folded May ᴺᵒ 30 Day."

Today the colonial almanac remains an important research source for students of history, science, sociology, economics, education, and literature. It is also the single most composite representation of the Puritan mind, for in its pages are reflected the earliest concerns and interests of Jonathan and Patience Doe, long before the advent of other popular reading matter. A study of almanacs reveals differences in regional outlook and changes in social attitudes, in currency, and in weights and measures. Historical and genealogical data are available in chronology tables and lists of "Remarkable Events," and on the handwritten interleaved pages where owners jotted down their own records of thoughts and happenings. From domestic budgets the social historian learns about current prices. Almanac-makers also played an important part in the fight for freedom of the press. The early roles of the Negro, the colonial woman, and the foreigner are illuminated through its study, for these people participated in its production. Perhaps the only historian who has recognized its true value has been the student of printing. Issued regularly and universally by almost all

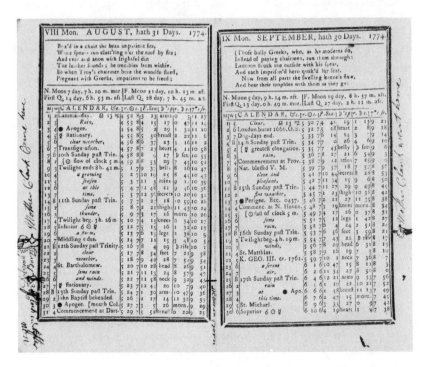

Marginal notes by a reader, indicating a birth and a visit by "Mother Clark." West's *The New-England Almanack* for 1774.

Paul Revere's depiction of the landing of troops in Boston Harbor in 1768.
Frontispiece, *Edes & Gill's Almanack* for 1770.

printing firms, the almanac is an excellent index of the history of printing and typography. It was the earliest consecutive colonial publication, preceding the newspaper by sixty-five years.

The almanac-makers themselves present a strong case for the importance of their product. Samuel Atkins, in the preface to his almanac for 1686, explains why he ventured to publish an "Ephemeris or Almanack":

> I having journied in and through several places, not only in this Province, but likewise in *Maryland*, and elsewhere, and the People generally complaining, that they scarcely knew how the Time passed, nor that they hardly knew the day of Rest, or Lords Day, when it was, for want of a Diary, or Day-Book, which we call, an *Almanack*. And on the other side, having in my Travels met with Ingenious Persons, that have been Lovers of the Mathematical Arts, some of which have wanted an Ephemeris to make some Practice thereon: I say, hearing this general Complaint from such abundance of Inhabitants, which are here. I was really troubled, and did assign, according to that small Knowledge that I had, to pleasure these my Country men with that which they wanted.

From this one book, the almanac, readers learned science, literature and art, history and current events, manners and morality, heavenly portents and warnings, the weather, and the time.

Instruction in science encompassed husbandry, astronomy, mathematics, the Copernican theory, Newtonian mechanics, natural history, geology, unexplained environmental phenomena (extraordinary occurrences and natural wonders), and health and medicine. Advice was given to the farmer on how to care for plants and animals, such as when and how to graft trees and geld cattle; and on home economy—from preserving gooseberries to "preserving Dung, so as to render it twenty times more useful than the Common Manner" (in William Andrews' *Poor Will's Almanack for* ... *1774*). Typical astronomical data were the dates of the eclipses, the positions of the sun and moon, the positions of the planets, and the moon's phases—all of which affected the weather and, according to some, man himself. The almanac taught Copernican and Newtonian science and may well have influenced the growth of deism, even rationalism, in America. Tables of interest, conversion tables for currency, and tables of weights and measures were common almanac fare. The life sciences were represented in essays describing plants, animals, and insects; the earth sciences, in maps and in essays dealing with geodesy. Common ecological problems also found expression, such as the impurity of city air and the strange mortality of little fishes. One of the most popular almanac features was the informative essay and the "receipt," or recipe, regarding health and medicine, where infallible cures were given for everything from a cold in the head to cancer.

Literature and art were introduced into the American home via the almanac. The farmer could read Pope, Dryden, and Bacon, sometimes on the same page where he found out when to plant his corn. British and American authors were advertised. The almanac also published the work of the earliest American engravers—John Foster, Alex Anderson, and Paul Revere.

Useful instruction in both historical and current matters was presented to the public in diverse forms: Chronological tables, essays and verse on famous persons and events, copies of legal forms, distances between towns, and meetings of the courts, the Quakers, and the Baptists. During pre-Revolutionary days, verse and essays

The LORD GOD Omnipotent reigneth.
Frontispiece, *Edes & Gill's Almanack*
for 1769.

fostered notions of liberty and furthered the cause of independence.

Readers also received a variety of miscellaneous information,
some of which was useful. The almanac instructed the reader on
how to behave, usually in pithy paragraphs on the calendar pages
and in sundry short essays found elsewhere. Many almanac-
makers warned God's people of impending disasters, explaining
the portents of the comets and meteors and the occultations of the
planets. For over 200 years, almanacs gave the American public
the information about weather and time that it later derived from
abundant newspapers, cheap watches, and free advertising calendars.

In addition to its role as educator, the almanac also served as entertainment for many who undoubtedly received it as welcome relief from tedious sermons and hard work. The successful almanac-maker had to study his ratings—the almanac business was obviously lucrative. (There were already several almanacs in Philadelphia when Ben Franklin started *Poor Richard.*[6]) The first few almanacs in America were almost completely utilitarian and this alone ensured a sale; but, as competition increased, so did the ingenuity of the compiler. He introduced anecdotes, proverbs, riddles, tales of the extraordinary, humorous poems and essays, and artwork of an entertaining nature.

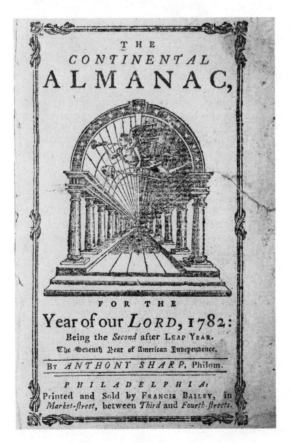

Title page, *The Continental Almanac* for 1782.

Toward the end of the eighteenth century, the almanac-maker Isaac Briggs, in his 1798 preface, paid tribute to his art, eulogizing its usefulness and underscoring its unique effectiveness as a versatile servant of the people, in what might be termed "The Credo of the Almanac-Maker":

PERHAPS few productions of Human Science are capable of being made of more general and important use to mankind than an ALMANAC. This, at first, may seem too bold an assertion; but deeper thinking will correct such a mistake. A good Almanac is, like *iron*, far more valuable (although much less valued) than *gold*, if we estimate its value by its *absolute* usefulness to the common purposes of life. I know not any way in which I can make this more convincing than by requesting thee, candid reader, to *lock up* thy Almanac as soon as thou hast purchased it, and take a resolution not to look at it, nor touch it, neither thou nor any of thy family, for some months; and, if I do not greatly mistake, thou wilt soon convince thyself on how many occasions an Almanac is useful. . . .

In addition to this consideration of the usefulness of an Almanac, its cheapness puts it in the power of the poorest citizen to possess one; it is, on these accounts, more extensively circulated throughout the country than perhaps any other publication, (the Holy Scriptures excepted) and is therefore the most proper vehicle I know of, for the diffusion of moral and natural science, and for exciting a spirit of scientific enquiry amongst our youth. In order to make my Almanac (which I propose to publish annually) answer these valuable purposes, as far as the size and price of one will admit of, I shall endeavour to the utmost of my power, that the moral pieces it may contain, both original and selected, shall appear in a pleasing dress; and that (although wit and humour shall be respected) low ribaldry and filthy jests shall be cautiously excluded—

> "Nor shall that have any place
> "At which a virgin hides her face."

In making selections, besides a strict attention to the purity of the moral, the correctness of science, and delicacy of wit, I shall endeavor to choose those pieces that are already in fewest people's hands. I expect that the *learned* will often meet with pieces they have read before. But this cannot be easily avoided—I do not presume to be the means of instructing them. It is to that valuable and important character, the plain, honest husbandman, I more particularly address this part of my publication.

Part One

The
ALMANAC'S
Development

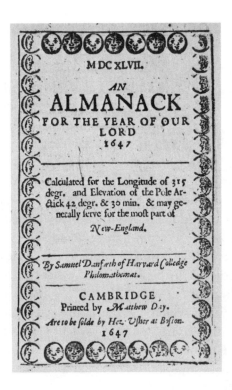

1 Early Almanacs

When early man began to cultivate his own food—and thus to depend upon the seasons—he found he needed to keep track of time. But there was no periodic cataclysm of sound or sight to mark its passage. Man had only the silent sun and the moon and the stars; from his observations of their risings and settings, he eventually constructed a crude calendar, the ancestor of the almanac.

The calendar is at least 5,000 years old. The Great Pyramid was a type of gnomon, which may be loosely defined as a tall object whose shadow is used for telling time. By observing the length of the shadows cast by the pyramids, the Egyptians were able to determine the true length of the solar year.

The ancient Greeks and Romans had great difficulty in delineating a calendar year which would coincide with the solar year. Various cycles of time were proposed. One of them, the Meton Cycle, consisted of 19 years, or 6940 days, divided into months. The Meton Cycle, also known as the Lunar Cycle, is reflected in almanacs to this day by the "Golden Number"—the number from 1 to 19 that shows the position in the cycle of a given year.

The Roman calendar, in the seventh century B.C., noted the "bissextile" and the "dominical letters" and placed "Martius" as the first month of the year. All these features persisted in early American almanacs; the bissextile and the dominical letters exist in almanacs today. The bissextile, or "twice six," originally referred to an extra day intercalated every fourth year by doubling the 24th of February, which was the sixth day before the "Calends of March," March 1st. This method of calculation was used in both the Julian and Gregorian calendars to designate leap year. Many American almanacs still refer to leap year as "bissextile." The seven dominical letters were introduced by the early Christians, who marked Sunday, the first day, as the day of rest rather than Saturday, the Jewish *shaboth*.

Subsequently, Pope Gregory found a difference of ten days between the Julian calendar and actual solar time. In 1582 he put the vernal equinox back to March 21st. Because the Julian year had 365-¼ days, the equinox had gradually fallen back, causing the length of the Julian year to exceed the length of the true solar year. Ten days were dropped from March, and a method of calculating leap year was devised that would make the calendar more nearly compatible with solar time. In England, however, the Julian vernal equinox (March 25th) continued to be the beginning of the year. It was 1752 before England officially adopted the New Style, or Gregorian, calendar by dropping ten days from September. Most of the European countries under papal rule had already changed their calendars.

Before America was settled, England, though fundamentally

opposed to papal decrees, was beginning gradually to designate January as the first month of the year. In America, however, both Old Style and New Style calendars continued to be used throughout the eighteenth century. To be exact, historians sometimes give both old and new dates.

The *Oxford English Dictionary* defines *almanac* as

> An annual table, or (more usually) a book of tables, containing a calendar of months and days, with astronomical data and calculations, ecclesiastical and other anniversaries, besides other useful information, and, in former days, astrological and astrometeorological forecasts.

An *ephemeris* is "an astronomical almanac," or,

> In wider sense: An almanac or calendar of any kind; in early use *esp.* one containing astrological or meteorological predictions for each day of the period embraced; also, a calendar of saints' days.

William Brattle, in his almanac for 1682, defines ephemeris as a "Day book, wherein the Heavenly minded Ephemeridist does keep an account of the Coelestial Motion." In the *British Museum Catalog*, "ephemerides" (ἐφήμερος—lasting one day) is still used as the general heading for almanacs and calendars. The word *calendar* seems to have been commonly associated with *almanac*. In 1590, Shakespeare wrote: "Doth the Moon shine that night wee play our play? A Calendar, a Calendar! looke in the Almanack, finde out Mooneshine" (*Midsummer Night's Dream*, III, i, 52-55).

There is a difference between *calendar* and *almanac*. A calendar refers to divisions of time, usually in tabular form, which may denote a particular year or a system of marking time in general, such as the Chinese or Gregorian calendars. The calendar may exist without an almanac, but the reverse is not possible. Even the most inventive almanac-maker leaves the calendar as it is: Friday the 13th always falls on Friday.

The term *calendar* may have derived from καλεῖν, to *call* or *proclaim*, probably referring to the ancient custom of publicly calling the beginning of the month in the market place. The origin of the

XI. NOVEMBER hath XXX Days.

Full Moon, 3d day, 5 h. 8 m. Morning.
Laſt Quarter, 10th day, 12 h. 41 m. Morning.
New Moon, 17th day, 5 h. 16 m. Morning.
Firſt Quarter, 25th day, 4 h. 47 m. Morning.

M D	W D	Remarkable Days, Weather, Aſpects, &c.		☽ riſe & ſets	☽ place		☉ riſes	☉ ſets
1	th	ALL SAINTS	*windy*	4 40	♈	18	6 39	5 21
2	fr			Moon	♉	1	6 40	5 20
3	ſa		*and*	riſes		15	6 41	5 19
4	G	21ſt paſt Trinity	*un-*	After.		29	6 42	5 18
5	m	Gunpowder Plot	*ſet-*	7 22	♊	13	6 43	5 17
6	tu	☍ ♃ ♂	*led*	8 25		27	6 44	5 16
7	w	☍ ♀ ♂ near ☽	*with*	9 29	♋	11	6 44	5 16
8	th	□ ♄ ☉ □ ♂ ♀	*rain,*	10 35		26	6 45	5 15
9	fr	♄ near ☽ Perigæon	*cold*	11 41	♌	10	6 46	5 14
10	ſa			Morn.		24	6 47	5 13
11	G	22d paſt Trinity ☿ ♍	*and*	12 44	♍	8	6 48	5 12
12	m	△ ♂ ☿	*wind,*	1 48		22	6 49	5 11
13	tu	♀ ſet 8 2	*unſet-*	2 52	♎	6	6 50	5 10
14	w	3*'s riſes 8 8	*led*	3 54		19	6 51	5 9
15	th	3*'s ſouth 2 4		4 56	♏	3	6 51	5 9
16	fr	☌ ☿	*fair*	Moon		16	6 52	5 8
17	ſa	Eclipſe of the Sun	*ſun-*	ſets		29	6 52	5 8
18	G	23d paſt Trinity	*ſhine,*	After.	♐	11	6 53	5 7
19	m	♃ near ☽ Apogæon		7 10		24	6 54	5 6
20	tu	☍ ♂	*rain*	8 3	♑	6	6 55	5 5
21	w	♀ near ☽		8 36		18	6 55	5 5
22	th		*wind,*	9 48	♒	0	6 56	5 4
23	fr	♂ ♊ ♊ ♄ ☿		10 44		12	6 56	5 4
24	ſa	☍ ♄		11 34		24	6 57	5 3
25	G	24th paſt Trinity	*rain,*	Morn	♓	6	6 57	5 3
26	m		*wind,*	12 32		18	6 58	5 2
27	tu	☍ ♃ ☿	*fair,*	1 27	♈	0	6 59	5 1
28	w	Dog Star riſes 9 2	*ſun-*	2 24		13	6 59	5 1
29	th	7*'s riſes 6 19	*ſhine,*	3 23		26	7 0	5 0
30	fr	St. ANDREW		4 22	♉	9	7 0	5 0

SOW peaſe, earth up cellery, and tie up endive for blanching. Sow parſley, ſpinage, radiſhes and lettuce of all kinds. Trim and dreſs your aſparagus beds, if neglected laſt month. Prune fruit trees, eſpecially vines, which may now be done with ſafety.

Calendar page from *The South Carolina and Georgia Almanack* for 1770.

word *almanac* is more uncertain. The most likely derivation is the Spanish Arabic *al manakh*, "the count." Samuel Briggs adds that the Arabic *almaneh* meant "New Year Gifts" and that the Teutonic *almaenachte* meant "observations on all the months"; Matthew Stickney quotes a more imaginative "Origin of Almanacks" from Low's Almanac for 1812.[1] Low's explanation, only slightly altered, had already been offered in Cotton Mather's 1683 almanac:

> Our English *Ancestors* used *annually* to engrave upon *squared sticks*, the *Courses* of the *Moon* for the whole Year. Such a little carved Instrument they called an *Almonaght*, i.e. *Al-moon-heed*, viz. the Heed, or *Observation* of all the *Moons*. And hence according to some *Antiquaries*, is derived the Name of *Almanack*. Though according to other *Philologists*, it may be an *Arabian* Word.
> We here offer thee an *Al-moon-heed*, and somewhat more: an *Ephemeris;* the composure of one who has endeavoured to give thee . . . [and there follows a description of the contents].[2]

Ainsworth Spofford's definition of the term, etymologically and semantically, is concise and comprehensive:

> The word is generally derived from the Arabic *al-manah*, the reckoning; and the book commonly embraces the calendar for one year, with a more or less extended ephemeris of the movements of the planetary system, and a record of the eclipses, festivals, or special days, etc., to which is sometimes added statistical matter or general information.[3]

Samuel Ellsworth, almanac-maker, deserves the last word in this learned word game. In the preface to his 1786 almanac he notes:

> I shall therefore only observe upon the subject, that as to the abilities requisite for composing an ALMANACK, the obvious etymology of the word is sufficient to convince us that in the opinion of the ancients they must be very extraordinary; ALMANACK, an evident abbreviation of ALL MY KNACK, or ALL MAN'S KNACK, plainly intimating, in the most expressive and laconic manner, that ALMANACK was the *ne plus ultra* of human genius, that this astonishing art engrossed all the powers and faculties of the mind, to that degree that a man that had a KNACK at this could not have a KNACK at any thing else.

Early almanacs were the Roman Fasti and the clogg (or clog) almanacs, also called log almanacs. The Fasti were calendars with

7

explanations of Caesar's festival days, illustrated on stone or marble slabs. The clogg almanac was known in England in the eleventh century. The same instruments were called *runstocks* or *runstaffs* in Scandinavia. These runic almanacs were wooden blocks, decorated and notched on all four sides to denote the day of the year, the seasons, the golden numbers, the dominical letter, etc. They may have been used as early as the seventh century in other parts of Europe. Sometimes found on the tops of pilgrims' staffs, cloggs also appeared on swords and agricultural tools.

Manuscript almanacs are believed to have been prepared by the Alexandrians as early as the second century A.D., but none exist today.[4] The earliest Christian almanac was written in A.D. 354, on parchment. Reconstructed from fragments, it was published in 1634 and again in 1850. References exist to manuscript almanacs by Solomon Jarchus, 1150; Roger Bacon, 1292; Walter de Elvendene, 1327; John Somers, 1380; and Nicholas de Lynne, 1386. The controversial Petrus de Dacia almanac (circa 1300) is perhaps the most famous of the manuscript almanacs. Though he may not have invented the Man of Signs, as some historians claim, de Dacia considered astrological influences important enough to warrant versification:

> *Jupiter atque Venus boni, Saturnusque malignus;*
> *Sol et Mercurius cum Luna sunt mediocres.*[5]

Early Books of Hours and prayer books (1200–1600) contained an ecclesiastical calendar, which, in turn, included many characteristics of the almanac. The earliest independent English calendar in the British Museum is dated 1431.

The first printed almanac may be the so-called Astronomical Calendar of 1448, printed by Gutenberg in Mainz.[6] Most authorities give Regiomontanus credit for originating (as calculator and printer) the almanac as we know it today. Regiomontanus was Johann Müller, originally from Königsberg (in Latin, Regiomontium). He started his printing press, however, at Nuremberg, in 1471. His *Kalendarium Novum* was supposed to have been printed in 1472; but the earliest existing copy is that for 1476, printed in

1796

I. THE calculations of this Almanack are made to folar or apparent time, to which, for the mean or clock time, apply the equation given in the fixth column, adding, when the fun is flow, and fubtracting when faft.

II. The time of high water at Philadelphia is fo computed as to ferve for either morning or afternoon, nearly enough for common ufe; the morning flood being about 12 m. earlier than the time in the tide column, and that of the afternoon as much later; but when there happens one flood only in the day, the true time is given, and diftinguifhed by this mark.*

III. The fun's declination is carefully fitted to the meridian of Philadelphia for every noon of the prefent year.

IV. The rifing, fetting, or fouthing of a ftar may be carried feveral days backward by adding, or forward by fubtracting, 4 m. per day: for inftance: on the 11th of the firft month (January) Sirius is fouth at 3 m. paft 11; adding 12 m. for 3 days fooner, we have 11 h. 15 m. for the fouthing on the 8th, and deducting 8 m. for 2 later, leaves 10 h. 55 m. for that of the 13th of the fame month, &c.

V. The time of Alioth's paffage over the meridian, or when a plumb-line apparently cuts both the Pole-ftar and Alioth, is given, for the firft fix months above, and the laft fix below, the pole, to five days in every month, and may be readily known for any day by the preceding note. Thefe two ftars will be vifibly coincident with a level eaft and weft line at 5 h. 59 m. before or after Alioth paffes the meridian, by which we may regulate time-pieces to a minute, or tell the time without them. The Pole-ftar is on the meridian five-minutes later than Alioth, when a true meridian line may be drawn by it, and the magnetic variation thereby determined.

Alioth is the firft ftar in the tail of the Great-Bear, viz. that next the fquare, or, it is the third ftar of the feven, commonly called the Waggon, or Plough, counting toward thofe two of them denominated the Pointers.

An explanation of astronomical calculations in *Poor Will's Almanack* for 1796.

Venice by Bernard Pictor, Petrus Loslein, and Erhardus Ratdolt—the latter a pioneer craftsman in the art of printing. The book was printed in both red and black, was ornamented and illustrated, printed on twelve leaves (twenty-four pages) quarto, and sold for ten gold crowns. It contained calendar, eclipses, and planets' places, and was also the first book to contain a complete—and ornamental—title page. Twenty years elapsed before a title page was used in another book.

The first almanac printed in England was *The Shepheard's Kalendar*, published in 1497 by Richard Pynson, who translated from the French *Grand Compost des Bergers* (1493).[7] An example of Pynson's almanac verse, reminiscent of the Petrus de Dacia Latin quotation mentioned above, furnishes some proof of the paternity of American almanac verse:

> *Saturne is hyest and coldest, being full olde*
> *And Mars with his bluddy swerde*
> *ever ready to kyll.*
> *Sol and Luna is half good and half yll.*[8]

The first genuinely English almanac was printed by Wynkyn de Worde in 1497, who used Pynson's translation from the French as a model.

Michael Nostradamus (1503–1566), of St. Remy, France, was probably the most famous almanac-maker of the sixteenth century. Royalty consulted him, for he foretold the deaths of kings, the Great Fire of London, and Cromwell's success in Flanders. In the sixteenth and seventeenth centuries astrology flourished, and so did prognosticators. In the reign of James I (1603–1625), the astrologers even formed a society and had annual meetings like trade guilds.

Prominent English almanac-makers in the seventeenth century included William Lilly (*Merlinus Anglicus Junior*, 1644–1681), John Gadbury, John Booker (*Bloody Almanack*, 1643; *Bloody Irish Almanack*, 1647), Richard Saunders, John Partridge, and Poor Robin, possibly the *nom de plume* of Robert Herrick, the poet. In his autobiography, William Lilly says that he conferred often with angels—Irish angels.[9] The title of Lilly's almanac derives from

Merlin Ambrosius, a fifth-century prophet and astrologist, who was supposed to have been born of a demon and a Welsh princess. His prophecies were published in Paris toward the end of the fifteenth century; and in London, in the sixteenth. John Partridge, a shoemaker who prepared *Mercurius Coelestis* in 1681 and *Merlinus Redivivus* later, is probably the best known of the English almanackers. Most students of eighteenth-century literature are familiar with Jonathan Swift's prediction, under the pseudonym Isaac Bickerstaff, of Partridge's death; and his insistence, despite Partridge's protests, that the almanac-maker was dead. Alexander Pope, too, helped to immortalize Partridge in "The Rape of the Lock," where he envisions Partridge scanning the skies for the sight of Belinda's lock in orbit. Francis Moore, a famous and prosperous charlatan, succeeded Lilly and Partridge with his *Vox Stellarum* or *Moore's Almanack* about 1700.

Royalty and the clergy interfered, for various reasons, with the almanac business. Henry III of France had decreed that almanacs could not contain political prophecies. Louis XIII reaffirmed this edict in 1628. In England, the Archbishop of Canterbury and the Bishop of London supervised the publishing of almanacs.

Most of the British almanacs were published by the Company of Stationers, to whom Elizabeth I had given the monopoly. James I had extended to Oxford and Cambridge the right to publish almanacs. Some say that the universities soon sold out to the Stationers, but Thomas Wright points out that it was an almanac published at Cambridge (Winter's almanac for 1636) that included the famous days-of-the-month rhyme:

> *Aprill, June, and September,*
> *Thirty daies have, as November;*
> *Ech month else doth never vary*
> *From thirty-one, save February;*
> *Which twenty-eight doth still confine.*
> *Save on leap-year, then twenty-nine.*[10]

In 1775, the Stationers' monopoly was 170 years old. At this time, Thomas Carnan, who had been imprisoned each of the three years he had published an almanac, filed a suit in the Court of

Common Pleas which ruled that Carnan could publish an almanac, thus ending the Stationers' monopoly and also striking a blow for free enterprise. For years after the Carnan case, the Stationers bought up competitors and remained in control of the almanac market. Although the government imposed an almanac tax of almost 30 cents each, more than 450,000 copies still sold annually.[11]

Almanacs remained popular and became more specialized. High Church almanacs concentrated on the saints; Gadbury's was Tory; the Whigs in 1684 put out one called *The Protestant Almanack*, which called attention in astrological jargon to "the Bloody Aspects, Fatal Oppositions, Diabolical Conjunctions and Pernicious Revolutions of the Papacy against the Lord and his annointed."[12]

Familiar with these British products, colonial Americans knew what to expect in an almanac. Early seventeenth-century American almanacs may have exceeded their expectations, for the literary and instructional quality of these almanacs was generally excellent. Almanac competition, which began in America in 1675 (a century before the Stationers' almanac-printing monopoly ended in England), may have helped to sustain the quality of the American almanac throughout the eighteenth century.

2 The American Almanac and the Printer

Since there was no American newspaper before 1704 and no American magazine before 1740, the colonial almanac served a dual literary purpose: topical items were blended with informative and entertaining essays, stories, and verse. The printer often furnished this literary material. His influence on the almanacs printed between 1675 and 1800 was prodigious. Throughout this period, the printer was a man of consequence in his community: he courageously engaged in battles for freedom of the press; and, what was more important to his countrymen, he printed their annual almanac, the only periodical in the colonies for over half a century.

On September 25, 1690, R. Pierce printed for Benjamin Harris *Publick Occurrences both Forreign and Domestick*, a journal to be issued monthly. It was immediately suppressed for being unlicensed, and it was 1704 before *The Boston News-Letter* became America's first regular newspaper—sixty-five years after the first almanac. Andrew Bradford (*The American Magazine*, January 1740/41) led Ben Franklin by three days in the race for recognition as America's first magazine editor, but Franklin's *The General Magazine* survived Bradford's.[1] Like many other colonial almanac printers, Bradford was printer, editor, and postmaster, as was Ben Franklin.

The almanac was published in book form. The Bodleian Library classifies almanacs as "printed books, as distinct from manuscripts, but they may fall within one or other of the subdivisions of 'book', such as broadside, single sheet, or pamphlet." Interleaved almanacs with diary entries, "both in this Library and elsewhere," are treated as manuscripts.[2] The almanac-makers themselves generally called their products "books." For example, John Tulley, in a letter to his printer (June 1695), referred to "a little booke . . . intitled New-England Almanack."[3] Neglecting sterile controversies for the moment, let us defer to the authority of Tulley's "little booke."

Most early American almanacs were probably printed on one sheet, eight pages to the side. The sixteen-page format was gradually expanded to more than twenty-four pages by the end of the seventeenth century. While Hixson notes that "Plain white or colored paper was used to cover the normal issue of the printing shop, e.g., almanacs, session laws and assembly proceedings, pamphlets, and sermons,"[4] an examination of many American almanacs reveals that they usually had no cover in the modern sense, save for the pocket almanac, which was generally protected with colored paper. *The Rhode-Island Almanack* for 1740 (*Poor Robin*) has a simple cover with the title and last page printed on heavier paper, apparently stamped to look like linen.

Isaiah Thomas's printing press, now in the possession of the American Antiquarian Society, Worcester, Massachusetts.

The dimensions of the almanacs varied from folio to pocket
size. The "sheet almanac" was a broadside, a large folio sheet
printed on one side only. Advertisements in newspapers show that
it was usually issued in January rather than in the preceding October or November. Used primarily for display in shops and other
public places, these almanacs have rarely survived to this day. A
standard almanac was roughly six by four inches, plus or minus an
inch in either direction. The pocket almanac averaged four and
one-half by two and three-fourths inches. It was usually interleaved with blank pages. Sometimes, instead of a paper cover, the
title page and last page were printed on heavier paper that had

The Anatomy of Man's Body as govern'd by the Twelve Constellations.

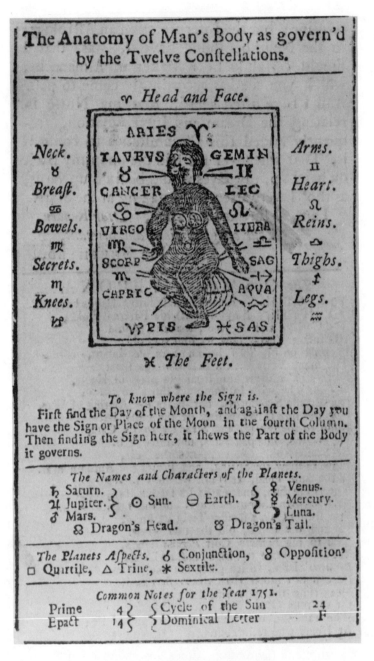

♈ *Head and Face.*

Neck.
♉

Breast.
♋

Bowels.
♍

Secrets.
♏

Knees.
♑

Arms.
♊

Heart.
♌

Reins.
♎

Thighs.
♐

Legs.
♒

♓ *The Feet.*

To know where the Sign is.
First find the Day of the Month, and against the Day you have the Sign or Place of the Moon in the fourth Column. Then finding the Sign here, it shews the Part of the Body it governs.

The Names and Characters of the Planets.

♄ Saturn.
♃ Jupiter. ☉ Sun. ⊖ Earth. ♀ Venus.
♂ Mars. ☿ Mercury.
☊ Dragon's Head. ☋ Dragon's Tail. ☽ Luna.

The Planets Aspects. ☌ Conjunction, ☍ Opposition,
□ Quartile, △ Trine, ✳ Sextile.

Common Notes for the Year 1751.
Prime 4 ⎱ ⎰ Cycle of the Sun 24
Epact 14 ⎰ ⎱ Dominical Letter F

Man of Signs from *Poor Job* for 1751.

16

already been stamped with a pattern such as linen or moire. The early James Franklin almanacs were anomolous; their text area was the size of the pocket almanacs, but the margins extended to about three by five and one-half inches, making them slightly narrower than the regular size. Paper cutting was apparently inexact, hence the variable page size often found within a single publication.

These early almanacs consisted of a title page, a preface with instructions for use, a discussion of the eclipses, the twelve calendar pages, and perhaps a timetable of local courts and fairs. One (late Victorian, and inaccurate) description of the almanacs reads: "Following the preface was the naked man bestriding the globe, the calendars of the months, the days of holding courts and fairs, a chronology that always went back to Adam, a list of British rulers in which Cromwell never had a place, verses destitute of feet and sense, and a serious prognostication of events as foretold by eclipses and the planets." [5] The "naked man" (Man of Signs) has often been shown sitting on a globe, but not "bestriding" it; the chronology rarely "went back to Adam"; the list of British rulers was a sometime thing; some verses did have "feet and sense" (certainly the borrowed verse of Pope); and many almanacs did not prognosticate at all.

At first there was one calendar page for each month, but this was later expanded to two. The earliest extant almanac (Danforth for 1646) shows March as the beginning of the calendar year, a custom practiced for many years. According to more than one source, John Tulley, in his almanac for 1687, was the first American author to use January as the first month of the year.[6] Many years before the official calendar change (1752), some almanac-makers had compromised between the Old Style and New Style calendars. Thus, January was *placed* first in the calendar, but it was designated "January, xi month." February was "xii month" and March was number "i" (for example, in the Daniel Leeds broadside almanac in 1687). However, the Rhode Island Historical Society has a copy of *Phillip's United States Diary* for 1796 with the March page placed first. Perhaps it was lingering anti-popery that caused the American almanac-makers to persist in using March as first month.

Although other information was added gradually—lists of roads, chronology tables, tables of interest and currency conversion, Quakers' and Baptists' meetings—the successful almanac-maker innovated with discretion. He was particularly cautious in regard to format. In saying "A man compiled an almanac as he pleased," Tourtellot suggests a total disregard for public opinion.[7] Actually, unless a man "pleased" to please his public, he would have been soon out of business. The public obviously enjoyed the occasional eccentricities of the authors, such as their personal feuds as related in prefaces, their satirical comments on weather prophecy, and their secular comments on sacred subjects. These humorous diversions may have served to brighten dull days for many stolid, hard-working Puritans who, in the words of Samuel Briggs, had "left 'Merrie England' to find a place where they could be miserable according to the dictates of their own desires."[8]

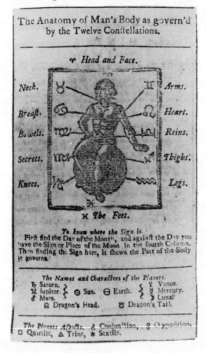

Poor Job,
1752.

West's *The New-England Almanack*, 1781.

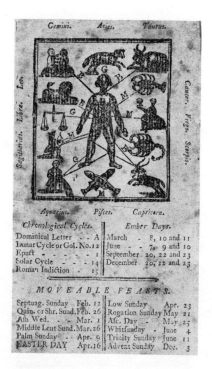

The North-Carolina Almanack, 1797.

A format for the almanac had been more or less established early in its history, with certain distinguishing features continuing from the first printed almanacs of the fifteenth century. Tyler points out that "From the first, they [almanacs] contained many of the traits that had become conventional in printed almanacs in Europe . . . particularly astrological prophecies."[9] Any later departure from established format would risk the loss of readers, who expected to find certain items in certain places. The American almanacs were therefore rather consistent in makeup.

A prominent feature of many almanacs is the *homo signorum,* also called the Man of Signs, moon's man, or "anatomy." Petrus de Dacia, fourteenth-century Danish astronomer and mathematician, included, but may not have originated, this drawing for his almanac; Littlefield believes that the moon's man may be much older than the fourteenth century. The Egyptians had a similar system

19

The Anatomy of Man's Body, as governed by the twelve Constellations.

♈ The head and face. G.

♉ Neck. B

♊ Arms. B

♋ Breast. M

♌ Heart. B

♍ Bowels M

♎ Reins. G

♏ Secrets M

♐ Thighs M

♑ Knees. B

♒ Legs. G

♓ The feet. G.

To know where the Sign is.
First, find the day of the month, and against that day you have the sign or place of the moon in the 7th column. Then finding the sign here, it shews the part of the body it governs.

The twelve Signs of the Zodiac.

♈ *Aries*, the Ram.
♉ *Taurus*, the Bull.
♊ *Gemini*, the Twins.
♋ *Cancer*, the Crab.
♌ *Leo*, the Lion.
♍ *Virgo*, the Virgin.
♎ *Libra*, the Balance.
♏ *Scorpio*, the Scorpion.
♐ *Sagittarius*, the Bowman.
♑ *Capricorn*, the goat
♒ *Aquarius*, the Waterman.
♓ *Pisces*, the Fish.

The Kentucky Almanac for 1800.

of noting the hourly positions of the stars around "some huge figure like the sphinx." [10] In almanacs, the "anatomy" was usually on the page following the title page and consisted of a figure of a man surrounded by astrological signs, or drawings illustrating the signs (figures of the "twins," the "archer," the "crab," etc.), with indicators to those parts of the body that are governed by these signs whenever the moon passes through their part of the heavens.

The Man of Signs had various guises, all artistically crude. Sometimes his moustache and beard are trimmed in current fashion; at other times he is clean shaven. He is usually nude and sometimes exposes his bowels. The Man in Briggs's almanac for 1798 is reclining in the center of a large oval that is oramented with garlands at the top and sides and with crossed swords at the bottom. This elaborate Augustan figure is clothed and surrounded by

20

signs; the Saggitarius archer resembles an Indian with feathers in his headdress and a Mohawk hair style. Charles Nisard reproduces a French illustration of a nude man directly decorated with the signs—one little geminus hangs on each arm, the crab grasps the chest, and a fish dangles from each foot.[11]

A key included with the Man of Signs explained the meaning of the diagram and its relation to the information in the relevant column on the calendar page. The usual explanation or caption underneath the drawing was a variation of that used by *Poor Richard Improved* for 1754:

> To know where the Sign is.
> First Find the Day of the Month, and against the Day you have the Sign or Place of the Moon in the 6th Column. Then finding the Sign here, it shews the Part of the Body it governs.

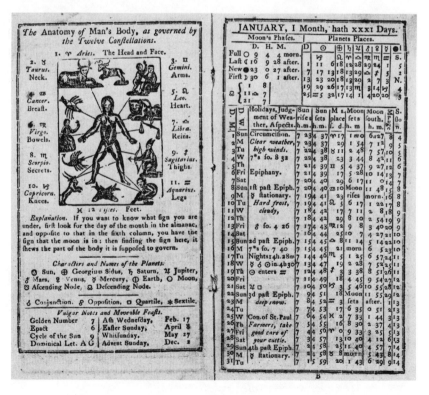

Double page from *The New Pennsylvania Almanac*, 1792.

21

Not all almanacs have included the Man of Signs. During the colonial period, the concept was both satirized and defended. Josh Billings' *Old Farmer's Allminax,* as late as 1870, satirized the Man of Signs and its explanation. Above Billings' figure of the "Man":

SIGHNS OV THE ZODIAK.

The undersigned is an American brave, in his grate tragick akt ov being attaked bi the twelve constellashuns.

—(*May the best man win.*)

Below the figure:

KEY TEW THE ABUV PERFORMANCE

Tew kno exakly whare the sighn iz, multiply the day ov the month bi the sighn, then find a divident that will go into a divider four times without enny remains, subtrakt this from the sighn, add the fust quoshunt tew the last divider, then multiply the whole ov the man's boddy bi all the sighns, and the result will be just what yu are looking after.

Almanac-makers apologized in verse for including the Man of Signs. Here is Daniel Leeds in 1710 borrowing from a Samuel Clough almanac of 1706 (who, of course, may have borrowed from someone else):

> *Here sits again the Old Anatomy,*
> *Which use to please the Country Peoples eye;*
> *For if they, in this place, don't see his Features,*
> *They'll not know at what time to Cut their Creatures.*

Similarly, Nathan Bowen in 1723 picks up a Clough verse for 1703:

> *The old Anatomy must still be in,*
> *Or else my Almanack's not worth a Pin:*
> *For Country-men regard the Sign,*
> *As tho 'twere oracle Divine.*
> *But do not mind that altogether,*
> *Have some Regard to Wind & Weather.*

In the 1725 *American Almanack,* Titan Leeds frankly concedes his commercial motives:

> *Should I omit to place this Figure here,*
> *My Book would hardly sell another Year.*
> *What (quoth my Country Friend) d ye think I'll buy*
> *An Almanack without th' Anatomy?*
> *As for its Use, nor he nor I can tell;*
> *However since it pleases all so well,*
> *I've put it in because my Book should sell.*[12]

In 1729 Ames writes, with less assurance:

> *The Blackmoore may as easily change his Skin,*
> *And men forsake the ways they'r brought up in;*
> *Therefore I've set the Old Anatomy,*
> *Hoping to please my Country men thereby,*
> *But where's the Man that's born and lives among,*
> *. . . . . Can please a Fickle throng?*

Expert opinion on astrology, however, was apparently divided. Dr. Nathaniel Ames's almanac for 1754 claimed emphatically that celestial powers exerted influences over the body (as

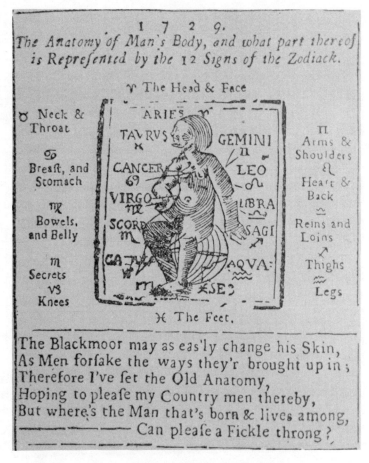

Ames's *American Almanack* for 1729.

23

The Anatomy of Man's Body, as said to be governed by the Twelve Constellations.

♈ Aries, the head and Face.

♉ Taurus, Neck.

♊ Gemini, Arms.

♋ Cancer, Breast.

♌ Leo, Heart.

♍ Virgo, Bowels.

♎ Libra, Reins.

♏ Scorpio, Secrets.

♐ Sagittarius, Thighs.

♑ Capricorn Knees.

♒ Aquarius, Legs.

♓ Pisces, the Feet.

To know where the Sign is. First find the day of the month, and against it the sign or place of the moon, in the eighth column. Then finding the sign here, it shews the part of the body it is said to govern.

We have inserted the above, and the prognostics of the weather, according to the most approved methods; but think it proper to inform our readers, that, in this enlightened age, the learned put but little confidence in them.

Characters explained.

● New Moon	☉ or ◉ Sun	☿ Mercury
○ Full Moon	♄ Saturn	✳ Geo. Sidus
☽ First Quarter	♃ Jupiter	☌ Conjunction
☾ Last Quarter	♂ Mars	☍ Opposition
☋ Moons's af. node	♀ Venus	▢ Quartile

Common Notes and Moveable Feasts for the Year 1796.

Dominical Letters	C B	Easter	March 27
Golden Number	11	Ascension	May 5
Epact correct	21	Whitsunday	May 15
Solar Cycle	13	Trinity	May 22
Ash Wednesday	Feb. 10	Advent	November 27

Poor Will's Almanack for 1796.

24

mediators only for the Almighty). George Andrews in *The South Carolina Almanack and Register* for 1760 said that only God ruled over man's body. Although its inclusion or exclusion has never determined the success or failure of any almanac, the Man of Signs has its devotees even today: the 1974 *Grier's Almanac, The Old Farmer's Almanac*, and *Ladies Birthday Almanac* contain the figure.

Whatever the popular demand for astrology, readers expected verse as early as 1667. Samuel Brackenbury writes:

> *My friends, you look for Verse, be pleas'd to know*
> *You'l miss,* URANIA *would have it so:*
> *Here's how the Sun his course in's Circle goe's:*
> *I write Celestial harmony in prose.*

Titan Leeds, in his *American Almanack* for 1718, tells the "Courteous Reader": "Because 'tis Common to put Verses at the top of the Months, therefore many People expect it; yet if I knew whether the Major number of Votes would be against it, I would Insert other things more useful to some." This utilitarian trend continued. Stearns says in 1773: "I have instead of poetical Lines inserted at the Head of each Monthly Page Tables of Chronology. . . ."

Other elements of the almanac had become standardized. In the *New England Almanack* for 1768 the author says: "I know a Preface to an Almanack is always Expected, and in compliance to the common mode, I have wrote one to this." Sagendorph tells of an incident that happened after he began editing the *Old Farmer's Almanac*. When a change was made in the calendar page format, one reader's emotion prompted this letter:

Dear Sir:
I have read The Old Farmer's Almanac for the last seventy-five years and I wish the damned fool that changed the heading of the Moon's place column had died before he done it.
Yours respectfully,
F. C. Crawford [13]

A unique characteristic of the early almanac is its manner of composition. It is the only American literature to be so much influenced by the printer, who was frequently the author; more frequently the co-maker; and, in the case of John Foster, the printer, author, and engraver. The printer-author combination is quite common. In no other literary form is the role of the printer so inextricably entangled with the product. Research in American almanacs involves the history of American printing.

It may have been the colonial printer who first recognized the public need for almanacs and who prevailed upon the Cambridge tutors to furnish him with material for the almanacs in the seventeenth century. Sometimes the printer bought the basic astronomical information and sold it to an editor who furnished the other material. The printer might then print and sell the almanac, thus making a profit with both his wholesale and retail merchandise. Printers paid in advance as much as thirty pounds a year for almanac computations. At the same time, the chief justice of Pennsylvania was receiving a salary of 100 pounds a year; the attorney general, 60 pounds; and the associate justice, 50 pounds.[14]

Pseudonyms were often used because the printers themselves were authoring the almanacs. Sometimes the printer did the calculations himself, as did John Foster and Benjamin Franklin, and also furnished the filler. Some of this material, of course, was the original work of a creative printer with an imaginative, literary bent (James Franklin, Benjamin Franklin, James Franklin, Jr.). Other articles were contributed especially for a particular almanac at the printer's request. Tulley's almanac for 1699 contained a brief essay by Cotton Mather, who recorded the incident in his diary:

> The Printer, wanting something to fill the last Leaf of his Almanack, for the year, 1699, came unto mee, to furnish him.
> . . . I took my Opportunity, and wrote a few pungent Lines, concerning the Changes, which may bee coming as a Snare upon the Earth. . . .[15]

Problems between the author and publisher are by no means a contemporary development. Similar disagreements were common between the early almanac compiler (author) and the printer-publisher. Except for the Cambridge Press (1639–1692), where the printer was hired by Harvard College, the colonial almanac printer was usually the publisher. Often it is he, rather than the author,

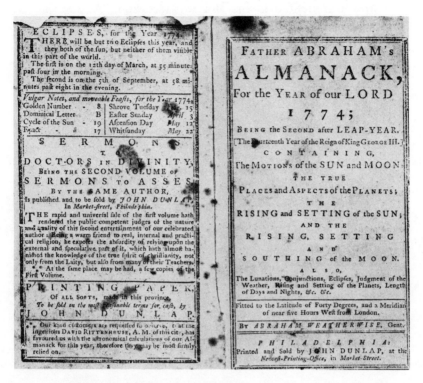

Title page and advertisements from Weatherwise's *Father Abraham's Almanack*, 1774.

who is given credit historically for the almanac. William Bradford, for example, the printer-publisher, is generally credited with Pennsylvania's first almanac, rather than Samuel Atkins, its compiler. Even when there were acknowledged authors, the printer would occasionally insert a notice to the reader (such as William Bradford's "The Printer to the Reader" in the *Kalendarium Pennsilvaniense* for 1686). When the author and printer sometimes disagreed, the printer magnanimously printed the author's derogatory comments directed at himself, and occasionally, these criticisms took the form of humor in the preface or in a light verse. Frequently, the author would react vehemently to the printer's choice of material, especially if the almanac had been criticized during the previous year.

Tulley commented in his almanac for 1696, "As for the late French King's Nativity, it was acted and put into my late almanack by the printer, unknown to me, for which I am much displeased with him for so doing."

An essay at the end of Titan Leed's *American Almanack* for 1727 appears to have been inserted by the printer, Samuel Keimer:

> As true Philosophy consists in the learning the true Original of things . . . the Printer hereof can't but think it must be acceptable . . . to give the World an Account how the several Days of the Week came to be called by the Appellations of *Monday, Tuesday.* . . .

William Bradford, printer in New York of Titan Leed's *American Almanack* for 1739, slyly inserted on the May calendar page: "The Printer born the 10th, 1663." No such comment appeared in Andrew Bradford's Philadelphia version for the same year.

De Foreest, the New York printer for Roger Sherman's *Almanack* for 1750, added some material that Sherman (who had furnished the tables and the calendar calculations, trusting the printer to fill in the rest) believed to be unfit for colonial family consumption. The offensive matter on the calendar pages was of this type:

> Comfortable candles warm, jellies and a kind she bed fellow, are three things very requisite all this month.

> Nights are premontriposterous long; now is the time for the tearing of sheets and begetting of bantlings.

In Low's almanac for 1767, "The following is inserted by the Printer to fill up a vacant Page." The page contained 1) "Advice to the Ladies" (a two-couplet verse), 2) "The Dimensions of Great-Britain," and 3) "Dick and his Spouse" (an anecdote).

Elisha Thornton in *The Rhode-Island Almanack* for 1791 explained the arrangement he had with Peter Edes, his printer, an arrangement which may have been common:

> The Printer having for three years' past condescended to print my Almanack in the plain and friendly style, which style, though adapted and agreeable to me and my friends, is not adapted nor so agreeable to his friends and customers in general; and he being desirous of inserting the courts in the

usual style, also the church days, in my Almanack for 1791; and my friends not having concluded on any way for taking off a sufficient number to encourage their being continued in the plain way, I have told my calculations to him, with my name subscribed as per title page, and he to publish said Almanack to his liking—believing he will publish nothing therein but what may be useful; and should it appear so, I hope said Almanack will not be less acceptable with my friends than other people.

I wish the kind patronage of every person understanding how to correct and mend my errors (the ignorant I hope to bear with) and acknowledge the general kind reception of my little performances. ELISHA THORNTON

Robert B. Thomas, in his *Farmer's Almanack* for 1797, apologized for

> . . . his indulging the printer, who took the liberty to retrench several useful matters to make room for a 'Sermon in favour of thieving'; and several ludicrous anecdotes, which were highly disgusting to many, and for which he himself asks forgiveness. . . .

Thomas resolved that he would henceforth "make all the arrangements himself" and that nothing that could offend his readers would ever be printed in the pages of his almanac.

Although the author blamed the printer for all kinds of error, the criticism was frequently good-humored and bantering. Daniel Leeds said in his 1711 almanac that, in the past, he and the printer had made errors, "But now, if you find any Errors in this Years Almanack":

> *You must therefore the Printer blame,*
> *For he did all those Errors frame,*
> *Thus if from Errors I myself can free,*
> *I'll think my self a better man then thee.*

Titan Leeds concluded in his *American Almanack* for 1714 (his first, written when he was not yet sixteen) with:

> *Now Readers, Both the learned and vulgar too*
> *I here Request you would me Justice do,*
> *In passing by what you may find amiss,*
> *And lay the Blame even Where the Error is;*
> *For being young, some may think me to blame*
> *Altho' the Printer may the Errors frame.*[16]

Titan attacked the printer again in the *American Almanack* for 1718:

> Note, that whereas my Preface Last year, gave Account that at least one Third of the Inhabitants of West-*Jersey*, were of the People call'd *Quakers*, but in my Copy I had written that there was not one third Quakers
>
> > *I Believe I may Venture,*
> > *To say this I do take,*
> > *For a wilfull mistake;*
> > *Of My Printer.*

The printer was even blamed for the weather predictions. In his anti-astrology preface, Freeman told the readers of his New York almanac for 1767:

> The Influence of the Planets is altogether imaginary, and the Almanack Makers are as utterly ignorant of all future Events as you are; . . . Indeed few of them pretend to know anything about it, but put in, or have to the Printers to put in something of the Weather, whenever there happens to be room for it. . . .

In 1790 a "Philomath N. Ames" (pseudonym) admitted that his predictions may fail and the weather may be unfortunate but "our Readers must attribute the *great evil* entirely to the Planets (certainly the Author is not in fault)—But alas for the *Printer*—tho' *Nobody*'s to blame!" The printer was either Philomath N. Ames himself or someone else who well knew the policy of blaming everything on the printer.

The cleverest fixing of the blame appeared in the 1754 issue of *Poor Job*, whose preceding number had been criticized by his greatest rival (Nathaniel Ames). "Poor Job" said: "[The error] was entirely owing to the Printer's Neglect; and that I am in no wise to be accountable, every Man having Faults enough of his own to answer for. . . ." James Franklin, Jr., was, of course, both author and printer.

By the time the first newspaper was printed (1704), the almanac business was prospering. Although the almanac, a household necessity, did not require advertisement to ensure sales, an occasional announcement would appear in a newspaper where several different almanacs were issued. Almanacs were sold in bookshops, by peddlers, and by the printers themselves. A cheaper rate by the dozen encouraged the wholesale trade.

Because almanacs were popular, hence profitable, and copyright was nonexistent before 1783, pirating flourished. The local dealer sometimes was a printer who would use the almanac material of a rival, changing only the title page.

James Franklin, Sr., published a spurious edition of Bowen's almanac for 1725.[17] Samuel Keimer printed an unauthorized version of Jacob Taylor's almanac for 1726, which Taylor, in a local newspaper, called "a lying Pamphlet, termed An Almanack." [18] Andrew Bradford, Leeds's printer, published a complaint against the same Keimer for printing a spurious edition of Titan Leeds's almanac for 1727.[19]

The Ames almanacs were frequently pirated. Notable offenders were the printers of New London, New Haven, and Hartford, Connecticut, who boldly purveyed copies in Boston, home of the genuine article. But pirated editions were even printed in Boston, and this outrage led young Dr. Ames to vilify the trade in his diary as "Knaves, Liars, and Villains." [20] In 1765, a rival delivered a successful coup with *Ames's Almanack Revised and Improved By a Late Student at Harvard-College*. The "Student," indexed by Charles Evans as Joseph Willard, claimed that "Mr. *Ames* (Son of the lately deceased Dr. *Ames*) declined furnishing the Public with an Almanack for the Year 1766." But young Ames's almanac was issued shortly thereafter—as soon as he had concluded bickering with his printers. The following year, readers were warned against *"spurious, pirated, and incorrect editions."* Piracy and idealism were not, apparently, irreconcilable. Some of the same printers who were involved in controversies over pirated almanacs were also active in America's fight for freedom of the press.

There was no effective legal protection for almanac authors and printers until 1790 when the Federal Copyright Act was passed. The Continental Congress in 1783 had passed a resolution recommending that all states make copyright laws, following the examples of Connecticut, Massachusetts, and Maryland. Although copyright statutes were enacted between 1783 and 1786 in every

31

state except Delaware, enforcement of these laws seems to have varied among the states, and even within a single state, depending upon its government officials.

In the seventeenth century, it was customary to submit material to the censor before publishing. Massachusetts appointed "licensers of the press" from 1662 to 1775. But each colony made its own laws, and dates of censorship duration vary for each colony. The censor was often listed on the title page. For example, Tulley in 1688 and 1689 listed "Imprimatur, Edw. Randolph Secr" on his title pages; in 1699, he printed "Licensed by Authority." Holyoke's almanac for 1715 included "Imprimatur, J. Dudley" (Dudley was governor of Massachusetts and himself the author of an almanac for 1668).

Although officially, the "imprimatur" (from the Latin, "Let it be printed") was required, the printer often used his own discretion. In 1700 Bartholomew Green of Boston refused to print an attack on Increase Mather, president of Harvard, unless the authors showed the article first to the lieutenant governor. The authors simply had their work printed in New York. Accused of being afraid of the Reverend Mr. Mather, Green pleaded that he was only abiding by the law.[21] The Reverend had himself been a "licenser of the press" in 1674.[22] Green's docility and discretion seem to have paid off, for in April 1704 he was duly permitted to publish the first newspaper in America, *The Boston News-Letter*. (R. Pierce and Benjamin Harris had failed in their attempt to publish a periodical in 1690 because they did not trouble themselves to obtain a license.)

Many printers were involved in disputes with the provincial authorities, although most of these conflicts did not involve almanacs. Political pamphlets and newspaper articles were generally supervised more closely by the government than were almanacs. Printers William Bradford, Andrew Bradford, James Franklin, Sr., John Peter Zenger, and Daniel Fowle were in trouble on more than one occasion.

In 1685 William Bradford's first issue from his Pennsylvania press, Samuel Atkins' *Kalendarium Pennsilvaniense*, included "The

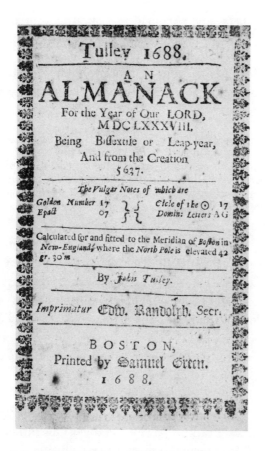

John Tulley's Almanac for 1688, with a prominent reference to the censor.

beginning of the Government here by ye Lord Penn" in a list of important events. The provincial Quaker council did not approve of titles like "ye Lord." Atkins was ordered to remove it and Bradford was told "not to print anything but what shall have lycence from ye Councill." [23] Four years later, Bradford printed the colony's charter, which angered the governor. The printer claimed that he was unaware that a censor had been appointed. Governor Blackwell said:

> Sir, I am "Imprimatur"; and that you shall know. . . . Sir, I have particular order from Governor Penn for the suppressing

of printing here, and narrowly to look after your press, and make you give in five hundred pounds security to print nothing but what I allow, or I'll lay you fast.[24]

Bradford, in his own account of the interview with the governor, claims to have made this impassioned plea for freedom of the press:

> Governour, it is my imploy, my trade and calling, and that by which I get my living, to print; and if I may not print such things as come to my hand, which are innocent, I cannot live. . . . If I print one thing to-day, and the contrary party bring me another to-morrow, to contradict it, I cannot say that I shall not print it. Printing is a manufacture of the nation, and therefore ought rather to be encouraged than suppressed.[25]

But more trouble was to come. In 1692, Bradford made the mistake of printing the unpopular side of a controversy among the Society of Friends. His press was seized, and he was promptly arrested and tried, the trial being, perhaps, the first in America involving freedom of the press. But the case was dismissed when one of the jurors dropped the chase of types being used as evidence. As soon as Bradford retrieved his printing equipment, he hurriedly moved to New York, where he introduced the first press in that colony.

Licensing in Pennsylvania lasted at least until 1722 when, in that year, Andrew Bradford, as intractable as his father, printed an article in his newspaper (the first in Pennsylvania) about the "dying Credit of the Province," an attitude the Council did not take kindly to. Andrew, when arrested, was ordered not to print anything else about the government "without the permission of the Governour or Secretary of this province."[26] He apologized ever so meekly for his transgressions, and then continued to do as he pleased. The ultimate reward for his courage was a jail sentence in 1729 for seditious libel.

In Boston, James Franklin, Sr., printed in 1722 some insinuating remarks about the government in his unlicensed newspaper, *The New-England Courant*. On one occasion he commented that the government was sending out a ship to capture pirates "sometime this month, wind and weather permitting."[27] Franklin was ordered not to publish his newspaper again. The order issued to him personally did not specify that his young apprentice Benjamin Franklin could not publish the newspaper, so Ben became the official publisher to circumvent the edict. James Franklin caused the colony so much trouble by his irrepressible antics that Massachusetts ceased trying to enforce an unenforceable law.

From the early part of the eighteenth century—despite these incidents of repression—governmental supervision of the press had definitely relaxed. By the 1730's, amateurs of astronomy and astrology, as well as those simply with an eye for the main chance, had a clear field, so "the almanack manufacturers increased and multiplied throughout the land." [28]

But the cause of freedom still needed defense. When censured for publishing an unpopular opinion, Benjamin Franklin wrote:

> Printers are educated in the Belief that when Men differ in Opinion, both Sides ought equally to have the Advantage of being heard by the Publick; and that when Truth and Error have fair Play the Former is always an over-match for the latter. . . .[29]

Then, with Franklinesque aplomb, he added this pragmatic defense: "I got Five Shillings by it. . . . None who are angry with me would have given me so much to let it alone." [30]

In 1757 the following verse was inserted in *Poor Richard Improved:*

> *While free from Force the Press remains,*
> *Virtue and Freedom chear our Plains,*
> *And Learning Largesses bestows,*
> *And keep unlicens'd open House.*
> . . . .
> *For those who use the Gag's Restraint,*
> *First Rob, before they stop Complaint.*

As revolutionary spirit heightened, expressions of free sentiments increased. In 1771 the Essex almanac argued that

> The Press is dangerous in a despotic Government, but in a free Country may be very useful, as long as it is under no Correction; for it is of great Consequence that the people should be informed of every Thing that concerns them; and, without Printing, such Knowledge could not circulate either so easily,

or so fast; and to argue against any Branch of Liberty, from the ill use that may be made of it, is to argue against *Liberty itself*, since all is capable of being abused.

The Essex almanac statement came exactly a century after Sir Willian Berkeley, Governor of Virginia, had spoken out sharply against such freedom:

> I thank God there are no free schools nor printing, and I hope we shall not have these hundred years; for learning has brought disobedience and heresy and sects into the world, and printing has divulged them, and libels against the best government.[31]

The almanac itself, apparently, was not greatly affected by censorship. William Bradford's indiscretion in his 1686 almanac, with "ye Lord Penn," had been attacked by the Quakers, not by the censors. Some almanacs were submitted to the censor; many were not, although the imprimatur was technically required. At any rate, almanac content was rarely political until the Revolutionary Period, at which time censorship was no longer in effect.

By the end of the seventeenth century, the colonial almanac had begun to resemble more closely the type of almanac that had been popular in England throughout that century. Until 1675, Harvard College had possessed the only printing press in the colonies. The "philomath," or Cambridge, almanac, a product of this press, had been scientific and academic in approach. After 1675, the philomath almanac gave way to the farmer's almanac, with its own distinctive character. This new type of almanac came to include a greater variety of material with popular appeal, such as astrological predictions, advice on husbandry and health, and humor. It is not, therefore, for chronological purposes alone that we mark a division between seventeenth-century and eighteenth-century American almanacs.

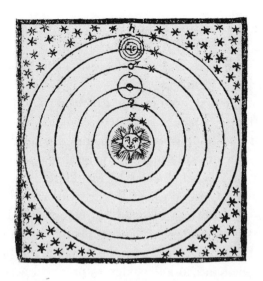

3 Seventeenth Century American Almanacs

From the following entry in John Winthrop's *Journal* we learn of the early beginnings of the American printing press and of the American almanac:

> Mo. 1 (March) [1640] A printing house was begun at Cambridge by one Daye, at the charge of Mr. Glover, who died on sea hitherward. The first thing which was printed was the freemen's oath; the next was an almanac made for New England by Mr. William Peirce, mariner; the next was the Psalms newly turned into metre.[1]

Both 1638 and 1639 have been claimed as the birthdate of the American press. The date may be further complicated by the fact that the Old Style calendar measured the year from March to

March; hence the last three months of 1638 would be, by New Style reckoning, the first three months of 1639. Samuel Danforth's 1647 almanac included "A Chronologicall Table," listing "1639—The first Printing at Cambridge."

No copy of the first issue of *The Freeman's Oath* is known to exist.[2] Nor is there a copy of Mr. Peirce's almanac. But we do have the *Bay Psalm Book,* published in 1640, and frequently referred to as the first book printed in America. By our criterion, however, the first book was the alleged almanac by Mr. Peirce. The compiler of this first almanac, Capt. William Peirce, was a celebrated ship's captain, well qualified to prepare an astronomical calendar, who, according to W. L. Andrews, "having abandoned his sea-faring life and cast his moorings ashore for the remainder of his days, was ready to turn his nautical knowledge to practical account."[3] But Winthrop mentions Peirce returning in the *Desire* in 1638 from the West Indies, where he had sold some captive Pequod Indians and had brought back "salt, cotton, tobacco, and Negroes."[4] Indeed, it may be asserted that Capt. Peirce was a precursor of American and British slave traders.

Rev. Jose Glover, who might have become the first president of Harvard, had returned to England to raise money for the new college, to purchase a printing press, and to arrange for his family's transportation to New England.[5] In September or October of 1638, Glover left London on the *John* with his wife, his steward, the Glovers' five children, household servants, Stephen Day, Day's two sons, and three menservants. Unfortunately, Rev. Glover did not survive the crossing. But his widow, Elizabeth Harris Glover, soon had a printing house ready for service in a Cambridge dwelling which she had obtained for Stephen Day's family. Stephen Day was a locksmith, an expert mechanic, not a printer; but his son Matthew had served an apprenticeship to an English printer, and Stephen, Jr., who died in December, 1639, may have also had some printing experience. The boys were minors, but Matthew, after directing his father how to set up the press, could proceed with the printing. Stephen, Sr., the nominal head of the press, expected to pursue his trade of locksmith and to prospect for iron ore.[6]

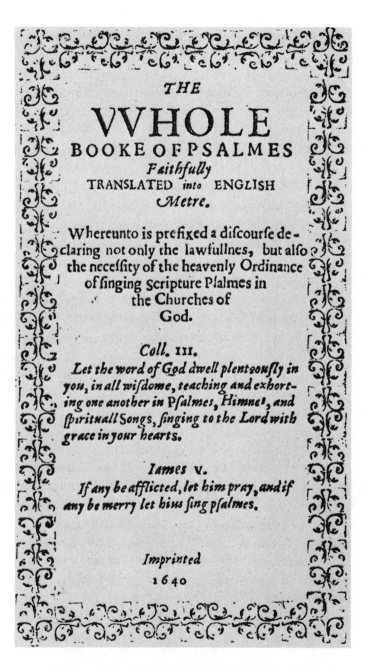

THE

VVHOLE

BOOKE OF PSALMES
Faithfully
TRANSLATED *into* ENGLISH
Metre.

Whereunto is prefixed a difcourſe de-
claring not only the lawfullnes, but alfo
the neceffity of the heavenly Ordinance
of finging Scripture Pfalmes in
the Churches of
God.

Coll. III.

*Let the word of God dwell plenteoufly in
you, in all wifdome, teaching and exhort-
ing one another in Pfalmes, Himnes, and
fpirituall Songs, finging to the Lord with
grace in your hearts.*

Iames V.

*If any be afflicted, let him pray, and if
any be merry let him fing pfalmes.*

Imprinted
1640

Stephen Day's *Bay Psalm Book*, Cambridge 1640,
the earliest extant book printed in America.

39

Stephen Day was certainly unskilled as a printer; his (or Matthew's) spelling in the *Bay Psalm Book* is sometimes as phonetic as that of Josh Billings. Stephen's character was no more impeccable than his printing: records of court cases reveal at least one term in the Cambridge jail and several run-ins with the local ministers.[7]

In 1641 Widow Glover married Henry Dunster, who, as her husband and as the first official president of Harvard, had charge of the printing press, which was Glover property. After Mrs. Dunster's death in 1643, the Day residence was sold to settle the Glover estate. The college provided a home for Mr. Dunster and his new wife, and the press was moved to the president's home.

The first extant almanac is that for the year 1646. Almanacs may have been issued every year from 1639, although George Parker Winship gives evidence, based on an account of expenses by Stephen Day and the fact that the Cambridge Press was no "ordinary commercial venture," to support "a belief that no other almanacs were issued until outside help was secured five or six years later." [8] "Outside help" referred to Gregory Dexter, a printer from London and a personal friend of Roger Williams, who went from Rhode Island to Cambridge in the 1640's to help Samuel Green with the Harvard printing business.

The almanac for 1646 apparently consisted of eight leaves (16 pages), though some leaves are missing in the extant copy.[9] The calendar pages obviously began with March as the first month and contained the usual calendars, including calculations for the sun, moon, and tides—in addition to miscellaneous information at the end. This format is typical of British almanacs of the same period.

Although American almanacs early developed special characteristics of their own, the seventeenth-century almanac-makers relied heavily for format and content on their British counterparts, particularly in the case of calendar pages. In 1646 there was scarcely an independent colonial tradition. Nevertheless, subtle differences were already detectable: the American almanacs were not so preoccupied with astrology as their British relatives. Consequently, satirical attitudes toward this subject developed much later in the American production than in the British.

The first American almanacs have been called the Cambridge almanacs, the "Philomath" almanacs, or the Astronomical almanacs. The scholarly editors frequently appended such titles as "Philomath," "Philomathemat," "A Lover of the Mathematics," "Φιλομαθὴς," or "Astrophil" to their names on the title pages, a practice occasionally imitated in quite different almanacs in the eighteenth century and even seen today in the *Farmer's Almanac,* "edited by Ray Geiger, Philom. . . . Successors to David Young, Philom."

Before 1687, Massachusetts had produced some forty-four almanacs. Forty-one of these were compiled by Harvard graduates, ten of whom were, at the same time, "tutors," or graduate students. Indeed, for many years, it seemed to have been the practice to assign—or award—the responsibility for the annual almanac to a tutor, thus providing him with a publication which exercised his mathematical skill and also encouraging his talent for versification. The list of early almanac-makers reads, as well, like a roster of First Families of Massachusetts: Samuel Danforth, Urian Oakes, Thomas and Jeremiah Shepard, Samuel Bradstreet, Zechariah Brigden, Samuel Cheever, Nathaniel and Israel Chauncey, Josiah Flint, John Sherman, Samuel Brackenbury, Joseph Dudley, Daniel and Noadiah Russell, Thomas and William Brattle, and Cotton and Nathaniel Mather—ministers, college presidents, and a governor of the colony. Eighteen of these early almanac-makers signed only their initials, but all except four have been identified.

The enigmatic four are "T.S.," "S.B.," "J.S.," and "H.B." Nichols believed that "T.S.," author of an almanac for 1656, was Thomas Shepard, a Harvard tutor and author of works on astronomy; that "S.B.," author of an almanac for 1657, was Samuel Bradstreet, although Samuel Brackenbury has also been considered; and that "H.B.," author of an almanac for 1692, was Benjamin Harris, the almanac's printer. In one of the two editions for 1692, the verses were signed "B.H." rather than "H.B." [10] The unidentified "J.S." (in an almanac for 1674) could have been Jeremiah Shepard, Thomas' half brother,[11] or John Sherman, although he was not a Harvard graduate.[12]

Youth was not a handicap to these early philomaths. It was not uncommon to find Harvard students producing almanacs between the ages of sixteen and twenty. Nathaniel Mather, who died at age nineteen, compiled his when only sixteen. Their successors, too, sometimes authored their works at an early age. Dr. Nathaniel Ames, III, and Titan Leeds were only sixteen when they began their almanac-making careers. Daniel George was seventeen. Briggs reported, with amusement, that a 1695 almanac was compiled by one Increase Gatchell, age sixteen, and another by the same Gatchell, age sixteen, in 1715.[13] Charles Angoff uses the 1695 date for the work of the precocious youth.[14] In fact, Increase Gatchell at age sixteen compiled only one almanac: *The Young American Ephemeris* for 1715.

Despite a few similarities, the philomath almanac differed considerably from the farmer's almanac developed towards the end of the century. Typically, the philomath almanac contained sixteen pages (eight leaves), of which twelve were the monthly calendars. It emphasized astronomy for over thirty years—as long as the Cambridge Press was the only press in the colonies—teaching Copernican theory and preparing the public to accept Newtonian science. That the new science might call into question the literal teachings of the Bible never seemed to enter the minds of most Puritan divines. It was accepted simply as one of the ways in which God worked; how He accomplished His miracles and established His cosmic order was not considered to be the province of theologians.

While Harvard was in control of the press, the astrology permitted in the almanacs dealt primarily with the portents of eclipses and comets. The Puritan's double vision allowed him to interpret cosmic phenomena both as omens of disaster according to God's providence, and as heavenly bodies obeying the natural laws of the universe. Minutest details and the most trivial happenings were seen as signs either of God's beneficence or of his displeasure; as such, they assumed a great importance and were duly recorded. It is difficult, if not impossible, to separate the astronomy and astrology of the seventeenth century since medieval superstition lingered, even in the works of the philomaths Samuel Danforth (*An Astronomical Description of the Late Comet or Blazing Star, 1665*) and Increase Mather (*Heaven's Alarm to the World, 1681*). The comets were believed to be signs sent by God to warn his people to repent of their sins.

After 1675, astrology and other popular interests began to transform the philomath almanac, which changed rapidly during the last decade of the century. An examination of some seventeenth-century almanacs that contained typical philomath matter clearly reveals the special character of the philomath almanac and its growing pains.

In 1646 Samuel Danforth, author of our earliest extant almanac, included historical information about timekeeping beneath the monthly calendars. This almanac was interleaved with blank sheets for personal records. Danforth's 1647 version, written when he was nineteen, was the first in America to contain 1) a decorated first page, 2) verse, and 3) a chronological table. The title page was attractively bordered with moon-faces, full, new, and profile.[15] Simple, original allegorical verse about New England appeared beneath the monthly calendars, and a chronological table of local events was placed last in the book. Danforth's next three issues followed the same format. In 1648 the verse was a more sophisticated allegory, featuring New England as a growing, fruitful tree. Local "memorable occurrences" included such items as "1638 Mrs. Hutchinson & her errors banished." [16]

In 1650 Urian Oakes, who signed his work "Astronomical calculations by a Youth," used the extra space beneath the calendar to summarize each century's events—a world history digest. This "youth" became president of Harvard. Recognized as a writer of merit by literary historians, he later used astronomical imagery in a frequently anthologized eulogy on the death of Rev. Thomas Shepard (almanac-maker), who died in 1677.

No almanacs are extant for 1651 through 1655. Beginning in 1656 with Thomas Shepard, the philomath almanac began one of its primary missions—teaching astronomy. Shepard followed the Danforth tradition but added the first scientific essay, "A Brief

Explication of the most Observable Circles in the Heavens," which was based primarily on Ptolemaic theory.

Zechariah Brigden in *An Almanack of the Coelestial Motions* for 1659 explained the Copernican theory, for the first time spreading the new science to the common people through a popular medium. Although Copernicus had published *De revolutionibus orbium coelestium* as early as 1543, his theory had not been widely disseminated and was by no means universally accepted. In his "Brief Explication and Proof of the Philolaick Systems," Brigden discussed three systems of the movements of celestial bodies—the Ptolemaick, the "Tychnick" (from Tycho Brahe, Danish astronomer), and the "Philolaick" (from Philolaus, a Pythagorean who antedated Kepler and Copernicus). His description of the latter system concluded with an authoritative reference:

> Further hence may the true places of the Planets be obtained and their several inequalities rectified to every point: as is evidently declared and proved by Mr. Vincent Wing in his "Astronomica Instaurata". . . .

Brigden, however, must have anticipated that these astronomical theories might conflict with some readers' religious beliefs. He cautiously proposed that reason be the basis of judgment for his sophisticated reader, while admitting the utility of a literal view of the scriptures for the uneducated:

> That the Scriptures being fitted as well to the capacity of the rudest mechanick, as of the [a]blest Philosopher, do not intend so much propriety and exactness, as playnes and perspicuity; and in Philosophical truths, therein contayned, the proper literal sense is always subservient to the casting vote of reason.

Rev. John Davenport, one of the founders of New Haven, disagreed with Brigden but calmly adopted a policy of wait-and-see. His comment to John Winthrop, Jr., was: "let him injoy his Opinion; and I shall rest in what I have learned, til more cogant arguments be produced." [17]

In 1660 Samuel Cheever chose for his almanac a historical essay on timekeeping, but, the following year, he contributed to the advancement of scientific learning with "A Brief Discourse of the Rise and Progress of Astronomy."

Nathaniel Chauncey, son of Harvard president Charles Chauncey, included in his almanac for 1662 an essay on the "Primum Mobile," presenting an original approach to the medieval system of Ptolemaic astronomy. Positing a cause of heavenly motion other than the locomotive soul, or Primum Mobile, Chauncey wrote that "The Sun . . . affixed to his Center so as not to move out of it . . . circumvolves his axis," emitting "electrical virtue, which is the prime cause (of motion)."

Nathaniel's younger brother, Israel, compiled the almanacs for 1663 and 1664 (at ages nineteen and twenty). In 1663 he wrote an essay on "Planetary Orbs," as well as one on eclipses and their portents. He illustrated his essay on eclipses with perhaps the first such illustrations to be found in an American almanac. In 1664 he added more specific weather prognostications, foretelling "rain" or "fair weather."

Alexander Nowell, in a 1665 almanac, continued the work of reconciling science and religion in "The Sun's Prerogative Vindicated": subjection to natural laws, in his view, did not disqualify comets as signs from God of approaching catastrophes.

Unlike his colleagues, Josiah Flint, in 1666, appeared almost untouched by the new philosophy. He quoted the scriptures, used Biblical personages in his verse relating the history of the Jews, and concluded with an essay on "The World's Eternity is an Impossibility." Making no attempt to be scientific, Flint displayed an almost evangelical fervor.

Although Samuel Brackenbury's almanac for 1667 lacked the usual philomath verse on the calendar pages, a rhyme appeared on the page with the eclipses. The last page contained a table of the sun's altitude at every hour of the day.

Joseph Dudley, later a Licenser of the Press and the governor of the colony of Massachusetts, wrote in the Cambridge almanac for 1668 a verse about the sun's eclipse and an essay, "The Beginning of the Year," accompanied by an illustration of the movements of the earth. In 1669 Joseph Browne emphasized local history with six pages of chronology on everything of importance that had happened in New England, in entries like that for May 7, 1647: "Mr. *Thomas Hooker,* that glorious Star, did set together with the Sun." Browne's almanac also contained the first advertisement which appears in an extant American almanac:

> Reader, in a few weeks will come forth to publick view, the History of New England, Entitled, New England Memoriall, or, a brief relation of the most Remarkable Passages of the Province of God manifested to the Planters of New England in America. By Nathaniel Morton.

John Richardson's 1670 contribution to the development of the almanac was the first humorous satire: a verse, "The Country-Mans Apocrypha," directed against astrology. Readers were usually given on the title page the longitude or meridian and "elevation of the pole" for which the almanac was calculated. Richardson parodied this information in the title of another verse satire, "A Perpetual Candor, fitted for the Meridian of Babylon, where the Pope is elevated 42 degrees."

Daniel Russell added a feature in 1671 which became commonplace thereafter—a table of the kings and queens of England. History was also stressed in Nehemiah Hobart's almanac for 1673, where he expanded previously published chronological tables. Among other notes of great local interest was a puzzling ecological problem dated 1670: "A strange Mortality [of] little Fish in a Pond near Cambridge, the manner whereof was very wonderful, and the number almost incredible, as many eye witnesses can testifie." His only concession to astronomy was an explanation of how to find the rising and falling of eleven fixed stars ("the Southing being first known") and thus tell the time.

"J. S." (possibly John Sherman or Jeremiah Shepard) returned to serious astronomy in 1674 with an essay on theories of planetary motion. In 1676 John Sherman presented his astronomical data in a moral context: catastrophes were occurring in New England because she was degenerate. This essay reflected a popular theme in contemporary sermons, which have been described as the "voice of a community bespeaking its apprehensions about itself," rather than descriptions of the facts.[18] In 1677 Sherman again connected science with religion, stating that natural events were evidence of God's omnipotence.

John Foster prepared the Cambridge almanac for 1675. By 1676 he had started his own press in Boston and considerably altered the American almanac. However, in 1675, he wrote, in the Harvard tradition, "A Brief Description of the Coelestial Orbs according to the Opinion of that ancient Philosopher Pythagoras, and all latter Astronomers," in which he reaffirmed the Copernican theory "that the Earth moves and the Sun stands still." A diagram called "A Figure of the Visible World according to the Opinions of Copernicus" may have been the first woodcut in American almanacs.[19] The illustration was reprinted by Foster and by other almanac-makers.

In the firſt Orb above the Sun is Mercury, who performeth his courſe about the Sun in 88 dayes.

In the next Orb is the glittering Star *Venus*, who finiſheth her Courſe about the Sun in 225 dayes.

In the middle of all the Planets is the Earth, who performeth her Revolution about the Sun in a year; and is turned round upon her own Axis in the ſpace of 24 hours. The Moon is a ſecondary Planet, retaining the Earth for her Center, about which ſhe performs her Revolution in 27 dayes, and returns to the *Sun* in 39. d. 12. h.

Next to the *Earth* is *Mars* accompliſhing his Revolution in two years.

Next is Jupiter, who hath ſeveral little Stars moving about him, as the *Moon* moveth about the *Earth*, he runs his Couſe in 12 years. *Saturn* the higheſt of the Planets finiſheth his Courſe in 30 years.

Far above all theſe is the Orb of the fixed Stars, who make their Revolution in no leſs then 25920 years, whoſe diſtance by reaſon that their Parallax is inſenſible, cannot be by any man determined.

John Foster's explanation of the Visible World according to Copernicus. The *Cambridge Almanack*, 1675.

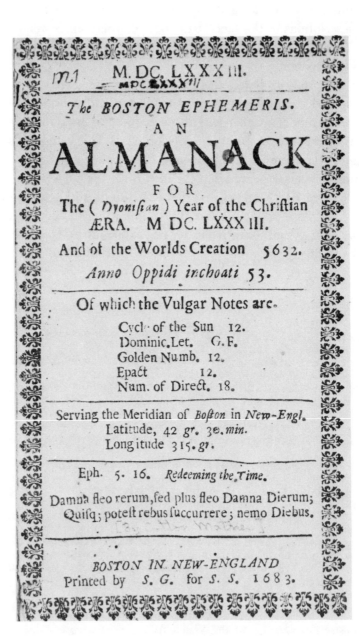

M. DC. LXXXIII.
MDCLXXXIII

The BOSTON EPHEMERIS.

A N

ALMANACK

FOR

The (*Dyonisian*) Year of the Christian
ÆRA. M DC. LXXX III.

And of the Worlds Creation 5632.

Anno Oppidi inchoati 53.

Of which the Vulgar Notes are.

Cycl of the Sun 12.
Dominic. Let. G. F.
Golden Numb. 12.
Epact 12.
Num. of Direct. 18.

Serving the Meridian of *Boston* in *New-Engl.*
Latitude, 42 *gr.* 30. *min.*
Longitude 315. *gr.*

Eph. 5. 16. *Redeeming the Time.*

Damna fleo rerum, sed plus fleo Damna Dierum;
Quisq; potest rebus succurrere; nemo Diebus.

BOSTON IN NEW-ENGLAND
Printed by S. G. for S. S. 1683.

A copy of
Cotton Mather's *Boston Ephemeris* for 1683.

The Reverend Cotton Mather
(1663–1728).

The most famous of the Harvard astronomers was Thomas
Brattle who prepared the 1678 edition, including a table showing
the length of the longest day of the year at all places in the world.
Brattle, a renowned scientist, subsequently made observations on
the 1680 comet with Harvard's three and one-half foot telescope.
These observations were both used and acknowledged by Newton
in deriving his theory of gravitation. Thomas Brattle reappeared
as almanac-maker in 1694 for the Boston edition, which included
a few meteorological notes on tides and weather. His brother William, an astronomer and logician whose *Compendium Logicae* was
later used as a text at Harvard, compiled the almanac for 1682. It
contained nine pages of astonomical notes and verse on the zodiac.

Another well-known Massachusetts family was represented by
Cotton and Nathaniel Mather. Although no author's name ap-

peared on *The Boston Ephemeris* for 1683, Judge Samuel Sewall wrote on his own copy, "By Cotton Mather." Sewall, who was at this time manager of the Boston press formerly operated by John Foster, employed the printer Samuel Green, Jr. The imprint is "Boston: Printed S.G. for S.S." In the 1683 *Ephemeris,* Mather wrote a scholarly, well-documented account of how the books of the Bible came to be written, a "serious Reflection on mans mortal and momentary life," and "A Description of Last Years Comet" (Halley's), which portended calamity. For the 1685 almanac, Mather's younger brother Nathaniel, who also showed scientific inclinations, wrote an essay on the planets or "a short view of the Discoveries that have been made in the Heaven with and since the invention of the Telescope." Nathaniel enthusiastically indulged his bent toward astronomy in *The Boston Ephemeris* for 1686 with two essays: "Concerning some late discoveries respecting the fixed Stars" and "Concerning late Marvelous Astronomical Discoveries in the Planets." He mentioned Robert Hook's discoveries as proof of the new system, further admitted that this system had not been popular, and expressed his faith that the new science would soon replace the old. The Mathers were Bostonians and friends of John Foster: all three of their almanacs were printed by Foster's successor in Boston.

Each of the two almanacs for 1684 contained innovations. Noadiah Russell, in Cambridge, introduced the first full-page almanac illustration, an unexplained drawing of a man with a harp in his hand. Russell also offered his readers a "scientific" essay on the effects of thunder and lightning:

> If lightning kill one in his sleep, he dies with his eyes opened, the Reason is because it just wakes him and kills him before he can shut his eyes again: If it kills one waking, his eyes will be found to be shut, because it so amazes him that [he] winketh and dies before he can open his eyes again.

Benjamin Gillam's *Boston Ephemeris* for the same year presented, for the first time, the meetings of the courts in a special table rather than on the calendar pages, a device which became fairly standard in subsequent almanacs.

Woodcut of King David with harp, the first full-page almanac illustration in America. Russell's *Cambridge Almanack* for 1684.

William Williams' *Cambridge Ephemeris* for 1685 included two scientific essays: one was "Concerning the Nature of Comets"; the other described, in true Puritan fashion, both the natural and supernatural causes of the rainbow. "The Natural," he wrote, "is either a sign of rain or a token of fair weather . . . the Supernatural end of the Rainbow is to be a sign or symbol of God's mercy to a world in never destroying it again by a deluge. . . ."

In *The New England Almanack* for 1686, Samuel Danforth, the son of the first Samuel Danforth, almanac-maker and minister of Roxbury, prepared the college almanac and presented his allusions to Copernican science in a long poem, "Ad Librum." The addition of "New England" to the title for this year reflects the fact that another almanac was printed in Pennsylvania in the same year.

Henry Newman compiled *Harvard's Ephemeris* for 1690. In an essay on the earth's motion, he perpetuated the stance taken earlier by the college that the new science of astronomy was compatible with theology—in celestial movements the Creator was showing his handiwork. Newman evidently had strong feelings about the new theory, for we can see him bearing down on the pen as he wrote: "He must have a larger Faith and be more credulous than any Female, that believes the Diurnal motion of the Sun and Immobility of the Earth." The following year, Henry Newman compiled the almanac printed in Boston, *News From the Stars,* and John Tulley prepared the almanacs at Cambridge for 1691 and 1692.

Harvard College (that is, the Cambridge Press) continued to produce "philomath" almanacs through 1692, but it was becoming difficult to compete in the growing almanac trade. These relatively staid almanacs were no match for the more versatile farmer's almanacs. In the last quarter of the seventeenth century, concurrently with Harvard philomath production, the printers John Foster and William Bradford began printing businesses elsewhere in Massachusetts and in two other colonies. Daniel Leeds also began the famous Leeds family almanacs of the eighteenth century, and John Tulley started his innovative almanac series.

The first of the new breed of almanac-makers was John Foster, Harvard graduate, who in 1675 was authorized by the Massachusetts government to set up the first printing press in Boston, thus ending the Cambridge monopoly.

Foster was author, printer, and engraver—an unusual combination in the history of American almanacs. He was also an amateur doctor, a sideline not uncommon for almanac-makers, and left a substantial library of "medicinal Books" on his death. Foster is generally credited with the operation of the first Boston press. However, one author contends that Marmaduke Johnson, a sometime partner of Samuel Green in Cambridge, was licensed in 1674 to set up a press in Boston, that he actually operated the press for a few months before his death on December 25, 1674, that he taught Foster the art of printing, and that Foster bought the Johnson press.[20] John Foster not only printed the first book with a "Boston" imprint (Increase Mather's *The Wicked Man's Portion*) but was also America's earliest wood engraver.[21]

The first of six issues in the Foster series was published in Cambridge for 1675. Though Foster's scientific purpose was paramount (typical of the Harvard philomaths), the almanac increased its calendar pages to two for each month and illustrations began to take on a new importance. John Foster probably made the woodcuts himself, for he had already exhibited skill as a wood engraver. Reflecting a growing awareness of the reader's needs, Foster added in his 1676 almanac (published on his own press, the first year that America had two almanacs) some meteorological advice for the farmer. The 1678 issue introduced another ingredient common in almanacs from that day to this: the first appearance of the illustration of the Man of Signs.[22] Accompanied by a humorous verse and a title, "The Dominion of the Moon in Man's Body," the Man of Signs was the first blatant affront to the Harvard astronomers, who had kept commercial astrology out of their almanacs. (Their portents of eclipses had been well synthesized with their theology.) In 1679 Foster concentrated on the tides; in 1680, on the planets; and in 1681, on the comets. The 1681 issue included Foster's scholarly essay "Of Comets, Their Motion Dis-

tance and Magnitude," as well as "Observations of a Comet seen this last Winter 1680." [23] Foster also printed his illustration of the Copernican system. Two editions of this popular almanac were required in 1681; one was "Printed by J. F. for Samuel Phillips"; the other, "Printed by J. F."

The following elegy on Foster's death was written by Joseph Capen and resembles the famous Benjamin Franklin epitaph by Franklin himself (see chapter 4, p. 85):

Thy body, which no activeness did Lack,
Now's laid aside like an old Almanack;
But for the present only's out of date,
'Twill have at length a far more active state.
Yea, though with dust thy body soiled be,
Yet at the resurrection we shall see
A fair EDITION, and of matchless worth,
Free from ERRATAS, new in Heaven set forth;
'Tis but a word from God, the great Creator,
It shall be done when he saith IMPRIMATUR.[24]

Spring-tides in the Year 1681.

March. From the eighth day to the eighteenth.

April. From the 6*th.* to the 14*th.*

May. From the 5 day to the 11.

June. From the 3 day to the 9.

July. From the 1. day to the 7*th.* and also the two last dayes in this moneth.

August. The four first dayes and the five last of this Moneth will produce high tides.

September. The two first dayes, and from the 17. to the end of the moneth, though not very high unless increased by the wind and weather.

October. From the 15*th.* day to the 30*th.*

November. From the 14*th.* to the 20*th.*

December. From the 12*th.* to the 18*th.*

January. From the 10*th.* to the fifteenth.

February. From the 8*th.* day to the 13*th.* the Tides will swell above their usual height.

THe Reader is desired to take notice that our Latitude here in *Boston,* hitherto reputed to be 42. *gr.* 30. *min.* is by better Observations found not to exceed 42. *gr.* 24. *m.* of which you may expect the certainty by the next opportunity. *The Author Dyed Sept. 9. 1681.*

ERRATUM.

In the first Page of our Observations of the Comet, and the first line, Read November the eighteenth.

John Foster's death is recorded in a copy of the *Cambridge Almanack* for 1681.

The year 1685, four years after Foster's death, marked another milepost in American almanac history. William Bradford, one of the greatest colonial printers, published the first almanac in Pennsylvania and the first to be printed outside Massachusetts: the *Kalendarium Pennsilvaniense* for 1686, prepared by Samuel Atkins in 1685. Evidence belies a claim that "The first Philadelphia almanac was put forth in 1686, edited by Daniel Leeds, and printed by William Bradford." [25] Bradford did print an almanac by Daniel Leeds, a broadside or "sheet" titled *An Almanack for . . . 1687*, but the Atkins almanac preceded Leeds's by at least one year. Atkins, in fact, was responsible for the earliest work printed in the Middle Colonies.[26]

William Bradford was also the first printer in New York, where he established his press in 1693. This colony's first almanac followed shortly after: *An Almanack for 1694*, by Daniel Leeds. Again, historians disagree about the "first almanac." [27] Leeds had prepared his almanacs for William Bradford while the printer was in Philadelphia, and when Bradford moved to New York, Leeds did not change printers. A few years later the Leeds almanacs were printed simultaneously in New York by William and in Philadelphia by his son, Andrew Bradford.

Before William Bradford left Philadelphia, Leeds prepared an almanac for 1693 that continued what Foster had begun in 1676—advice for farmers. Leeds's almanac, largely agricultural, gave farmers monthly reminders. A sharp departure from the philomath style and content, this was a genuine farmer's almanac. To justify his subject matter, Leeds remarked in verse that, while the subject of politics tends to be controversial:

> I'm safe while moving in my proper sphere,
> In Plowing, Planting, there's no treason there.

Leeds's 1693 almanac also contained aphorisms, forty years before *Poor Richard:* "As this Country makes Rich men poor and Poor men rich, so it very well fits all People but Beggars and Gentlemen, so called."

Leeds also made a major contribution to almanac format in 1695 when he added "A Short Description of Highways," delineat-

Kalendarium Pennsilvaniense,

OR,

America's Messinger.

BEING AN

ALMANACK

For the Year of Grace, 1686.

Wherein is contained both the English & Forreign
Account. the Motions of the Planets through the Signs, with
the Luminaries, Conjunctions, Aspects, Eclipses; the rising,
southing and setting of the Moon, with the time when she
passeth by, or is with the most eminent fixed Stars : Sun rising
and setting, and the time of High-Water at the City of *Philadelphia, &c.*
With Chronologies, and many other Notes, Rules,
and Tables, very fitting for every man to know & have ; all
which is accomodated to the Longitude of the Province of
Pennsilvania, and Latitude of 40 Degr. north, with a Table
of Houses for the same, which may indifferently serve *New-
England*, *New York*, *East* & *West Jersey*, *Maryland*, and most
parts of *Virginia.*

By *SAMUEL ATKINS.*
Student in the Mathamaticks and Astrology.

And the Stars in their Courses fought against Sesera, Jndg. 5. 29.

Printed and Sold by *William Bradford*, sold also by
the Author and *H. Murrey* in *Philadelphia*, and
Philip Richards in *New-York* ; 1685.

The first American almanac published outside Massachusetts, 1685.

ing the distance from New York to Philadelphia. John Clapp listed distances from New York to Boston in 1697, and John Tulley gave road distances in 1699 from Boston to several other cities. Tulley is credited with the first list of roads by several authors who ignore Leeds and Clapp.[28] Tulley's lists were more extensive, but the feature itself was added by Leeds. Road lists became standard in later almanacs.

Astrology, popular with the farmers, had a firm grip on Leeds. When John Clapp said in 1697 that eclipses did not affect people, Leeds retorted in 1698 with ". . . Tis true, eclipses are Natural, as he says. So likewise Meat and Drink are Natural, and that Nourishes Mankind; so is poison Natural, but yet that destroys them. . . ." Astrology was definitely in fashion, and the Leeds family were leaders in the field for more than forty years.

One anomalous almanac during the last decade of the century had elements of both philomath and farmer's almanacs, as well as its own unique characteristics. *The Boston Almanack* for 1692, attributed to its printer, Benjamin Harris, was America's first color printing. The title appeared in fancy red letters, and another page was printed almost entirely in red. With the exceptions of a poem addressed to William and Mary and a useful article on blood-letting, Harris devoted his almanac to legal affairs: the local courts, names of debtors and their debts, and copies of legal forms such as indentures, letters of attorney, and wills. January, the first month, was designated simply as "January," with no "xi mo." or "i mo." following, suggesting that readers had accepted the new calendar change instituted in the 1687 almanac by John Tulley. Harris followed Tulley in mentioning weather predictions, but omitted the holidays.

The philomaths had begun their decline with John Foster; they completed the fall with John Tulley, the most notorious almanac-maker of the seventeenth century. The publications of John Tulley were the most notable exceptions to the general high seriousness and religio-astronomical tone of the early almanacs. Tulley was born in England, settled in Connecticut, and was not a Harvard graduate. A teacher of mathematics, astronomy, and navigation, he attained through his almanacs a wide reputation as a prognosticator—in fact, as a conjurer. Between 1687 and 1702 he almost revolutionized the character of the American almanac, although it may not be entirely accurate to say that he compiled the "first humorous almanack in the Colonies," [29] for John Richardson's of 1670 contained some leg-pulling.

Tulley's style was lively and entertaining; the contents were varied and diverting, as well as useful. Possibly he can be credited with the first bawdy almanac. In 1688 he predicted on the May calendar page: *"Many Weddings this Month: but the people coupled very unequally, a sneaking Woodcock joyned to a wanton Wag-tail, a Henpeckt Buzzard to a chattering Magpie."* In June:

> *The Sun is entered now into the Crab,*
> *And days are hot, therefore beware a Drab;*
> *With French diseases, they'll thy body fill,*
> *Being such as bring Grist to the Surgeon's Mill.*

July's verse was written in the same spirit:

> *Now wanton Lads and Lasses do make Hay,*
> *Which unto lewd temptation makes great way,*
> *With tumbling on the cocks, which acted duly,*
> *Doth cause much mischief in this month of July.*

Tulley in 1687 was responsible for a number of "firsts"—the first officially to use January as first month of the year, thus bringing American almanacs more in line with their British counterparts, which had followed this practice for many years,[30] and the first to insert the feast and fast days of the English church (such as Valentine's Day, New Year's Day, Shrove Sunday, Easter), a notion considered anathema to the orthodox Puritan clergy. He also introduced weather forecasts.[31] In 1691 he added a "table of expence"—the first of many similar tables that included interest and currency conversions. Mr. Tulley was daring, but not too daring. It is not quite accurate to say that John Tulley "did not care a shilling what his public thought of him. He cared less about his confreres. "[32] True, Tulley poked fun at almanac-makers who took themselves seriously (a sport popular in England for over a century). But the public obviously liked what Tulley did and they bought his almanacs. He was just bawdy enough to be refreshing and just shrewd enough to know what his audience wanted and needed: so he gave them smiles. Attitudes were changing, and Tulley's almanacs reflected these changes.

During the time Tulley was in business, the conservative philomaths and astrophils, desperately trying to hold on to a sober mein that was fast going out of fashion, attacked the astrological almanacs zealously. One of Tulley's chief critics was Dr. Christian Lodowick, who in 1695 may have been the first to include cures for disease in an almanac, such as how to prevent toothache and how to care for "pyles." In the same issue he spoke "Against certain Impieties and Absurdities in Tully's Almanacks"; weather forecasts, for example. Tulley in turn had little respect for Lodowick's products. In a letter to Vavasour Harris, son of Benjamin Harris, printer, on June 4, 1695, Tulley wrote that he had received Lodowick's *New-England Almanack* from Harris "which will be no help or advantage to me in the makeing of my Almanacke, for I can make a better then that which would be more usefull without the help of it." [33] He did, however, "humbly" apologize in his 1696 almanac for the offenses publicized by Lodowick. Tulley was really unperturbed and irrepressible, and his audience doubtless delighted in his antics. English almanacs at this time were filled with foolish prognostications, and Tulley's were no more ridiculous; yet his frequent satire may have been lost on many in his audience, who took his astrology seriously. Like many almanac-makers, John Tulley had a better education than most of his readers, but he seems to have been the first to use this advantage to educate by entertaining. He was a genuine popularizer.

Tulley's 1687 almanac began with a table of the kings and concluded with two pages of weather and eclipses. The 1688 edition sagely told the readers: "For all predictions do to this belong/That either they are right, or they are wrong." This almanac, one of Tulley's best, included advice for farmers, humorous predictions on the calendar pages, and entertaining verse. It also was the first to have an imprimatur ("Edw. Randolph, Secr.") on the title page. Tulley was taking no chances. Essays on various aspects of weather

60

such as thunder and lightning were popular Tulley items. In 1693, in an essay called "Source of the Watery Meteors," he expressed an old theory of earthquakes: "Plenty of Winds gotten in the Bowels, holes and corners of the Earth bursting out of the Earth and closing again causes the shaking of Earthquake, and is a token of ensuing war." [34]

Tulley's almanacs also advertised books: *Ornaments for the Daughters of Zion* in 1692; Cotton Mather's *The Wonders of the Invisible World* in 1693; *A Present to be given to Teeming Women* in 1695; *Hannah Swarton's Account of her Captivity* in 1697.[35]

Although Tulley at times may have affronted the Mathers and their highly solemn brethren, he was sure to have pleased them with his 1695 story of the Protestant martyrs, "The Cruelty of the Papists." In 1698 Tulley advertised "Womens Hair and Perriwigs" for sale, which may have been the first advertisement for such fripperies. The 1702 almanac, called *Tulley's Farewel* because he "dyed as he was finishing this Almanack," carried on the first page a one-quatrain epitaph on the ingenious John Tulley.[36]

Tourtellot notes that "From their tables of computations of moons . . . the almanac makers were naturally led to an absorbing interest in astronomy and thence to astrology and every variety of natural phenomena." [37] But the earliest almanac-makers were Harvard mathematicians and astronomers whose work in their fields may have led them to a collateral interest in making an almanac, rather than the reverse. Astrology and natural phenomena followed, just as Tourtellot says, but not in the typical philomath almanacs. Astrology, as John Foster suspected and John Tulley knew, was good for sales. Successful British almanacs had emphasized it for years.

Generally the philomath almanacs included explanatory notes for the calendar, a discussion of the eclipses, the calendar pages, verse, and approximately two pages of astronomical, religious, or historical essays. To this basically astronomical format, John Foster added astrological material, notably the Man of Signs; John Tulley added humor and satire, and Daniel Leeds added practical material for farmers. By the end of the century, the almanac had taken on most of the characteristics that we regard as typical of a farmer's almanac: astrology, humor, cures for disease, and weather predictions.

The Cambridge almanac dynasty had practically ceased to exist by 1700. The college itself had suspended printing operations in 1692, but some of its graduates continued to prepare almanacs, which were then printed in Boston. The last of the Harvard tutors as almanac-makers were Edward Holyoke, who later became President of Harvard, and Thomas Robie, who became its librarian.[38] Both men began their almanac series in 1709; Holyoke's lasted until 1716, and Robie's ended in 1720. By 1700 almanacs were printed in Boston, Philadelphia, and New York; and the innovations of John Foster, John Tulley, and Daniel Leeds had led to the farmer's almanacs of the eighteenth century.

The Arms of the Family of LEEDS.

4 Eighteenth Century Almanacs

In its astronomical heyday during the seventeenth century, the philomath almanac served primarily as calendar and educator. Although some of the eighteenth-century almanac-makers continued to call themselves *philomaths*, they were printers, physicians, and practical men of affairs rather than scholars. Both informative and entertaining, their products were general miscellanies of useful facts, not mere exercises in celestial mechanics. Reason and science had come down to earth.

The farmer's almanac retained the basic philomath format but added more verse, aphorisms, and humor—and even some romantic tales. The preface was often amusing, and it frequently publicized feuds between rival almanac-makers. The calendar pages usually contained verse and aphorisms and, sometimes, notes of advice or scientific information. The last pages were devoted to essays and poems or to miscellanenous tables and lists, or to both. The list of roads became almost indispensable. There were "how to" articles and there were more "receipts" and anecdotes. The place and time of courts were almost invariably included. Even the meetings of the Friends (or Quakers) were announced in almanacs serving those areas where such meetings might be of interest. Chronological lists of important events continued to be popular. Tables of interest, tables of currency conversions, and lists of public officials kept the reader abreast of the times. As watches and clocks became available, some almanacs added "Sun fast and slow" so that timepieces could be adjusted accordingly. There were short biographies and other historical notes. Later in the century, some of the almanacs became propaganda pamphlets for the American Revolution. Essays and poems were sometimes "continued next year," and the solutions to mathematical problems were given in the succeeding issue—a foretaste of future commercial sophistication.

During the last half of the century, the almanac-maker became increasingly aware of the females in his audience and aimed some of his material (and his "arrows"—only slightly barbed) at them. Almanacs appeared with titles like *The Lady's and Gentleman's Almanac* and *The Lady's Almanac* (extant in today's *Ladies Birthday Almanac*).

A notable change is evident in style. As early as 1670 the general tone had been lightened by John Richardson and, shortly after, by John Foster and John Tulley. Almanacs continued to serve their basic function as calendar and weather guide, but predictions were often satiric and humorous. Levity became a common ingredient. The times were changing, and the almanacs, as usual, reflected the changes. Only 37 of the 230 books printed between 1700 and 1776 were religious as compared with 58 of the 157 publications from the Cambridge press from 1639 through 1670. The old order was yielding: the Puritans were becoming increasingly worldly. (Increase Mather died in 1723; Cotton Mather, 1728; John Wise, 1725; and Samuel Sewall, in 1730.)

Two new kinds of almanac appeared in the eighteenth century, the pocket almanac and the register. Neither philomath nor farmer's, these almanacs were used as handy little reference books.

The pocket almanac contained no essays or poetry and specialized in current affairs; such as the names of government officials, the members of organizations, and copies of laws and regulations. Although these almanacs were particularly popular in New York, they were also published in the other colonies (for example, by Benjamin Franklin in Philadelphia). It was not at all uncommon for the same almanac-maker to print both regular and pocket almanacs for the same year. The register was of the same character as the pocket almanac, was of larger size, had no literature *per se,* and contained even more miscellaneous governmental data. These registers were the forerunners of modern compendia such as the *Reader's Digest Almanac* and the *World Almanac.*

Paper remained expensive, and the almanac printers frequently advertised for rags for paper-making, more and more as the Revolution approached and emphasis was placed on using home products. The familiar, though possibly apocryphal, picture of Franklin pushing a wheelbarrow loaded with paper down a Philadelphia street may reveal more than the fact that he had rather do it himself: paper was too scarce to be entrusted to delivery boys. Partly because of this scarcity and the high price of paper, both writer and printer used all available space, adding aphorisms to their calendar pages and filling space in the manner of Nathan Bowen in *The New England Almanack* for 1733, who used the four lines left over on the last page to list the days when courts were held in South Carolina. But the paper remained of good quality, and the type was fairly clear, until the Revolution, when paper, ink, and type were poorly made and in short supply.

The content was fairly standard, except for the work of a handful of outstanding personalities who managed to project something of their idiosyncrasies onto the unpromising printed page. Their prejudices, attitudes, and humors occasionally colored their otherwise humdrum pages. Such almanac-makers as Leeds, Franklin, and Ames are interesting from the point of view of originality, as well as for the significance of their contributions to the development of the almanac's form and content. Printers, too, assume their usual importance. Interesting, if relatively minor, contributions to almanac-making during this period include those of six women printers, the printers and authors of foreign-language almanacs, and a Black almanac-maker.

THE LEEDS FAMILY

By the beginning of the eighteenth century, Daniel Leeds had already been compiling almanacs for twelve years. He and his sons, Titan and Felix, issued almanacs for over fifty years. The most famous of the three was Titan, partially because of the public badinage between him and Benjamin Franklin. But it was Daniel who developed an almanac superior to those of his contemporaries and one that was to become the model for his successors. Samuel Atkins had prepared the first Pennsylvania almanac in 1685 (for 1686), but Daniel Leeds, then a Quaker, began his publication the following year and managed to discourage competition for many years. One of his very first actions was to alienate himself from the Friends. His 1688 issue was entirely too satirical at the expense of the good brethren, although Leeds may have intended only to have a little fun. The Friends were not amused and bought up all copies of the almanac for that year. Leeds defected from the Quaker movement, turned Episcopalian, and fought his former colleagues with a vengeance. One of his favorite targets was Jacob Taylor, a Quaker almanac-maker who proved a worthy adversary. The feud between these two probably sold Leeds and Taylor to the same readers—like Titan Leeds's and Ben Franklin's public feud later.

In his 1704 almanac, Leeds directed verses against William Penn, George Fox, and Quakerism generally. He contended that the "unworldly" Friends were altogther too much interested in cash and that their preachers were salaried like any others. In general, however, his almanacs contained an excellent variety of material: astronomical essays; advice for farmers and homemakers; serious verse (philosophical and religious) and light verse (satirical-political), tables of currency conversions; book advertisements; chronologies; customs in foreign lands; lists of meeting places and dates of courts, fairs, and Quakers' meetings; lists of distances from town to town, often including the condition of the roads; aphorisms; and predictions that were humorous and serious (when dealing with portents). When Daniel Leeds made his farewell address to the reader in 1714, he explained that, having served his public for twenty-seven years, he was to be succeeded by his son Titan, already a proficient philomath

> whose natural inclination leads him to Science Mathematical, insomuch that tho he is not sixteen Years of age, he has calculated the Planets Places from *Wings Astronomical Britannica*, and taken their Aspects, and calculated the great Eclipse of the Moon to be in May next, and performed all the Mathematical part of this Almanack himself. Wherefore I have acquitted my self of this Work, and leave it to him, not doubting but he will perform his annual Service to the Satisfaction of the Publick.

Titan continued his father's general format, but announced in the 1715 almanac (now thirty-two pages rather than his father's usual twenty-four) that he was changing the format of the calendar pages. All extraneous information would now fall in the third column (formerly used only for weather predictions): aphorisms, birthdates of famous people, Saints' Days, etc. At the top of the second January page was a brief table showing the sun's place and the planets' motions. "Of Eclipses" appeared below, explaining when and where, and whether their effects would be ill or good. But in 1716, Titan's calendar pages again closely resembled his father's. He dispersed aphorisms in both last and second columns and returned to twelve calendar pages rather than twenty-four.

The ornate title page for Leeds's almanac for 1725 contained "LEEDS" in large Old English script, enclosed in a banner-type block. In 1726 two cherubs bore this banner against a background of sun and stars. Titan reminded his readers that, although almanacs were flourishing, his "Father was the first that appeared to serve his Country [Pennsylvania] in that respect," a statement that coincides with the belief of some historians who, overlooking Sam-

The *American* Almanack

For the Year of Chriſtian Account, 1728.

Unto which is Numbred,

From } By the *Orient* and *Greek* Chriſtians, 7236
the } By the *Jews, Hebrews* and *Rabbins,* 7488
Creation } By the late Computation of *W. W.* 5737

Being the Biſſextile, *or* Leap-Year.

Wherein is contained,

The *Lunations, Eclipſes, Judgment* of the *Weather* the *Spring-Tides, Planets Motions* and *Mutual Aſpeɛts.* With the Birth-Days of the Succeſſive Heirs to the Crown of *Great Britain,* Time of SUN and MOON's *Riſing* and *Setting,* Length of *Days,* the Seven Stars *Riſing, Southing,* and *Setting,* Time of *High-Water, Fairs, Courts,* and *Obſervable* Days.

Fitted to the Latitude of 40 Degrees, and a Meridian of Five Hours Weſt from LONDON, but may without ſenſible Error, ſerve all the adjacent Places, even from *New-found-land* to *Carolina.*

By *TITAN LEEDS,* Philomat.

Printed by S. KEIMER in *Second-ſtreet Philadelphia,* and ſold by *W. Heurtin* Goldſmith in *New York,* David Humphreys *at* Fluſhing on *Long-Iſland.* (Beware of the Counterfeit One.

Printer's warning (on last line) of a counterfeit Leeds almanac for 1728.

uel Atkins, agree with Titan that Daniel Leeds prepared the first almanac in Pennsylvania.

Professional almanac-makers and printers were doubtless accustomed to unscrupulous business practices, for spurious editions of the Leeds almanac had been printed before 1728. But, in this year, the trouble came from within the family. The Titan Leeds almanac for 1728, published by Samuel Keimer in Philadelphia, had a printer's note: "Beware of the Counterfeit One." Andrew Bradford, who had been publishing Titan's work, was now printing an almanac purported to be by brother Felix. Felix, too, has a fancy title page with "LEEDS" in large type, decorated with cherubs. Titan countered with "The Arms of the Family of Leeds." Although it had only twelve calendar pages, this 1728 almanac totaled thirty-two pages in all and was filled with useful information—and a one and one-half page poem "On Drunkenness." Titan frankly confessed to the "Courteous and Candid Reader" that he had changed printers because serving his country was not enough: he wanted to make a profit.

In 1729 and 1730 there was even more confusion about authorship of the Leeds almanacs. In the Titan Leeds almanac for 1729 (printed by Keimer), Leeds added this note to the end of the chronology table: "*Felix Leeds* was hir'd to sign his Name to an Almanack he never wrote one Page of, and has contin'd that base Practice." The charge was unsupported, and we may never know whether it was true. There were *four* Leeds almanacs for 1730—three by Titan and one by Felix. One version of Titan's was printed by both William Bradford in New York and Andrew Bradford in Philadelphia; two others were printed in Philadelphia, one by Nearegress and Arnot, the other by D. Harry. The Felix Leeds edition, also printed by William Bradford in New York, had the same title as Titan's *American Almanack* (the Nearegress and Arnot edition). These two were quite similar, some of the material being identical. The verse and the courts sections, however, were different. D. Harry's publication introduced an embellished coat of arms and a new title: *The Genuine Leeds Almanack*. Again, some items were identical with items in the other almanacs.

In the Felix and Titan *American Almanacks,* the printers shared either manuscripts or printed pages. Regardless of details, it appears that Felix was indeed in cahoots with a rival printer. In *The Genuine Leeds Almanack,* D. Harry set the type differently and printed a better product, although the content of one table, verse, calendar information, and an article on the eclipses were the same as in the *American Almanacks.* D. Harry explained in a preface that he had bought Samuel Keimer's press and that he and Titan had an agreement giving him sole rights to Leeds's almanac copy for 1730 and for 1731. Any edition from anyone else was counterfeit. He piously concluded with a stanza on honor:

> *Honour's a sacred Tye, the Law of Kings,*
> *The noble Mind's distinguishing Perfection,*
> *That aids and strengthens Virtue when it meets her*
> *And imitates her Actions where she is not:*
> *It ought not to be sported with.*

But 1730 was D. Harry's only year to print a Titan Leeds almanac, despite the announcement that the printer had a contract with Titan for 1730 *and* 1731. In this comedy of pirated editions, the honorable man is hard to find.

Titan apparently was reconciled to the Bradfords, for they both were printing his almanacs for 1731: William, in New York; and William's son Andrew in Philadelphia. There were two versions, by the same author and by the same printers. The information was generally the same, but verses in one were homiletic; in the other, mythological and Christian. In the latter version, Titan admitted:

> *Many people do me blame*
> *My Printer for to change,*
> *But I do not think it so,*
> *For all the World's the same.*

Andrew Bradford was again publishing Leeds's *American Almanack for . . . 1736.* The conflict over, Titan no longer was compelled to specify "GENUINE" in his title, although the banner still retained the word. Two separate editions with similar contents appeared in 1737, but William Bradford was clearly a better printer than his son; there were fewer printing errors in William's edition.

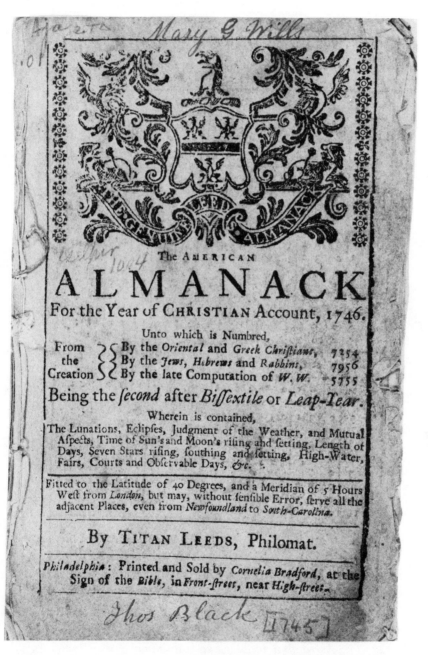

The AMERICAN
ALMANACK
For the Year of CHRISTIAN Account, 1746.

Unto which is Numbred,

From	By the *Oriental* and *Greek Christians*,	7254
the	By the *Jews*, *Hebrews* and *Rabbins*,	7956
Creation	By the late Computation of *W. W.*	5755

Being the *second* after *Biſſextile* or *Leap-Year*.

Wherein is contained,

The Lunations, Eclipſes, Judgment of the Weather, and Mutual Aſpects, Time of Sun's and Moon's riſing and ſetting, Length of Days, Seven Stars riſing, ſouthing and ſetting, High-Water, Fairs, Courts and Obſervable Days, &c.

Fitted to the Latitude of 40 Degrees, and a Meridian of 5 Hours Weſt from *London*, but may, without ſenſible Error, ſerve all the adjacent Places, even from *Newfoundland* to *South-Carolina*.

By TITAN LEEDS, Philomat.

Philadelphia: Printed and Sold by *Cornelia Bradford*, at the Sign of the *Bible*, in *Front-ſtreet*, near *High-ſtreet*.

"The Genuine Leeds Almanac," 1746; printed by Cornelia Bradford.

71

In the two versions for the following year, the printers added prefaces (signed "W.B." and "A.B." in Philadelphia, "W.B." in New York), announcing that Titan Leeds was now truly dead, but that he had supplied them "with his Calculations for an Almanack for seven Years to come." Ben Franklin, of course, had announced Titan's "death" six years before. The Leeds family had finished writing almanacs, but the Bradfords continued to use the Titan Leeds name. In 1744 William whimsically titled his edition *The Dead Man's Almanack.*

NATHANIEL AMES, FATHER AND SON

For seventy years of the eighteenth century, the almanacs of the Ameses edified and entertained a prodigious number of readers. The spelling on the title pages alternated between Nathanael and Nathaniel, but the latter was more common. There were three Nathaniel Ameses—grandfather, father, and son. The two who were almanac-makers can be easily distinguished by referring to "the elder" or "Dr. Ames, II," and to "the younger" or "Dr. Ames, III." The dates of their almanacs also indicate the authors: after his father's death in 1764, Nathaniel III prepared subsequent editions. One authority erroneously states that the first Nathaniel Ames prepared an almanac until his death in 1764 and that "His son carried the almanac on until 1795 when it was then continued by his son, Nathaniel the third. All three men were certainly cut from the same cloth and by now it is hard to tell one from the other." [1] It was the second Nathaniel Ames who died in 1764. This second Nathaniel was the first Ames almanac-maker; the first Nathaniel was an astronomer. When the second Nathaniel Ames died in 1764, the work was continued by Nathaniel the third until 1775, not 1795.

Nathaniel Ames, II, was born in Bridgewater, Massachusetts, in 1708. He published the first of his popular almanac series in 1725: *The Astronomical Diary and Almanack for . . . 1726.* In 1732 he moved to Dedham, Massachusetts, and his name has since been them difcover her, they give notice to thofe near them and then to the reft, and in a few minutes they all collect them-felves round her, and are fo happy at having found this fole fupport of their ftate; that they will long remain quiet in their fituation. Nay the fcent of her body is fo attractive, that the flighteft touch of her body along any thing will attract the bees to it, and induce them to purfue any path fhe takes.——My attachment to the Queen and tender regard for her precious life, makes me ardently wifh I might here clofe the detail of this operation, which I am afraid when attempted by unfkilful hands, will coft many of their lives.'

Mrs. CATHARINE M'CAULAY.

Mrs. Catherine McCaulay, English author. Illustration from Ames's
Astronomical Diary for 1772.

73

associated with this city, as physician, astronomer, almanac-maker, and tavern-keeper. Dr. Ames's father, Nathaniel, I, had been deeply interested in astronomy and had imparted his knowledge and his interest to his son. In 1735 Dr. Ames married Mary Fisher of Dedham, who did not live long after their marriage. In 1740 he married Deborah Fisher (the women were not sisters) and they had five children, two of whom attained distinction: Nathaniel, III, a Harvard graduate, physician, and almanac-maker; and Fisher, who entered Harvard when he was twelve, graduated at sixteen, became a famous lawyer, and helped draft the Constitution.

Although it was the fashion to denigrate lawyers in colonial almanacs, Dr. Ames, II, probably had the best personal grounds of all the almanac-makers. Dr. Ames was generally amiable; but he was especially vituperative toward lawyers. His first wife had owned a tavern. After her death in 1737, her mother tried to recover the tavern property. In the ensuing lawsuit, Dr. Ames claimed his wife's estate through a son (who had died as an infant, about a year after his mother) according to Province Law;

The tavern belonging to Nathaniel Ames, II., in Dedham, Massachusetts.

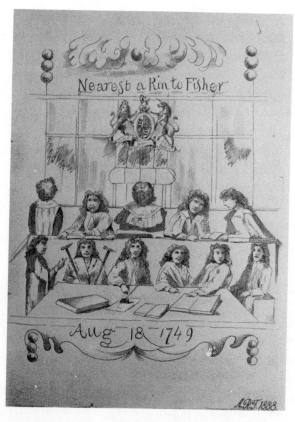

Ames's cartoon of the Supreme Court Judges.

his wife's family claimed the property by English Common Law. Ames won the case, but two of the eleven judges of the Supreme Court were against him. Ames took down his tavern sign and substituted a cartoon of the judges, in which all were easily identifiable. Each man was shown studying the Province Laws—except for the two dissenters, who had their backs turned to their law books. One of the dissenting judges—no less than the Chief Justice —sent the sheriff to arrest Ames and confiscate the libelous portrait. But Ames was warned and quickly managed, with the help of Matt. 16:4, to substitute another sign for the sheriff: "A wicked and adulterous generation seeketh after a sign, and there shall be no sign given unto it." [2]

<hr>

75

The second Dr. Ames (Nathaniel, III), who continued his father's almanac until 1776, was not the genial gentleman that his father was. In fact, his diary shows him to have been rather testy at times, a man who seemed to have a genuine liking only for farmers. His pet peeve was printers: "for they are all Knaves, Liars, Villains to serve their interests and when they appear most Friendly have most of the Devil in their Hearts." [3] Tourtellot says that Dr. Ames the younger finished his almanac early in the year and then fought with his printers the rest of the year.[4] Ames the younger did, however, continue his father's good work, patterning almanacs after those published by Ames the elder from 1725 to 1764, with contents comparable in variety and quality.

THE FRANKLIN FAMILY

The combination role of printer-author is particularly noteworthy in the Franklin family, for all four of those who published almanacs were, at some point in their careers, both printer and author.

James Franklin, born in 1697, was the first almanac-maker in the Franklin family. He began the "Poor ——" almanacs in America with *The Rhode Island Almanack* for 1728 by "Poor Robin." The ancestor of this type of almanac was the 1663 British *Poor Robin*, the first humorous almanac in England, "Written by Poor Robin, Knight of the Burnt Island, a well-willer to the Mathematicks."

To the British "Poor Robin" nothing was sacred: science, religion, weather predictions, and prognostications in general were targets for ridicule. The contents were those usually found in almanacs but were burlesqued. For example, the saints' days were offset with a list of "sinners' days" or "saints of the Roundheads": Cesar Borgia, Moll Cutpurse, Robin Hood, the Knave of Clubs, and Friar Bacon. The prognostications parodied those of the serious astrologer: in December 1684, "Saturn and Mercury are in conjunction with Venus, and meet every night at a club to invent mischief; therefore it is ten to one if some shops be not broke open before they part." [5]

James Franklin was a worthy heir to this kind of foolishness. Even before he printed his first almanac, he had already caused some excitement in Boston. Franklin's contract to print the local newspaper, which included the job as local postmaster, had been given to a rival printer, so Franklin started a newspaper of his own, *The New-England Courant*. He and a group of friends, called "The Hell-Fire Club of Boston" by the Mathers, printed exposés of political shenanigans and consistently opposed whatever the establishment favored. Franklin even took on Cotton Mather, speaking out against smallpox inoculation—mainly because Mather was for it. To operate within the Bay Colony's stringent legal restrictions, James often resorted to stratagems, such as the time when he temporarily turned over his editorship to his brother Ben. After about five years of battling the local leaders and the government (and a month in jail for tangling with Mather), James left Boston in 1726 for Newport, Rhode Island.

The Rhode Island Almanack for 1728 was the second issue from his Rhode Island press. James Franklin had served an apprenticeship in England and had learned to be a good printer. From the very beginning of Franklin's journalistic career with *The New-England Courant*, his writing had exhibited characteristics later known as "American"—fresh, lively, natural, and easy. James Franklin's prefaces exhibit the same brand of sprightly humor that his brother Ben later used in *Poor Richard*, the world's most famous almanac. Between 1728 and 1741 *Poor Robin* was published regularly, except for 1736, the year after James died. Samuel Maxwell had compiled the 1731 edition, but "Poor Robin" was back in 1732 as author. Joseph Stafford compiled the almanacs for 1737 and for 1738 at the request of James's widow, Ann, who was then in charge of the printing house. From 1739 to 1741 the almanac was prepared by "Poor Robin, revived" (the widow Ann herself, perhaps).

Ann Franklin (discussed in more detail later in this chapter) was the first New England woman printer and one of the six women printers in America before 1800 who printed almanacs. As early as 1730 she is supposed to have helped with the printing of a broadside (a *Perpetual Almanack*) which involved difficult typesetting.[6] Ann was the colony printer, printing all the official governmental forms, such as laws and ballots for election. She also printed legal forms, pamphlets, and books.

James Franklin, Jr., carried on the almanac-printing tradition of his family. His Uncle Ben relates in his autobiography how he went to Newport and returned with his ten-year-old nephew, sent the little boy to school, taught him the printing business, and "assisted him with an assortment of new types, those of his father being in a manner worn out. Thus it was that I made my brother ample amends for the service I had deprived him of by leaving him so early."[7] James, Jr., managed the family press from 1748, when Ann retired, until his death in 1762. However, as late as 1758 bills were still made out to "Ann & James Franklin."[8] James, Jr., printed Rhode Island's currency and also established a newspaper, *The Newport Mercury*, in 1758. The most important of his publications, for our purposes, were his *Poor Job* almanacs, published from 1750 to 1758. He carried on the tradition of his parents' *Poor Robin* and his uncle's *Poor Richard* in his humorous prefaces and in the excellent overall quality of his work. As in *Poor Robin* and *Poor Richard*, the good-humored and informal prefaces were the most entertaining part of *Poor Job*. The 1751 edition has the distinction of being the first in Rhode Island to include an illustration, and the 1752 *Poor Job* contained one of the best explanations of the official changeover to the New Style calendar given in any almanac that year.

In 1760 James, Jr., printed the last almanac published by his firm. The author, Nathaniel Whitefield, told the reader "That a Kinsman of mine, George Whitefield has employ'd all his latter Years in travelling . . . for the good of Souls." George Whitefield, British evangelist, was a real person. But "Nathaniel Whitefield," like "Poor Job," was probably a fictitious name, for no such person has been found in Newport's historical records.[9]

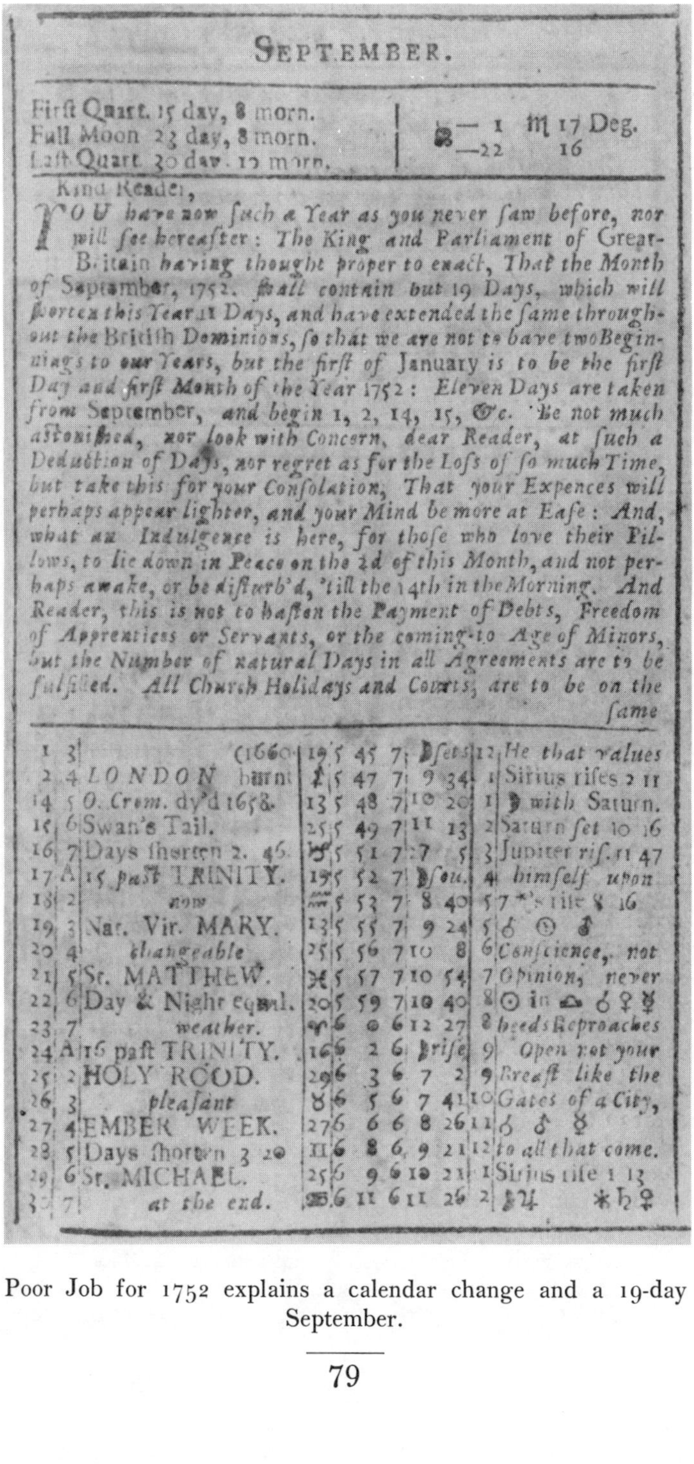

SEPTEMBER.

First Quart. 15 day, 8 morn.	☊ — 1	♏ 17 Deg.
Full Moon 23 day, 8 morn.	—22	16
Last Quart. 30 day, 10 morn.		

Kind Reader,

YOU have now such a Year as you never saw before, nor will see hereafter: The King and Parliament of Great-Britain having thought proper to enact, That the Month of September, 1752. shall contain but 19 Days, which will shorten this Year 11 Days, and have extended the same throughout the British Dominions, so that we are not to have two Beginnings to our Years, but the first of January is to be the first Day and first Month of the Year 1752: Eleven Days are taken from September, and begin 1, 2, 14, 15, &c. Be not much astonished, nor look with Concern, dear Reader, at such a Deduction of Days, nor regret as for the Loss of so much Time, but take this for your Consolation, That your Expences will perhaps appear lighter, and your Mind be more at Ease: And, what an Indulgence is here, for those who love their Pillows, to lie down in Peace on the 2d of this Month, and not perhaps awake, or be disturb'd, 'till the 14th in the Morning. And Reader, this is not to hasten the Payment of Debts, Freedom of Apprentices or Servants, or the coming to Age of Minors, but the Number of natural Days in all Agreements are to be fulfilled. All Church Holidays and Courts, are to be on the same

1	3	(1666	19	5	45	7	☽ sets		12	He that values
2	4	LONDON burnt	♐	5	47	7	9	34	1	Sirius rises 2 11
14	5	O. Crom. dy'd 1658.	13	5	48	7	10	20	1	☽ with Saturn.
15	6	Swan's Tail.	25	5	49	7	11	13	2	Saturn set 10 16
16	7	Days shorten 2. 46	♑	5	51	7	7	5	3	Jupiter ris. 11 47
17	A	15 past TRINITY.	19	5	52	7	☽ sou.		4	himself upon
18	2	now	♒	5	53	7	8	40	5	7 *'s rise 8 16
19	3	Nat. Vir. MARY.	13	5	55	7	9	24	5	☌ ☉ ♂
20	4	changeable	25	5	56	7	10	8	6	Conscience, not
21	5	St. MATTHEW.	♓	5	57	7	10	54	7	Opinion, never
22	6	Day & Night equal.	20	5	59	7	10	40	8	☉ in ♎ ☌ ♀ ☿
23	7	weather.	♈	6	0	6	12	27	8	heeds Reproaches
24	A	16 past TRINITY.	16	6	2	6	☽ rise		9	Open not your
25	2	HOLY ROOD.	29	6	3	6	7	2	9	Breast like the
26	3	pleasant	♉	6	5	6	7	41	10	Gates of a City,
27	4	EMBER WEEK.	27	6	6	6	8	26	11	☌ ♂ ☿
28	5	Days shorten 3 20	♊	6	8	6	9	21	12	to all that come.
29	6	St. MICHAEL.	25	6	9	6	10	21	1	Sirius rise 1 13
30	7	at the end.	♋	6	11	6	11	26	2	☌ ☽ ♃ ✱ ♄ ♀

Poor Job for 1752 explains a calendar change and a 19-day September.

When James, Jr., died in 1762, Ann Franklin again was in charge of the business.[10] This time she was newspaper publisher and editor, as well as colony printer.

Benjamin Franklin, the most famous of the Franklins, was early exposed to the almanac business. As an apprentice, he ran away from his brother James and sought work first in Philadelphia, then in New York with William Bradford, who kindly referred him to his son Andrew in Philadelphia. Ben worked for Samuel Keimer, who was printing Jacob Taylor's almanacs, and for Andrew Bradford, who was printing Titan Leeds's. Ben finally opened his own press in Philadelphia. Thomas Godfrey, Franklin's partner, prepared the almanacs published by their firm for 1729, 1730, and 1731. They also printed John Jerman's almanacs and imported the British *Poor Robin.*[11]

As Richard Saunders, Franklin began a series of almanacs under the title *Poor Richard,* which he prepared from 1732–1758. Phenomenal success resulted in three printings of the first issue. *Poor Richard's Almanack* is by far the best known of all American almanacs, although it may not be the best. Having spent eighteen months in London in 1725 and 1726, Franklin was familiar with the British *Poor Robin* and with *The English Apollo (Apollo Anglicanus)* by Richard Saunders, noted eighteenth-century almanac-maker and physician.

The first issue of *Poor Richard* contained twenty-four pages and was printed both plain and interleaved. Franklin tells about this project in his *Autobiography:*

> In 1732 I first publish'd my Almanack, under the name of *Richard Saunders;* it was continu'd by me about twenty-five years, commonly call'd *Poor Richard's Almanack.* I endeavor'd to make it both entertaining and useful, and it accordingly came to be in such demand, that I reap'd considerable profit from it, vending annually near ten thousand. And observing that it was generally read, scarce any neighborhood in the province being without it, I consider'd it as a proper vehicle for conveying instruction among the common people, who bought scarcely any other books; I therefore filled all the little spaces that occurr'd between the remarkable days in the calendar with proverbial sentences, chiefly such as inculcated industry and frugality, as the means of procuring wealth, and

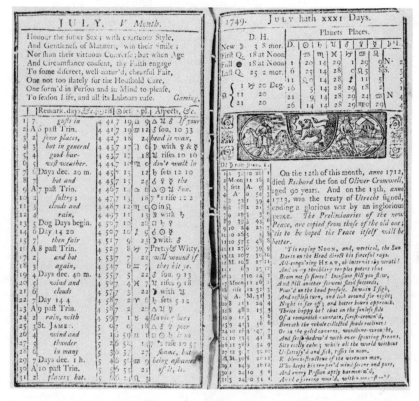

Poor Richard Improved for 1749 included first example of pictorial illustrations on calendar pages.

thereby securing virtue; it being more difficult for a man in want, to act always honestly, as, to use here one of those proverbs *it is hard for an empty sack to stand upright.*[12]

Benjamin Franklin adopted the format and general style of the Titan Leeds almanacs of Philadelphia.[13] It was quite common to "borrow," and much of Franklin's material was taken from other almanacs and from foreign writers. (The prediction of the death of his rival, Titan Leeds, in his very first issue, is the most famous of his borrowings—a replay of the Swift-Partridge hoax.)

Franklin's major contribution to the almanac was not the addition of any particular feature, despite his introduction of the pictorial calendar page that still exists in many of today's almanacs.

81

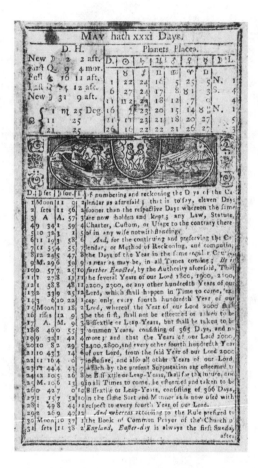

Gemini and seasonal art in *Poor Richard Improved* for 1752.

Aphorisms had long been interspersed on calendar pages; prefaces had been amusing; and humor was by then a fairly common commodity in almanacs. What Franklin did was to create two characters, Richard and Bridget Saunders, and to write his borrowed maxims in a more quotable style than any of his predecessors. His almanac was outstanding for its scope. There was hardly a subject on which Poor Richard did not comment. "Poor Richard says" became an American expression and, although his wisdom was not original, Poor Richard did "say" it better than anyone else.

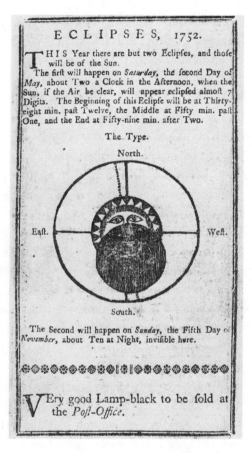

An eclipse of the sun, from *Poor
Richard Improved*, 1752.

Using the same kind of humor that had been so successful in the Mrs. Silence Dogood series that Ben had written for his brother's newspaper, Richard and Bridget Saunders made outspoken, shrewd, and comical observations, staying in character as struggling tradespeople. As Faÿ says, Poor Richard could speak Ben's mind.[14] Beneath the pseudonym was a real person with whom readers could identify. The upshot of the creation of this famous character was that Ben Franklin actually became Richard Saunders in the eyes of those who knew him.

As Franklin became more urbane and more cosmopolitan, his almanacs took on a different tone. The humor was less broad. After 1748, as *Poor Richard Improved,* the almanac was not only decorated with woodcuts but had, in general, a more sophisticated air.[15] The volume increased from twenty-four pages to thirty-six. The reader was still getting his money's worth, but the character of the prefaces changed, as did the quality. The strength of Franklin's early almanac had been a peasant strength, a rustic's enthusiasm; as Franklin became more polished, the almanac developed more gentlemanly restraint. Of course, it is an open question whether the "improvement" was anything but a concession to Franklin's more genteel milieu.

Franklin's last *Poor Richard* was the 1758 edition. Opinions differ regarding the length of Franklin's association with his almanac, despite the author's claim in his *Autobiography* that he wrote the almanac until 1757, at which time he prepared the 1758 issue just before leaving for England on government business. From 1758 to 1766, Franklin's name continued to appear as co-printer with Hall. After 1766 the almanac was published by Hall and Sellers.

In the 1758 almanac appeared one of Franklin's most famous (if not the most famous) short pieces: "Father Abraham's Speech" or "The Way to Wealth" or "The Sayings of Poor Richard." "Father Abraham's Speech" was a collection of sayings from twenty-five issues of *Poor Richard* and *Poor Richard Improved.* Poor Richard attended an auction and supposedly heard an old man's wise reply to the question of what was wrong with the world. Franklin, famous for almost everything except his modesty, wrote of the work:

> The piece, being universally approved, was copied in all the newspapers of the Continent, reprinted in Britain on a broad side, to be stuck up in houses; two translations were made of it in French, and great numbers bought by the clergy and gentry, to distribute gratis among their poor parishioners and tenants. In Pennsylvania, as it discouraged useless expense in foreign superfluities, some thought it had its share of influence in producing that growing plenty of money, which was observable for several years after its publication.[16]

According to Spofford, there were seventy-five editions of "Father Abraham's Speech" in English; sixty in French; and fifteen in German.[17] There were, in all, fifteen different translations and more than four hundred reprintings. As "La Science du Bonhomme Richard," it was very popular in France. The *Bonhomme Richard* of John Paul Jones was named for Franklin's *Poor Richard*. The story is that Jones was in France waiting for a ship promised by the French government when he saw in *Poor Richard*, "If you would have your Business done, go; if not, send." Jones went to see about his ship himself and got it.[18]

Franklin's prefaces and his maxims are considered in detail in Part II. Let it suffice here to say that "Richard Saunders, the Philomath of the *Almanack*, was the Sir Roger de Coverley of the masses, pilfering the world's store of aphorisms, and adapting them to the circumstances and the understanding of the poor." [19]

Although Ben Franklin could have claimed several vocational titles, he chose to refer to himself as printer. This version of the "Premature Epitaph" that he wrote for himself in 1728 appeared in Ames's almanac for 1771, differing slightly from the famous copy of the epitaph in Franklin's own handwriting reproduced in many works on Franklin:

> Mr. FRANKLIN's Epitaph on himself curious for conveying such solemn Ideas in the Stile of his Occupation.
>
> The Body of BENJAMIN FRANKLIN
> Printer,
> Like the Covering of an old Book
> Its contents torn out
> And stript of its Lettering and Gilding,
> Lies here, Food for Worms;
> But the Work shall not be lost,
> It will (as he believ'd) appear once more
> In a New and more beautiful Edition
> Corrected and amended
> By the Author.
> He was born January 6th 1706 and
> died ——— 17–

NATHANAEL LOW

There were many excellent almanacs in the last half of the eighteenth century. Although those of the Ameses are generally conceded to be the most outstanding, another Nathanael started a remarkably successful almanac series which lasted from 1762 to 1827. Nathanael Low, born in Ipswich, Massachusetts, in 1740, eventually settled as a physician in South Berwick, Maine. He prepared almanacs from 1762 until his death in 1808, except for the year 1766. The series was continued by his son, also named Nathanael, for another twenty years. The first Low issue, *An Astronomical Diary or an Almanack*, was signed "Nathanael Low, Professor of Astronomy in Ipswich."

Notable characteristics of Low's almanacs were literary erudition and patriotic fervor. These, with the usual variety of miscellaneous information expected by readers, made a winning combination. In his political essays, Low was generally original; but he drew upon many sources for his non-political verse and articles. He acknowledged sources or used quotation marks, and he specifically stated in the 1764 issue that his verse was entirely original. The general tone of his material was patriotic, but sometimes his literary inclinations won out: the frontispiece for 1773 is a woodcut portrait of John Dryden.

Low courageously printed original political articles in his almanacs under his own name during the Revolutionary period, when many essayists and pamphleteers were using pseudonyms. In the 1767 issue of the *American Calendar* he apologized for not having produced an almanac for 1766 because of the "perplexed" political situation. A featured article was "Recapitulation of Events Which Happened in Consequence of the Late American Stamp Act."

Low was as frank as Benjamin West and Nathaniel Ames when it came to liberty for the colonies, and may even have outspoken them when he wrote on the March page of his almanac for 1771 of "A horrid infernal massacre most inhumanly and barbarously com-

An Astronomical DIARY; Or,
ALMANACK
For the Year of Christian Æra,
I 7 7 4.
Being the second YEAR after BISSEXTILE or LEAP YEAR.
And the 14th Year of the Reign of K. GEORGE IIId.
Containing, besides the usual Astronomical Calculations
&c. many curious, useful and entertaining Particulars.

By NATHANAEL LOW.

UNgrateful those, who would no Tears allow
To him, who gave them Peace and Empire too!
Princes who fear'd him, griev'd; concern'd to see
No Pitch of Glory from the Grave is free.

BOSTON: Printed and Sold by j. KNEELAND, in Milk
Street:—Sold also by the Printers & Booksellers. 1774.

Portrait of Oliver Cromwell on the cover of a Low almanac for 1774.

mitted by the British troops, on the inhabitants of Boston—5th day 1770."

In the same year he condemned the use of tea; in 1776 he included an address to the Army, an account of the Lexington battle, and a letter to the Tories. For two crucial decades, his almanacs, like those of Nathaniel Ames and Benjamin West, made important contributions to the revolutionary cause.

BENJAMIN WEST AND "BICKERSTAFF"

One of the most prolific almanac-makers of the last half of the century was Benjamin West (1730–1818), mathematician and Brown University professor. He was a member of the American Academy of Arts and Sciences and the American Philosophical Society, a graduate of Harvard (A.M., 1770) and of Brown (LL.D., 1792).

West published almanacs at Providence, Rhode Island, from 1763 through 1781. The first three of the West series were printed by William Goddard (1763–1765). The initial issue included a table of kings and queens of Europe and its capital cities, a common ingredient in almanacs; but West added an uncommon parenthesis: "(Clement XIII, Pope of Rome)." Sarah and William Goddard printed West's almanac for 1766; in 1768 the firm was Sarah Goddard and John Carter. In 1769 Goddard and Carter published a rival almanac, *The New-England Town and Country Almanack* by "Abraham Weatherwise," and Mein and Fleeming of Boston printed the West almanac, "Sold by Benjamin West (the author) in Providence." In 1781, the West almanac became *Bickerstaff's New-England Almanack* and continued until 1814. From 1781 to 1787 he authored *The North American Calendar; or Rhode Island Almanack.*

Meanwhile, West also used the pseudonym "Isaac Bickerstaff" in *Bickerstaff's Boston Almanack* for almost every year between 1768 and 1793. "Bickerstaff" could teach history as well as mathematics. The first issue in the Boston series included a modest undertaking called "A General View of the Whole World" (four pages). For 1778 there was a *Bickerstaff's New York Almanack*. West repudiated one edition of *Bickerstaff's Boston Almanack* for 1786 and put out another with the word *Genuine* in the title. Benjamin may not have written all the almanacs attributed to "West," as there was very probably more than one "Bickerstaff." [20]

West furnished the calculations for more than one almanac, sometimes during the same years; he changed the name of his almanacs; and he changed printers. It is therefore difficult to assess the quantity of his production. West was also involved in squabbles with printers and was the cause of others. He apparently had no serious disagreements with the Goddards, but he seems to have had considerable difficulties with John Carter. As early as October 18, 1766, Carter stated in the *Providence Gazette* that West had

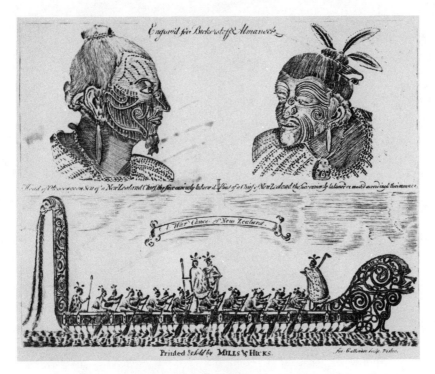

Frontispiece from West's *Bickerstaff's Boston Almanack*, 1774.

89

Man with jacob staff, from *Bickerstaff's Boston Almanack*, for 1786.

sold him sole rights, but that the same almanac was being printed in Boston:

> Charity bids us hope, that those Gentlemen of Boston have more Virtue and Honor, than to persue under-handed measures to obtain the Property of others, and that Mr. West could not be deluded by any Consideration, to deviate from the Paths of Rectitude, and risque the Loss of his Credit, by selling a second Time what he had already disposed of.[21]

Prof. West, who seems to have spent more of his time publishing than teaching, must have been somewhat chagrined by this public innuendo—particularly if it were true. (West's *The New England Almanack* was also printed in 1772 by Ebenezer Campbell in Newport. Pirated, or sold "a second time"?) In 1781, Carter brought out two almanacs, differing only in the title page: *The New-England Almanack* by Benjamin West and *Bickerstaff's New-England Almanack* by Isaac Bickerstaff, Esq., the latter published probably in a fit of pique after the first had been issued. Compounding his vengeance by using the same pseudonym from the series that West had begun in 1768, Carter continued his Bickerstaffs until 1799. West, who was calculating Ezekiel Russell's *American Almanack*, retaliated by also furnishing the material for Russell's Bickerstaff almanacs from 1783 to 1793.[22]

West authored the *North American Calendar*, published by Bennett Wheeler from 1780 to 1805. Isaiah Thomas' almanac for 1784 tells us why: ". . . West was the original Bickerstaff and had ceased to publish his annuals in 1779 because of those persons who had brought the name into disrepute." This almanac was in great competition with Carter's Bickerstaff almanacs. And so the feud continued on a commercial basis.

Benjamin West prepared some of the best almanacs of the eighteenth century, combining dependable almanac calculations with literary excellence and topicality. Printed during a most interesting period of American history, West's almanacs also reflect the political unrest from 1763 until after the Revolution, as seen by an outstanding American patriot.

NATHAN DABOLL

Nathan Daboll (1750–1818), of Groton, Connecticut, began a series of almanacs in New London in 1773. Daboll was a mathematician, and a teacher of navigation and nautical astronomy. Although he received little formal education, his remarkable aptitude for mathematics enabled him to master the subject while he earned his living as a cooper. In 1799, Daboll published a textbook on arithmetic, *Daboll's Complete Schoolmaster's Assistant*. Later he prepared a navigation guide for seamen, *Daboll's Practical Navigator*, which was published posthumously.

For several years Timothy Green had published almanacs by Clark Elliott, who had in 1770 begun using the pseudonym "Edmund Freebetter." Under the Freebetter pseudonym, Daboll calculated almanacs for Green from 1773 to 1793. During Nathan Daboll's career as almanac-maker, he occasionally prepared sheet almanacs (broadsides) and registers, as well as standard almanacs.

Titles for his works varied. Two major series are evident: Daboll as Freebetter from 1773 to 1793, and Daboll signing his own name from 1793 to 1818. During these years his almanacs included: *The Connecticut Almanack* for 1773; *Freebetter's New-England Almanack* for 1773, 1776, and 1777; *Freebetter's Connecticut Almanack* for 1774; *Daboll's New-England Almanack* for 1775; *The New-England Almanack* (as Freebetter) for 1777 through 1792, and for 1793 until after the turn of the century as Nathan Daboll. He also prepared sheet almanacs for 1791 through 1801 (except for 1793 and 1794). From 1785 through 1795 (except for 1787 and 1788), he calculated *Green's Register*, which in 1785 was called *A Register for the State of Connecticut*.

Daboll made occasional allusions to the Revolution. Some of his almanacs completely ignored the political conflict; others included references that were usually either satirical or factual. Stirring patriotic essays, like those of Ames and West, were nonexistent in his work. The title page of *Freebetter's Connecticut Almanack* for 1774 featured "a curious cut of his M——y's WIG" (George III). The owner of the Boston Public Library copy added in his own handwriting: "The 31 of this [August] was a fast on the account of the danger we were in from the king's Troops." In *Daboll's New-England Almanack* for 1775 was a cut of "The Patriotic BISHOP, Dr. JONATHAN SHIPLEY" and the text of Shipley's speech, which the bishop had intended to present to the House of Lords. "Boston Cannonaded" was the subject of the title page cartoon in Freebetter's for 1776. A man with a "Port Bill" protruding from his pocket is pouring tea down the throat of a woman (America) forcibly held on the ground by one man, while a third at her feet lewdly lifts her skirts.

In *The New-England Almanack* for 1777 (New London: Timothy Green), a dialogue between two Britishers, called "The Politicians," ridiculed England's plan to conquer America: close their ports, dig a ditch to keep the Americans from escaping, set the air afire, and "let the clouds down upon their heads." Peter, the "newsmonger and Politician," tells Dick, "a Country Man," that England has "a grander scheme" than the one to conquer America: send horse regiments to the moon; board a comet there; land on Mars, Jupiter, Saturn, and the other stars and planets; "and take them every one, and bring them to England, and make them pay taxes." *Freebetter's New-England Almanack* for 1777 (Hartford: N. Patten) had a map, "A VIEW of the Present Seat of WAR, at and near NEW YORK." "*A few Thoughts on the* TIMES," primarily on tax burdens, appeared in *The New-England Almanack* for 1778. Daboll included a five-page biography of George Washington in 1782, the Articles of Confederation in 1783, and the complete text of the Treaty between Great Britain and the United States of America, in *A Register for the State of Connecticut* for 1785.

Daboll's almanacs contained a balanced mixture of typical material: the usual calendar information (including weather predictions); tables of interest, currency values, and distances between towns; meeting places and dates of courts; "Freemen's Meetings"; seasonal and moralistic calendar verse; homiletic essays and maxims; a few humorous poems, songs, and anecdotes; household how-to's; and occasional cures. Daboll did not stress astrology and rarely printed the Man of Signs. His almanacs, ex-

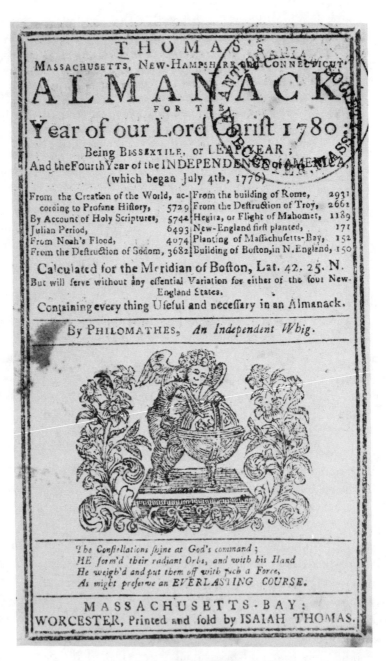

THOMAS's
MASSACHUSETTS, NEW-HAMPSHIRE and CONNECTICUT
ALMANACK
FOR THE
Year of our Lord Christ 1780:
Being BISSEXTILE, or LEAP YEAR;
And the Fourth Year of the INDEPENDENCE of AMERICA,
(which began July 4th, 1776)

From the Creation of the World, according to Profane History,	5729	From the building of Rome,	2931
		From the Destruction of Troy,	2662
By Account of Holy Scriptures,	5744	Hegira, or Flight of Mahomet,	1189
Julian Period,	6493	New-England first planted,	171
From Noah's Flood,	4074	Planting of Massachusetts-Bay,	152
From the Destruction of Sodom,	3682	Building of Boston, in N. England,	150

Calculated for the Meridian of Boston, Lat. 42. 25. N.
But will serve without any essential Variation for either of the four New-England States.
Containing every thing Useful and necessary in an Almanack.

By PHILOMATHES, *An Independent Whig.*

The Constellations shine at God's command;
HE form'd their radiant Orbs, and with his Hand
He weigh'd and put them off with such a Force,
As might preserve an EVERLASTING COURSE.

MASSACHUSETTS-BAY:
WORCESTER, Printed and sold by ISAIAH THOMAS.

Isaiah Thomas' almanac for 1780.

tremely popular throughout New England, were continued by members of the Daboll family in Connecticut for nearly a century.

THE THOMASES: ISAIAH AND ROBERT B.

There were two "Thomas" almanacs: one printed by Isaiah Thomas, Sr., of Boston and Worcester from 1772 to 1803 (and subsequently by his son Isaiah, Jr.); and one by Robert B. Thomas, from 1793 to 1856 (and continued to the present day by other editors). Unrelated, the two Thomases were serious rivals, and their almanac prefaces reveal a heated feud.

Isaiah Thomas is famous for publishing *The History of Printing in America* in 1810 and for founding the American Antiquarian

Portrait of Isaiah Thomas
by Ethan Allen Greenwood.

The flying days and months are hurrying on,
Years press on years, impatient to be gone,
With eager steps to bring th' important hour,
When angry fires this system shall devour.

Man with jacob staff, from *Thomas's
New-England Almanack* for 1775.

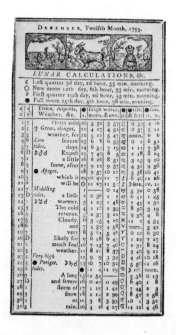

Calendar pages for December and April, from *Thomas's Massachusetts, Connecticut, Rhode-Island, New Hampshire, and Vermont Almanack* for 1797.

Society in Worcester, Massachusetts, in 1812. He began his almanacs with the *Massachusetts Calendar* in Boston in 1772 and had published several almanacs before he moved to Worcester in 1775, including the first to bear his name in the title: *Thomas's New England Almanack, or the Massachusetts Calendar* for 1775. Thomas, in his letters, credits Benjamin West with the calculations for 1775 to 1786; Dr. Samuel Stearns with those from 1787 to 1790; and Daniel George with those from 1791 to 1794. The remainder may have been calculated by West.[23]

As postmaster of Worcester, Isaiah Thomas followed the traditional combination of postmaster-publisher. His newspaper, *The Spy*, was delivered by post-riders who also served as couriers for the Patriots. Only two days after he moved to Worcester (April 19, 1775), the famous battle at Lexington took place, and the "Patriot Printer" helped Paul Revere warn the countryside.[24] The 1775 almanac included, on its first page, a rather distorted woodcut illustration of a man with a jacob staff, and an illustration of Hannah Snell, female soldier, which accompanied her life story. The 1789 edition was notable for illustrations on the calendar pages. For example, for March, there are a boy and girl en route to school, and a ram; for September, the scales, some reapers, and a mother and child. This type of illustration appears in some almanacs today.

The Lawer's Pedigree,

Tune, *Our Polly is a sad Slut.*

A Beggar had a Beadle,
  A Beadle had a Yeoman ;
A Yeoman had a prentice,
  A prentice had a Freeman :
The Freeman had a Master,
  The Master had a Leafe ;
The Leafe made him a Gentleman,
  And Justice of the peace.
The Justice being rich,
  And gallant in Defire,
He marry'd with a Lady,
  And fo he had a Squire :
The Spuire had a Knight
  Of Courage bold and stout ;
The Knight he had a Lord,
  And fo it came about.
The Lord he had an Earl ;
  His Country he forfook,
He travel'd into Spain,
  And there he had a Duke :
The Duke he had a prince,
  The prince a King of Hope
The King he had an Emperor
  The Emperor a Pope.
Thus, as the Story fays,
  The pedigree did run;
The Pope he had a Friar,
  The Friar had a Nun :

The Nun, she was with Child
  And fo her Credit funk
The Father was a Friar,
  The Iffue was a Monk.
The Monk he had a Son,
  With whom he did inhabit,
Who when the Father died,
  The Son became Lord Abbot :
Lord Abbot had a Maid,
  And catch'd her in the Dark,
And fomething did to her,
  And fo he had a Clerk.
The Clerk he had a Sexton,
  The Sexton had a Digger ;
The Digger had a Prebend,
  The Prebend had a Vicar ;
The Vicar had an Attorney,
  The which he took in Snuff ;
The Attorney had a Barrifter,
  The Barrifter a Ruff.
The Ruff did get good Counfel,
  Good Counfel get a Fee,
the Fee did get a Motion
  That it might Pleaded be :
the Motion got a Judgment,
  And fo it came to pafs,
A Beggar's Brat, a fcolding **Knave,**
  A crafty Lawyer was.

BOSTON : Printed and Sold below the *Mill-Bridge.* 1755

The Lawyer's Pedigree, set into type by Isaiah Thomas at the age of six.

———

Thomas' career as a printer had begun when he was apprenticed at age six to Zechariah Fowle, with whom he formed a partnership in 1770. Thomas describes Fowle as a dolt. A story is told that Fowle once set a ballad in type, using the punctuation from another ballad—line by line—regardless of sense.[25] Perhaps because he could not read at age six, little Isaiah stood on a bench eighteen inches high to set the type for a rather bawdy broadside ballad, "The Lawer's Pedigree," in 1755. A copy of the ballad, the story of Thomas' precocious printing skill, and Thomas' printing press are on exhibit at the American Antiquarian Society.

Isaiah Thomas' almanac was perhaps the most widely distributed almanac of the last quarter of the eighteenth century. Thomas, in his diary, mentions selling as many as 29,000 in 1797.[26] In addition to the usual publications (books, pamphlets, and his own almanacs), he also printed the almanacs of Drs. Nathanael Low and Samuel Stearns.

Robert B. Thomas did not begin his *Farmer's Almanac* until 1792 (for 1793), but he soon became the leader in the almanac field. In 1832 he changed the title to the *Old Farmer's Almanac*, to distinguish it from its many imitators. It bears this title today. So successful were the *Farmer's Almanacs* that Isaiah Thomas was obliged to add "Isaiah" to the title of his "Thomas" almanac in 1798, to prevent being mistaken for "Robert B."

Robert was from Boylston, Massachusetts, only a few miles from Worcester, Isaiah's home. Robert implies that he published his own almanac because Isaiah Thomas would not sell him any of his. Besides, he thought he could prepare a better one than Isaiah Thomas.[27] The two Thomases engaged in spirited competition, providing Massachusetts (and the neighboring colonies) with superior almanacs as each tried to better the other.

Robinson says that "The Farmer's Almanack is the oldest living periodical in America."[28] But Nichols, a better authority on almanacs, grants it the distinction of being "one of the oldest almanacs now in existence," giving Webster's of Albany, begun in 1787, first place for being the oldest, still-published almanac in America.[29]

[No. II.]

THE
FARMER's ALMANACK.

Calculated on a new and improved Plan;

FOR THE YEAR OF OUR LORD
1794:

Being the Second after Leap Year, *and Eighteenth of the* Independence *of* America.

Fitted to the town of BOSTON, but will serve for any of the adjoining States.

Containing, besides the large number of *Astronomical Calculations* and *Farmer's Calendar* for every month in the year, as great a variety as are to be found in any other Almanack,

Of New, Useful and Entertaining Matter.

BY ROBERT B. THOMAS.

" The various ord'nances of the sky
Witness the great ARCHITECT on high :
Summer and winter, autumn and the spring,
For him, by turns, their attestation bring."

PRINTED AT THE Apollo Press, IN BOSTON.
By BELKNAP and HALL : Sold by them, at No. 8, Dock Square, *Boston ;* by the Author, and M. Smith, *Sterling ;* and by the principal Booksellers in Town and Country.
Price 4os. per groce, 4s. per dozen, 6d. single.

Illustrated title page from Robert B. Thomas' *The Farmer's Almanac.*

100

Portrait of Robert B. Thomas by William Talcott.

BENJAMIN BANNEKER

A unique place in the history of almanacs is held by Benjamin Banneker, America's only Negro almanac-maker. His ancestry can be traced to Molly Welsh, an Englishwoman who chose to be transported to Maryland rather than imprisoned in England for the alleged theft of a pail of milk. After completing seven years of indentured service, she bought a small farm and acquired two Negro slaves. Molly eventually set the two men free and married one of them, Banaky, who claimed a chieftain's parentage in Africa. Mary, one of their four children, married Robert, a free African, who chose to be called by his wife's surname.

Benjamin, born in 1731, was the eldest child of Robert and Mary. The surname was spelled *Bannaky, Banneky,* and *Bannaker,* before *Banneker* became the accepted version. Benjamin's father eventually bought a 120-acre farm near Baltimore, which his oldest son inherited. The farm was productive, and provided Benjamin Banneker with a good livelihood. Even before he became known for his almanacs, Banneker had already gained fame in the community through the construction of a clock that struck the hours.

George Ellicott, a Quaker and one of the proprietors of the flour mills of Ellicott City, established business dealings with Banneker for his agricultural produce. Later, Ellicott recognized the farmer's unusual computational ability and let him borrow Ferguson's *Astronomy,* Mayer's *Tables,* and Leadbetter's *Lunar Tables.* Through the study of these texts, Banneker was soon able to make his own astronomical calculations. Several authors have stated that Banneker noted errors in the texts lent to him, but according to Banneker himself what he thought were errors in his sources was actually due to his initial inability to understand two different methods of deriving the same results.[30] Inspired and fascinated by astronomy, Banneker began to spend most of his time studying celestial mechanics. In 1791, at Andrew Ellicott's suggestion, Banneker was appointed a member of a commission for a survey of the Federal Territory (District of Columbia).[31] In

102

the same year, he issued an almanac for 1792, the first of a series that lasted until 1797.

Banneker's first almanac contained a brief sketch of his own life in the form of a letter to the printers signed by Dr. James McHenry, military surgeon and politician, who became Secretary of War under Washington and Adams. The "Anatomy" was included, followed by the twelve calendar pages. Miscellaneous material included *"The* Planetary *and* Terrestrial Worlds *Comparatively considered,"* "On the Swiftness of Time," "Origin *of the* Gray Mare's *being the better* Horse," "The Two Bees," *"Extracts from the Writings of the* Ancients *of distinguished fame,"* and "Effusions on a Town and Country Life." On the practical side, there were some cures for disease in humans and in trees; dates of court sessions and meetings, tables, road information; as well as verse on health, religion, and nature. A notable item appeared at the bottom of the "Tide-Table for Chesapeake Bay":

> Needles first made in London, by a Negro, from Spain, in the reign of Q. Mary; but he dying without teaching the art, it was lost till 1566, when it was taught by Elias Groro . . . a German.

Also included was *"On* Negro Slavery, *and the* Slave Trade. An Extract from the Columbian Magazine."

Banneker's first publisher was the printing firm of William Goddard and James Angell. When Goddard insisted that he had exclusive rights and refused to allow any other printer to use Banneker's calculations or the McHenry sketch, a member of the anti-slavery Ellicott family came to the rescue. Elias Ellicott wrote to James Pemberton, an influential member of the Maryland Society for the Abolition of Slavery, who in turn wrote to Goddard.[32] The Baltimore publisher finally agreed to furnish copies for three other printers: Joseph Crukshank and Daniel Humphreys of Philadelphia, and Hanson and Bond in Alexandria.

Ellicott and Pemberton then prepared a "certificate" in support of Banneker signed by eleven men, all members of the Ellicott family or their friends:

To the Public.
In Order to clear up any doubt that may Arise as to Benjamin Banneker (a Black man whose Father came from Africa) being the Author of the Prefixed Almanac We whose Names are hereunto Annexed to Certify that we for several Years have been Acquainted with him and that his knowledge in Astronomy and the Mathematicks was of his own Acquiring Assisted only by Astronomical Tables which he with much Difficulty procured.

Andrew Ellicott	Michael Pue, M.D.
James Gillingham	George Ellicott
Daniel Carroll	Gerard Hopkins
Elias Ellicott	Jonathan Ellicott
Wm. Dillworth	James Carey.[33]
Joseph Evans	

In addition to obtaining the certificate, Pemberton sent a copy of the almanac to David Rittenhouse, America's foremost astronomer, also a calculator of almanacs, and Ben Franklin's successor as president of the American Philosophical Society. Rittenhouse promptly replied:

I think the papers I herewith return to you a very extraordinary performance, considering the Colour of the Author. Though I have had leisure to make but few comparisons I have no doubt that the Calculations are sufficiently accurate for the purposes of a common Almanac. Every Instance of Genius amongst the Negroes is worthy of attention, because their oppressors seem to lay great stress on their supposed inferior mental abilities.[34]

Pemberton also sent a copy to William Waring, calculator of *Poor Will's Almanack,* published by Joseph Crukshank for several years. Waring, a mathematics teacher, a competent astronomer, and a member of the American Philosophical Society and the Pennsylvania Society for the Abolition of Slavery, replied: "I have examined Benjamin Banneker's Almanac for the Year 1792, and am of the Opinion that it well deserves the Acceptance and Encouragement of the Public." [35]

Meanwhile, Banneker sent a copy of his manuscript to Thomas Jefferson, then Secretary of State. The manuscript was accompanied by a letter soliciting Jefferson's support, which was pub-

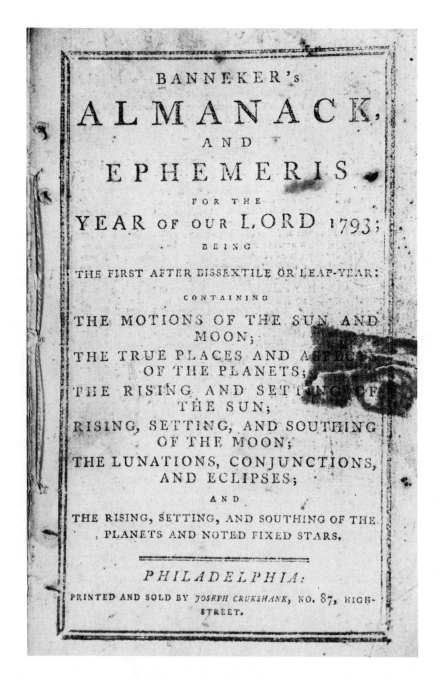

BANNEKER's
ALMANACK,
AND
EPHEMERIS.
FOR THE
YEAR OF OUR LORD 1793;
BEING
THE FIRST AFTER DISSEXTILE OR LEAP-YEAR:
CONTAINING
THE MOTIONS OF THE SUN AND MOON;
THE TRUE PLACES AND ASPECTS OF THE PLANETS;
THE RISING AND SETTING OF THE SUN;
RISING, SETTING, AND SOUTHING OF THE MOON;
THE LUNATIONS, CONJUNCTIONS, AND ECLIPSES;
AND
THE RISING, SETTING, AND SOUTHING OF THE PLANETS AND NOTED FIXED STARS.

PHILADELPHIA:
PRINTED AND SOLD BY *JOSEPH CRUKSHANK*, NO. 87, HIGH-STREET.

Banneker's second publication, printed by Joseph Crukshank, prominent abolitionist.

lished in the 1793 almanac (Goddard and Angell edition) with Jefferson's appreciative reply.

Banneker, like many other almanac calculators, probably had little to do with the miscellaneous contents of his almanacs. Pemberton, in his original letter to William Goddard, says that he "made a collection of some instructive essays to be published as usual in an Almanac." [36] The 1792 preface (by Goddard?) ambiguously refers to "editors." After praising Banneker and mentioning the "Approbation" of David Rittenhouse, the preface concludes:

> Though it becomes the Editors to speak with less Confidence of the miscellaneous Part of his Work, they yet flatter themselves, from their Attention to the variegated Selections in Prose and Verse, that their Readers will find it both USEFUL and ENTERTAINING. . . .

Almost all selections are carefully enclosed in quotation marks, even when the author's name is withheld.

The most prominent editions of Banneker's almanacs for 1793 were by Goddard and James Angell in Baltimore and Joseph Crukshank in Philadelphia. This year Crukshank repeated part of the McHenry sketch; Goddard published the letter to Thomas Jefferson and Jefferson's reply. These almanacs are quite different from each other, even to weather forecasts, which were probably selected by the printers. Goddard's had typical almanac fare. Crukshank was an active abolitionist. In his 1793 version of the Banneker almanac, he printed an "abstract from the speech of William Pitt, esq. on the motion for the Abolition of the Slave-Trade," an exhortation to Christians on doing their duty, "Extract from *Jefferson's* Notes on Virginia," "On Liberty, and in Praise of Mr. Howard Cowper," and "Extract from Wilkinson's Appeal to England on Behalf of the Abused Africans," the latter written in verse. The extract from Jefferson's *Notes* shows that his objections to slavery were not so much to the condition of the oppressed Negro as to the baseness of character induced in the master and the master's sons by such an arrangement. Crukshank's edition also contained the famous "Plan of a *Peace-Office*, for the United States," a work often attributed to Banneker. The plan, however, was written by an entirely different Benjamin: Dr. Benjamin Rush.[37]

William Prentis of Petersburg, Virginia, printer of *The Virginia Almanack* for 1794, refers in the title to his calculator, "that ingenious self taught Astronomer, *Benjamin Banneker,* a black man." This almanac, like many of the Southern ones, is filled with anecdotes, more ironic than moralistic. There is also a section for the "Compleat Gardener," and satiric anecdotes directed against doctors and the military.

Goddard eventually sold out his interest in the Baltimore firm to James Angell, who mentions Banneker in his 1794 preface. Referring to Phyllis Wheatley, a slave woman who became a poet, he points out that Banneker, the *"African descended* self-taught Astronomer," is not the only African who has achieved eminence.

Banneker almanacs flourished in 1795. Samuel and John Adams printed several editions in Baltimore and Wilmington. One edition, printed for John Fisher in Baltimore, had the same text as William Gibbons' in Philadelphia. S. and J. Adams printed a portrait of Banneker on the title page but omitted it in their copy to be sold by Frederick Craig. The almanac contained many anecdotes, receipts for cures, helpful household advice, and some riddles. Fisher printed the portrait of Banneker with part of McHenry's sketch. There were anecdotes, receipts, and hints for farmers. There were also editions by Jacob Johnson & Co. in Philadelphia and by Matthias Day in Trenton, New Jersey. A poem in the 1795 editions was signed by an unidentified "G.H.," who compared the almanac calculator with Newton in sixty-two laborious lines of heroic couplets such as the following:

> *Fain would the muse exalt her tuneful lays,*
> *And chant in strains sublime BANNEKER's praise;*
> . . . .
> *What tho' thy skin be of the blackest hue,*
> *Such as the sable sons of Afric' shew;*
> *What tho' descended from that sable race,*
> *Which nature's fairer sons hold in disgrace;*
> *Ah! foul disgrace! disgraceful to mankind,*
> *To those whose narrow minds are thus confin'd!*
> *Talents thou hast superior to most,*

Cover of Banneker almanac for 1795.

No matter what complexions *they boast,*
In arts, in sciences, or in philosophy,
Or in the myst'ries of astronomy;
The abstruse secrets of great nature's *plan,*
Like Newton, *thou presumed had to scan,*

. . . .

Hail! genius great! astronomer self-taught!
Thy ideas from nature's self *are brought . . .*

"G.H." may have been Gerard Hopkins, an educated minister of the Society of Friends who, a few years earlier, had added his signature to the Banneker "certificate."

In an unsigned preface, probably written by the printers (Baltimore: Philip Edwards, James Keddie, *et al.*), Banneker's 1796 almanac tells the "Gentle Reader":

> *To make an ALMANAC is not so easy a matter as some people think—like a well furnished table, it requires to have a variety of dishes to suit every palate . . . but there is one dish we invite you to partake of, and we are prouder of it than of all the rest put together; and to whom do you think are we indebted for this part of our entertainment? Why, to a* Black Man—*Strange! Is a* Black *capable of composing an Almanac? Indeed, it is no less strange than true; and a clever wise long-headed Black he is: It would be telling some whites if they had made as much use of their great school learning, as this aged philosopher has made of the little teaching he has got.*

The preface concludes with Thomas Gray's quatrain beginning *"Full many a gem of purest ray serene,"* followed by a quatrain of the author's making:

> *Nor you ye proud, impute to these the blame*
> *If Afric's sons to genius are unknown,*
> *For Banneker has prov'd they may acquire a name*
> *As bright, as lasting as your own.*

In 1797 Christopher Jackson in Baltimore printed one Banneker almanac for himself and one for George Keatinge. Samuel Pleasants' edition in Richmond contained much that was in Jackson's. In Petersburg, Prentis and Murray reprinted some of the old 1796 Edwards *et al.* material and some of the same new pages as Christopher Jackson. The appearance of the "Epitaph on a Watch-Maker" in all four versions indicates to one author that Banneker may have written this epitaph.[38] However, since many other selections were exactly the same in all four almanacs, it is more likely that the printers exchanged text. Admittedly, Banneker was interested in timepieces and had a modicum of literary ability, but the same epitaph can be found on an 1802 gravestone in Devonshire, England, with the name "George Routleigh" substituted for "Peter Pendulum." [39] All we know for sure is that the epitaph was not written expressly for George.

EPITAPH on a WATCH-MAKER

HERE lies, in a *horizontal* position;
The *outside case* of
Peter Pendulum, Watch-Maker,
Whose abilities in that line were an honour
To his profession,
Integrity was the *main spring*,
And prudence the *regulator*
Of all the actions of his life,
Humane, generous and liberal,
His *hand* never *stopped*,
Till he had relieved distress.
So nicely *regulated* were all his *motions*,
That he never *went wrong*,
Except when set a *going*,
By people
Who did not know
His key:
Even then he was easily
Set right again.
He had the art of disposing his *time*
So well,
That his hours glided away,
ın one *continual round*
Of pleasure and delight,
Till an unlucky *minute* put a period to
His existence.
He departed this life
Wound up
In hope, of being *taken in hand*
By his *Maker*,
And of being thoroughly *cleaned*, *repaired*,
And set a *going*
In the world to come.

The rest of Benjamin Banneker's story is relatively uneventful. He sold his land to the Ellicotts for an annuity to last the rest of his life, remained a bachelor, and devoted himself to the study of astronomy. When the annuity expired eight years before he did, someone remarked that this error in calculating was the only one that Benjamin Banneker ever made.[40] He lived until 1806, supported by his patrons, the Ellicotts, to whom he willed his papers.

For almost a century, writers have repeated the errors in the sparse early material on Banneker, or have invented facts where they were lacking.[41] A more recent biography of Banneker has separated fact from legend, and added much new material.[42]

Banneker, as a person, remains elusive. We know for sure that he acquired considerable computational skill late in life. But we know very little about his mathematical and literary capabilities, still less about his personal views on color, race, and slavery. He can be justly acclaimed as an unusually able self-taught technician. His era was remarkable for the production of such men and women (in Europe and in North America)—"village Newtons" experimenting with clockwork and with the new calculus, and sometimes with literary conventions as well. Banneker's almanacs are especially interesting because they were the only ones in American almanac history that were calculated by a black man, a man who doubtless possessed unusual abilities, and whose achievements, in relation to his background and the social conditions and beliefs of the time, were particularly noteworthy.

HUGH GAINE AND
THE POCKET ALMANAC AND REGISTER

Although several almanac-makers prepared more than one type of almanac, Hugh Gaine printed the broadside, the register, and the pocket almanac in his name (and in that of Thomas Moore, pseudonym), as well as an almanac ordinary in format but exceptional in content by John Nathan Hutchins, Yale University professor.

Gaine began, in his own name, the register and the pocket almanac with *Gaine's New York Pocket Almanack* for 1760 (by Thomas Moore, pseudonym) and Gaine's *Register* for 1775. Gaine was not the first to print registers; Mein & Fleeming had published the *Massachusetts Register* from 1767 through 1769. *Gaine's New York Pocket Almanack* for 1775 contains eighty-four pages, including the usual astronomical calendars; a tide table; Quakers' meeting dates; the times and places of courts in New York, New Jersey, Connecticut, Rhode Island, and Philadelphia; eight pages of currency conversion and gauging tables ("gauging" inches of barrels of liquor for duty tax purposes); ten pages of the officials of the North American Army and Civil Establishment, seven pages of His Majesty's Forces, and one of the delegates to the American Congress in Philadelphia; lists of court officials for each county in New York, fairs in New York, duties on imported goods, stagecoaches from Montreal to Quebec, colleges and American seminaries; "Genealogical List of the Royal Family of Great Britain"—and more.

Gaine's Universal Register, or, American and British Kalendar, for the Year 1775 has 168 numbered pages. The list of contents covers two and one-half pages. A two-page preface explains Gaine's first attempt at this type of publication. His information section begins with the Royal Family of Great Britain, and is followed by the Royal Families of France, Spain, Portugal, Denmark, Norway, Sweden, Germany, Poland, Prussia, Sardinia, Orange, Italy, and Turkey. His roster of the Royal Navy and Army includes each man's salary. Organizations and their officials include the American Philosophical Society in Philadelphia, with Benjamin Franklin as president. Other features are the American Bill of Rights, the Association of the Continental Congress, and a list of holidays ordered by England to be observed in the colonies.

Hugh Gaine, as publisher of two newspapers, vacillated between Tory and Whig, but finally decided on Loyalism. Although neither side could really trust him, the only retaliation by the patriots was verbal abuse. Gaine generally managed to keep his varying political views out of his almanacs (with a few exceptions), but his journal occasionally reveals his true feelings of the moment. An entry dated "Oct. 1781" mentions an acquaintance "who brought an account, that Lord Cornwallis had surrendered to General Washington on the 17th." A few days later, he says that "the Misfortune of Lord Cornwallis has been confirmed." [44]

In his register for 1778, Gaine's passion erupts in an unrestrained expression of his loyalty to Britain:

> Let every thinking Mind duly reflect upon the repeated Benevolences of the Parent State, and only ask, When will the Colonies be able to do for themselves what she has done for them in the Way of *Supplies;* and how is it possible that a Nation, which has lavished (as it seems) so much Expence upon its Provinces in their infant State, should after all, be desirous of their Destruction, though, at the same Time (as the Congress has owned) the Prosperity of the Colonies is the Welfare of Britain?

He presents tables of expenses and concludes that, besides two wars which Britain fought for "70,000,000 *Sterling*," she has spent 34,696,867 pounds sterling—"An unequivocal Testimony of her Affection and Regard, and a full Refutation of the slandering Falsehoods of a licentious Congress!"

The closest approach to verse occurred in Gaine's weather prediction for December 13 and 14 in the register for 1779: "It may snow / for what I know." He was evidently pleased with his rhyme, for he also used it on December 12 and 13 in his pocket almanac for the same year and in the register for 1780. In the 1782 register he wrote for February 22 and 23: "If it don't snow / Perhaps 'twill blow"; and for June 20–22: "Like for rain and / thunder / or I wonder."

Gaine's publications are typical of the pocket almanac and the register, which specialized in lists and tables rather than subjective essays and verse.[45] *Gaine's Universal Sheet Almanack* for 1788, a broadside in folio size, contained five rows of six frames each.[46] In the pocket almanac for 1792, Hugh Gaine himself is named as Treasurer of the St. Patrick's Society. Even the Hook and Ladder men are listed for the fire department.

"ABRAHAM WEATHERWISE" AND PSEUDONYMS

Pseudonyms were especially prevalent among eighteenth-century almanac-makers. Readers were treated to "Poor ——" productions in epidemic proportions: *Will, Tom, Ned, Robert,* and *Roger,* as well as the Franklins' *Robin, Richard,* and *Job.* There were Copernicus Partridge (and Copernicus Weather-guesser), Andrew Aguecheek, Father Richard, Father Tammany, Philopatria, Edmund Freebetter, and Timothy Trueman. But the single most popular pseudonym used by more than one author (other than "Isaac Bickerstaff," discussed above) was "Abraham Weatherwise." *Father Abraham's Almanack* for 1759, compiled by "Abraham Weatherwise" and published by W. Dunlap in Philadelphia, was the first. A novel format placed the essays under the calendar pages, continued from page to page, rather than at the beginning or at the end of the calendar material. Another series begun in Philadelphia was *Weatherwise's Town and Country-man's Almanack* for (1781). Nichols comments on the excellence of the illustrations in this series and in the Weatherwise almanacs printed in Boston, which included in 1781 a woodcut of George Washington ascribed to Paul Revere. The 1785 issue began with an illustration of a burning aerial balloon.[47] The public was apparently interested in the balloon experiments, for the year 1786 saw a new series of *Balloon Almanacks* published in Philadelphia. In this same year several other printers used the Abraham Weatherwise name.[48]

FOREIGN-LANGUAGE ALMANACS

The eighteenth century was well on its way before an almanac was published in America in a language other than English. By the end of the century, foreign-language almanacs were becoming quite popular. One of the most skillful printers in America, Christopher Sauer, was a German, and one of the first things he printed was an almanac. Another almanac, in French, was printed for only

Cover woodcut of a burning balloon,
from *Weatherwise's Town and Countryman's Almanack*,
1785.

one year. Its interest lies in the unusual circumstance of its publication—and its just claim to a historical "first."

The most distinguished of the foreign-language almanacs was *Der Hoch-Deutsch Americanische Calender,* begun in 1738 for the year 1739 by Christopher Sauer (Saur or Sower), German printer and almanac-maker of Germantown, Pennsylvania. This almanac was not the first in German that was printed in America, despite

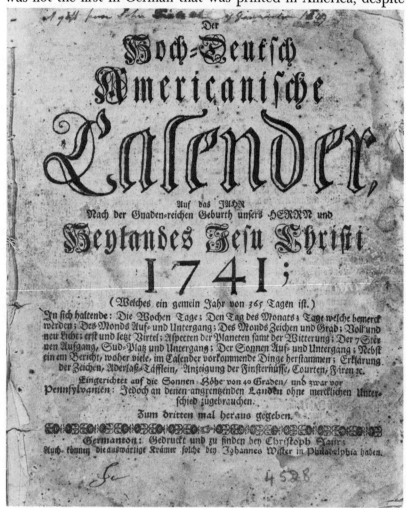

Sauer's *Der Hoch-Deutsch Americanische Calendar* for 1741.

Man of Signs from Sauer's
Americanische Calender, 1740.

the claims of two authorities.[49] Andrew Bradford of Philadelphia
had printed a German almanac for three years—1731, 1732, and
1733—about seven years before Sauer. There were three Christopher Sauers (father, son, and grandson), but only the first two de-
serve attention as almanac-makers. The popular Sauer almanac,
compiled and printed by the Sauers for thirty-nine years, sold
10,000 copies annually.[50]

Christopher Sauer, Sr., was a religious man, generally associated with the Dunker sect. The Dunkers closely resembled the
German Mennonites and the English Quakers. Christopher Sauer,
Jr., a Dunker bishop and pacifist, refused to fight in the Revolution on religious grounds, but his son, Christopher, III, was openly
pro-British.

A Microprint copy of the first Sauer almanac shows twenty-
four printed pages and several blank sheets. Measuring about eight

by seven inches, it has no cover or title page. Evans' bibliographical entry, however, mentions thirty-six pages. There are twelve calendar pages, with the phases of the moon at the bottom of the pages and weather predictions in the calculations columns. The other pages contain lists of eclipses, courts and fairs; chronology of events; tables (roads and distances, interest); books for sale; and some advice on health.

By 1755 the almanac had reached forty-eight pages, accommodating, for the most part, religious literature written by Sauer. During the 1740's an engraved emblem was added: an angel with a wand and a scroll, on which was printed a motto which changed from time to time. First, it was "To the honor of God and my neighbor's good." Subsequently, it became "War and Rumors of War" and, in 1765, "Troublesome Times." From 1767 on, the motto was "Hope for Better Times." [51]

Christopher Sauer, Sr., was an unusually talented printer. In 1743 he printed the Bible in German, advertising it the preceding year in his almanac. This Bible was 1248 pages long, the largest work up to this time from an American press, and preceded the first English Bible printed in America by forty years.

For several years Sauer omitted the saints' days from his calendar, not wanting to encourage "popery" among the Protestants. But in 1748 he capitulated, rationalizing that, since a great many people were worshipping neither God nor Christ, they would be hardly likely to worship the saints.[52] From 1748 to 1754 he printed the saints' days in red ink, as was the custom in Europe. The price of the two-color almanac was raised from ninepence to one shilling. In 1749 he printed two editions—one in two colors for one shilling and the other in black for ninepence. The following year the price was the same for either issue. In 1754, Sauer discontinued the color printing.

Sauer printed an almanac in English, *The Pennsylvania Town and Countrymen's Almanack*, in 1755, with his son's name listed as publisher. This English edition was not so successful as the German; likewise, Benjamin Franklin's German almanac in 1748 was not a financial success.[53] There were, however, other German

118

Illustrated cover of Sauer's *Americanische Calender* for 1744.

(1)

ARTICLES PRINCIPAUX
DU
CALENDRIER
Pour l'Année Commune 1781.

Année de la période Julienne............... 6494.
 depuis la p. Olymp. d'Iphitus, jusq. Juillet. 2555.
 de la fond. de Rome, selon Varon (Mars) 2534.
 de l'époque de Nabouassar depuis Février. 2528.
 de l'Hégire ou époque des Turcs (Julien.) 1195.

		QUATRE-TEMPS.
Nombre d'Or...... 15.		
Epacte............ iv.	Mars......... 7, 9 & 10.	
Cycle Solaire....... 26.	Juin.......... 6, 8 & 9.	
Indiction Romaine... 14.	Septembre... 19, 21 & 22.	
Lettre Dominicale ... G.	Décembre... 19, 21 & 22.	

FESTES MOBILES.

Septuagésime..... 11 Févr.	Ascension........... 24 Mai.
Les Cendres...... 28 Févr.	Pentecôte........... 3 Juin.
Pâques........... 15 Avril.	La Trinité......... 10 Juin.
Les Rogations. 21, 22 &	La Fête-Dieu..... 14 Juin.
23 Mai.	Pr. Dim. de l'Av. 2 Déc.

De l'Epiphanie à la Septuagésime.... cinq Dimanches.
De la Pentecôte à l'Avent.... vingt cinq Dimanches.

Eclipses de l'Année 1781.

Il y aura cette année deux éclipses de Soleil, dont la premiere sera visible seulement dans l'Amérique septentrionale : il n'y aura point d'éclipse de lune.

La premiere éclipse de soleil arrivera le 23 Avril, la seconde arrivera le 17 Octobre.

Newport 1781.

Page one of *Calendrier Français*, 1781, the first French-language almanac in America.

almanacs in Philadelphia: Anton Armbrüster's, which began in 1760; and Heinrich Müller's, in 1762.

The Sauer almanacs were consistently of high quality, and were oriented toward religion, health, and history—probably in that order. After his father's death in 1758, Christopher, Jr., operated the press. One of the new features was the publication of excerpts from a German manual on medicinal herbs, beginning in installments in 1762 and culminating in 1778 with an index. From 1763 to 1778 the Sauer almanac carried installments of a history of England.

Christopher, Jr., retired in 1777, and his sons, Christopher and Peter, managed the press. After the property of Christopher Sauer, Jr., was confiscated by the Revolutionaries in 1778, John Dunlap became the owner of the engraved plate used for the cover of the almanac. He printed the traditional Sauer almanacs until 1784; successive printers continued them until 1835.[54]

Unusual circumstances precipitated the printing at Newport in 1781 of the first French almanac in New England. A French fleet, anchored at Newport during the winter of 1780–81 to help defend the colonists, possessed a printing press. The press, set up *"pres le Parc de la Marine,"* issued the *Calendrier Français*, which included the usual calendrical information, but with saints' names for each day—the first Roman Catholic almanac printed in New England. The remainder of the *Calendrier* consisted mainly of a list of the French ships, their cannon, and their officers. Handwritten notes in the copy owned by the Rhode Island Historical Society describe the condition of many of the officers: *"mort," "Tué à Chesapeak," "blessé aux jambes,"* and so forth.

THE LADY'S ALMANACK

A sporadic feature of the last half of the eighteenth century was the appearance of Ladies' Almanacks. *The Lady's Almanack* of 1786 was authored "By a Female. Being her First Public Production of the Nature." It was quite similar to others of the same period, including the conventional, stilted verse about Phoebus Apollo and his courtship of Tellus; some Persian fables; verse from Sterne, Fielding, and Pope; the usual astronomical information; and a few articles of domestic science. In the preface the author explained her motives "to the uncandid Critick, and the base Assassin of literary Merit."

All almanacs with *Lady* in the title were not of this type: some of the contents of the 1792 *Lady's Almanack* were bawdy, and the author's real name was withheld. The almanac began conventionally, with the usual calendar verse. In May, "Fair-handed spring embosoms every grace." In November, "Fled is the blasted verdure of the fields . . . The desolated prospect thrills the soul." But all the verse was not so bland: "Materials for a Jemmy" describes the fop's costume, says "Jemmy" has money "unless robbed," and adds that Jemmy's sex was determined in this manner:

> *Nature whilst Jemmy's clay was blending,*
> *Uncertain what the thing would end in,*
> *Whether a Female or a Male,*
> *A Pin dropt in, and turn'd the scale!*

The almanac's title had advertised that it contained "Besides Everything Necessary for a Work of the Kind, a Variety of Entertainment." And so it did. An anecdote about a lady in New York at a "Fly-Market" notes the surprise of a country woman to learn that the city woman's hands are soft and white because she wears "dog skin" gloves. The country woman retorts that her "husband's _____ is as brown as nutmeg" despite his wearing "dog skin small clothes these three years."

WOMEN PRINTERS

Several American women ran their own printing shops during the eighteenth century. These included Ann Franklin and Sarah Goddard in Rhode Island; Elizabeth and Ann Timothy (Timothée) and Mary Crouch in South Carolina; Cornelia Bradford in Pennsylvania; Catherine Zenger and Elizabeth Holt in New York;

Dinah Nuthead, Mary Katharine Goddard and Anne Catherine Green in Maryland; Clementina Rind in Virginia; Margaret Draper in Massachusetts; and Hannah Watson in Connecticut. Some actually set type and ran the presses; some served only as managers. All these women except Dinah Nuthead published newspapers, and six of them also printed annual almanacs: Franklin, Bradford, Zenger, Green, and Sarah and Mary K. Goddard. During two years, 1746–1748, there were three separate women printing almanacs—C. Zenger, Cornelia Bradford, and Ann Franklin.

Most of these women became printers through necessity. Their husbands had died, leaving them with little means of support but the family printing press. It was, of course, a common practice in colonial America for women to carry on the businesses of their deceased husbands. But the printing business seems to have been one in which many women did particularly well.

As we have seen, the first press to arrive in America was owned by a woman, the Widow Glover, who later married Henry Dunster, the first president of Harvard University. But the Widow Glover never operated a press, nor, probably, did Dinah Nuthead, who owned the Annapolis press in 1695. The first colonial woman actually to operate her own printshop was Ann Franklin, widow of Benjamin's older brother James.

Ann Franklin engaged in a general printing business intermittently between 1735 and 1763, serving the colony of Rhode Island, the clergy, and the general public. She printed the laws, government forms, sermons, and the *Rhode Island Almanack* ("Poor Robin") sometimes in partnership with her son, sometimes with other printers, and sometimes alone. The widow's problem of finding help appears to have been solved by her own daughters, who were probably the first females in American printing history employed as typesetters. They seem to have been capable:

> Her daughters were correct and quick compositors at case; and were instructed by their father whom they assisted. A gentleman who was acquainted with Anne Franklin and her family, informed me that he had often seen her daughters at work in the printing house, and that they were sensible and amiable women.[55]

123

Perhaps Ann's most remarkable production was a 340-page folio edition of the laws of Rhode Island, an unusual feat for any colonial printer. Her publications were varied: a proclamation by Governor William Greene to raise troops to send to Canada (a broadside); such sermons as John Callender's ". . . Occasioned by the Death of the Reverend Mr. Nathaniel Clap, Pastor," Joseph Fish's "Love to Christ a Necessary Qualification in a Gospel Minister"; as well as the popular *Rhode Island Almanack* by Poor Robin, begun by Ann's husband in 1728. This almanac, the first of the "Poor _____" series, was in circulation five years before brother Benjamin's better-known *Poor Richard*. Ann continued "Poor Robin" in the style of her husband—satirical, humorous, and chatty. The filler on the calendar pages was especially lively and gossipy.

Ann's son, James, Jr., eventually took over the press, but when he died in 1762, Ann, at age sixty-five, again became the official printer for the colony of Rhode Island, as well as the publisher of *The Newport Mercury*, her son's newspaper. Samuel Hall, her son-in-law, was her partner. (Coincidentally, in Philadelphia, there was also a printing firm of Franklin and Hall—Benjamin and his partner, David Hall.) On April 19, 1763, Ann died, and *The Newport Mercury* carried her obituary in its next issue:

> . . . She was a Widow about 29 Years—And tho' she had little to depend upon for a Living, yet by her Oeconomy and Industry in carrying on the Printing Business, supported herself and Family, and brought up her Children in a genteel manner. . . .[56]

In Pennsylvania, the first woman printer was Cornelia Bradford, whose husband, Andrew, was the well-known publisher. From 1744 to 1750, the Widow Bradford ran a bookstore, a common adjunct to a printing business, and published the *American Weekly Mercury*. In 1746 she printed "New-Year Verses of the Carriers of the *American Weekly Mercury*" and almanacs by Titan Leeds, John Jerman, Jacob Taylor, William Ball, and William Birkett. For several years she printed Birkett's *Poor Will's Almanack*, one of the most popular almanacs of that time.

A New York printer, Anna Catherina Zenger, took up and continued her husband John Peter Zenger's *New York Weekly Journal* in 1746, as well as the printing of pamphlets and John Nathan's almanac. Mrs. Zenger had learned how to operate the printshop in 1735 when her husband was imprisoned for criticizing the government. Allowed to communicate solely with his wife, Zenger instructed her from his cell. The paper missed only one edition. After her husband's death, the Widow Zenger also ran a stationery store, and was apparently well acquainted with the competitive business practices of her time, for in 1747 she announced in her paper:

> This is to acquaint the Public that some Evil minded Persons have been pleased to spread a Report abroad that the Widow Zenger, Publisher of this Paper, had entirely dropped the Printing Business, &c. This is therefore to give Notice, that the said Report is Notoriously False, and that the said Widow still continues the Printing Business, where any Person may have their work done reasonable, in a good Manner, and with Expedition.[57]

Mrs. Zenger's work was well done indeed and technically surpassed that of her Dutch-born husband, whom Isaiah Thomas describes as "a scholar, but . . . not correct in the English language, especially in orthography." [58]

Maryland had three colonial women printers of unusual interest: the first—Dinah Nuthead, about whom very little is known, and the best—Mary Katharine Goddard. Between these two was Anne Catherine Green, born in Holland. Anne Catherine's husband, Jonas, died in 1767 and from 1767 to 1775 she ran the press in Annapolis, sometimes singly and sometimes in partnership with her son. She had fourteen children, six of whom survived her; annually printed almanacs (*The Maryland Almanack* and Robert Cockburn's *Poor Robert Improved*); did the official Government printing for eight years; published the *Maryland Gazette;* and printed political pamphlets and satirical pieces. This was no mean achievement for a life of fifty-five years.

Mrs. Green's *Bye-Laws of the City of Annapolis,* a volume of fifty-two pages, is one of the best examples of colonial printing.

The Maryland Assembly, pleased with her work, voted to pay her the same salary they had paid her husband: 48,000 pounds of tobacco annually for those years in which the Assembly met, and 36,109 pounds during the interim years. Although she worked with her sons, they always took second place. It was "Anne Catherine Green" alone who was appointed printer to the Province. Immediately after her husband's death she was assisted by one of her sons, whose help she mentions in an appeal to the public. She reminds readers of her husband's faithful service and adds, "I flatter myself that, with your kind Indulgence and Encouragement, Myself, and Son, will be enabled to continue it on the same Footing . . . Your grateful and faithful humble Servant, A.C. Green." [59]

Mrs. Green was a good printer—and a good woman. Notice of her death in the *Maryland Gazette* for March 30, 1775, says: "She was of a mild and benevolent disposition, and for Conjugal Affection, and Parental Tenderness, an Example to her Sex." [60]

Two of our women printers were Goddards. But the Goddard women were not widows carrying on the work of their husbands. Sarah Goddard (née Updike) "received a good education; acquired an acquaintance with several branches of useful and polite learning, and married Dr. Giles Goddard of New London, who left her a widow." [61] Sarah became involved with printing because of her son, William, who operated the printing press in Providence, Rhode Island. William, a peripheral political figure, was a wanderer. Leaving his mother and sister in charge of his press in 1765, he went to Philadelphia. While in Providence, Sarah printed (among others) *The New-England Almanack, or, Lady's and Gentleman's Diary* for 1768. She soon sold "Sarah Goddard and Company," and followed William to Philadelphia. When Sarah died in 1770, her daughter Mary Katharine took over the printing duties in Philadelphia, and William set out for Baltimore, to found the *Maryland Journal*.

In 1774 Mary Katharine went to Baltimore to manage the Goddard press and edit William's newspaper while he organized the Constitutional Post Office. She efficiently conducted her brother's business. For many years all publications of the press were "Printed by Mary K. Goddard, at the Post-Office in Baltimore-Town." Technically expert, she employed unusual type fonts. She also ran a dry goods and stationery business, and may have had a financial interest in the local paper mill. During the war years, when printing supplies were scarce, she published the only newspaper in Baltimore.

William and Mary Katharine Goddard each printed the Ellicott almanacs. In those produced by Mary Katharine, the printing is excellent. The calendar pages, a real test of the printer's art, are neat; the symbols are clear, and the spelling and capitalization are generally more consistent than in most of the other almanacs of the time. Her Ellicott almanacs disclose that she may have been a better printer than William. Nor did she ever quarrel with the eminent astronomer, Andrew Ellicott, as William did. (Accused by the latter of "fallibility in astronomical calculations" in the al-

Pastel Portrait of William Goddard
by Benjamin Blyth.

Mary K. Goddard.

manac for 1787, Ellicott retaliated in a paid advertisement, in the same almanac, that these errors were the printer's rather than the calculator's.)

Mary Katharine's almanacs were of relatively high literary quality. Her *Maryland and Virginia Almanack* for 1782 included a serious and formal preface; eclipses; "Explanation of the Type of the Transit of Mercury," accompanied by an illustration; an advertisement that offered (from the printer) cash and merchandise in exchange for rags and "empty vials"; an "Account of the Allegany Philosopher"; fables, anecdotes, maxims; "Some remarkable Observations and Reflections on that Remarkable Bird the STORK"; "A Concise Character of the Indians from Capt. Carver's Travels"; "An Account of the River Mississippi"; and verse, including a translation from the French. Of special interest to feminine readers were "The Art of dying Worsteds, Cottons, Linens, &c, &c of Vari-

128

ous Colours" and "An excellent water for taking out spots in cloth, stuffs, &c." *Mary K. Goddard's Pennsylvania, Delaware, Maryland, and Virginia Almanack for . . . 1785* contained advertisements for patent medicines. (Miss Goddard frequently used her name as part of her almanac title—the only colonial woman printer to do so.) In other issues, "Receipts" (a more familiar component of

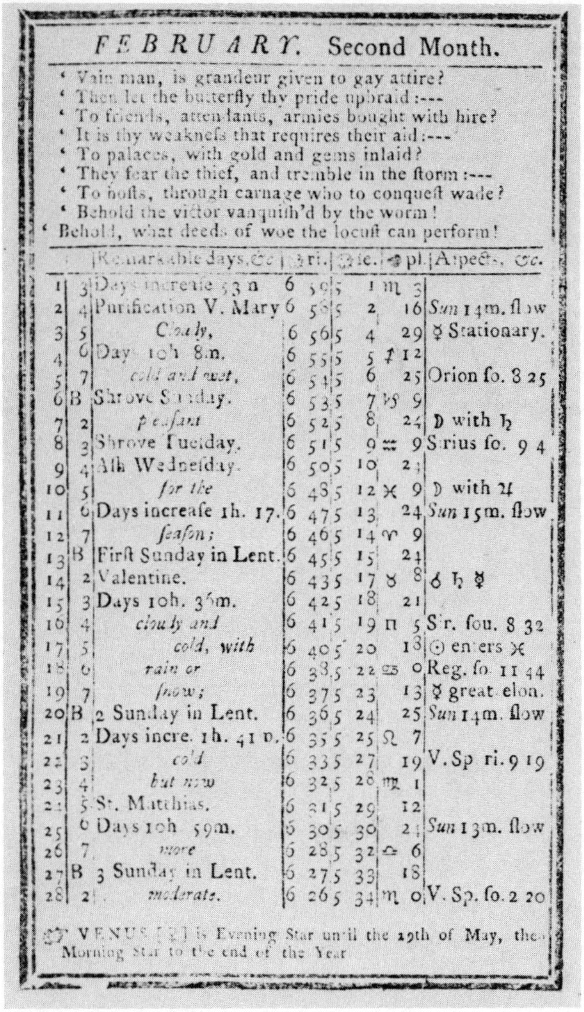

FEBRUARY. Second Month.

'Vain man, is grandeur given to gay attire?
'Then let the butterfly thy pride upbraid:---
'To friends, attendants, armies bought with hire?
'It is thy weakneſs that requires their aid:---
'To palaces, with gold and gems inlaid?
'They fear the thief, and tremble in the ſtorm:---
'To hoſts, through carnage who to conqueſt wade?
'Behold the victor vanquiſh'd by the worm!
'Behold, what deeds of woe the locuſt can perform!

		Remarkable days, &c.	☉ ri.	☉ ſe.	☽ pl.	Aſpects, &c.
1	3	Days increaſe 53 m	6 59	5 1	♏ 3	
2	4	Purification V. Mary	6 58	5 2	16	*Sun* 14m. ſlow
3	5	*Cloudy,*	6 56	5 4	29	☿ Stationary.
4	6	Days 10h 8m.	6 55	5 5	♐ 12	
5	7	*cold and wet,*	6 54	5 6	25	Orion ſo. 8 25
6	B	Shrove Sunday.	6 53	5 7	♑ 9	
7	2	*pleaſant*	6 52	5 8	24	☽ with ♄
8	3	Shrove Tueſday.	6 51	5 9	♒ 9	Sirius ſo. 9 4
9	4	Aſh Wedneſday.	6 50	5 10	24	
10	5	*for the*	6 48	5 12	♓ 9	☽ with ♃
11	6	Days increaſe 1h. 17.	6 47	5 13	24	*Sun* 15m. ſlow
12	7	*ſeaſon;*	6 46	5 14	♈ 9	
13	B	Firſt Sunday in Lent.	6 45	5 15	24	
14	2	Valentine.	6 43	5 17	♉ 8	☌ ♄ ☿
15	3	Days 10h. 36m.	6 42	5 18	21	
16	4	*cloudy and*	6 41	5 19	♊ 5	Sir. ſou. 8 32
17	5	*cold, with*	6 40	5 20	18	☉ enters ♓
18	6	*rain or*	6 38	5 22	♋ 0	Reg. ſo. 11 44
19	7	*ſnow;*	6 37	5 23	13	☿ great elon.
20	B	2 Sunday in Lent.	6 36	5 24	25	*Sun* 14m. ſlow
21	2	Days incre. 1h. 41 m.	6 35	5 25	♌ 7	
22	3	*cold*	6 33	5 27	19	V. Sp. ri. 9 19
23	4	*but now*	6 32	5 28	♍ 1	
24	5	St. Matthias.	6 31	5 29	12	
25	6	Days 10h 59m.	6 30	5 30	24	*Sun* 13m. ſlow
26	7	*more*	6 28	5 32	♎ 6	
27	B	3 Sunday in Lent.	6 27	5 33	18	
28	2	*moderate.*	6 26	5 34	♏ 0	V. Sp. ſo. 2 20

☞ VENUS [♀] is Evening Star until the 29th of May, then Morning Star to the end of the Year

Typically neat calendar page from Mary K. Goddard's almanac for 1785.

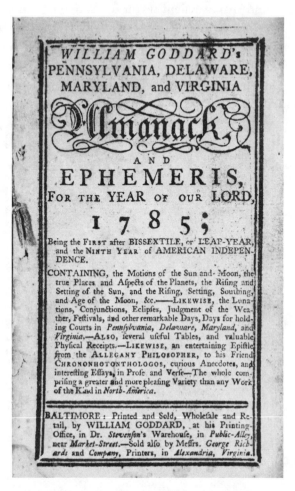

WILLIAM GODDARD's
PENNSYLVANIA, DELAWARE,
MARYLAND, and VIRGINIA

Almanack

AND

EPHEMERIS,
FOR THE YEAR OF OUR LORD,

1 7 8 5;

Being the FIRST after BISSEXTILE, or LEAP-YEAR,
and the NINTH YEAR of AMERICAN INDEPEN-
DENCE.

CONTAINING, the Motions of the Sun and Moon, the
true Places and Aspects of the Planets, the Rising and
Setting of the Sun, and the Rising, Setting, Southing,
and Age of the Moon, &c.—LIKEWISE, the Lunations, Conjunctions, Eclipses, Judgment of the Weather, Festivals, and other remarkable Days, Days for holding Courts in *Pennsylvania, Delaware, Maryland*, and
Virginia.—ALSO, several useful Tables, and valuable
Physical Receipts.—LIKEWISE, an entertaining Epistle
from the ALLEGANY PHILOSOPHER, to his Friend
CHRONONHOTONTHOLOGOS, curious Anecdotes, and
interesting Essays, in Prose and Verse—The whole com-
prising a greater and more pleasing Variety than any Work
of the Kind in *North-America*.

BALTIMORE: Printed and Sold, Wholesale and Retail, by WILLIAM GODDARD, at his Printing-
Office, in Dr. *Stevenson's* Warehouse, in *Public-Alley*,
near *Market-Street*.—Sold also by Messrs. *George Richards* and *Company*, Printers, in *Alexandria, Virginia*.

Rival almanacs published by William Goddard . . .

nineteenth-century almanacs) were given for the cure of the
"Dysentery or Bloody-Flux," the "Bite of a Mad-dog," and a
"Cramp of the Stomach."

Humorless, ambitious, and intellectual, Mary Katharine never
married. Records show that she excelled in every business she un-
dertook; that she ranked high in the public regard; and that she
seems to have devoted her life to serving her country, her customers—and her brother. Yet despite the historical portrait of a

130

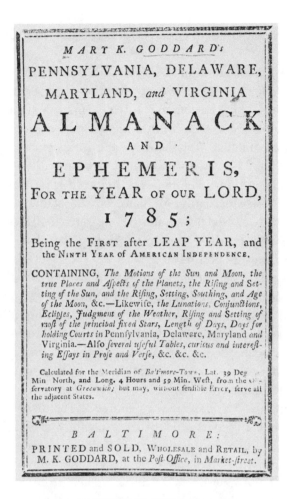

. . . and Mary K. Goddard, 1785.

dignified, dedicated, and exemplary woman, some of her actions
show that she was not totally devoid of passion. She was an early
advocate of liberty of the press. The minutes of a meeting on
June 3, 1776, of the Baltimore County Committee relate her claim
that "Mr. George Somerville came to the office and abused her
with threats and indecent language on account of a late publication [against him] in her paper." Refusing to obey an official sum-
mons, Mr. Somerville was forcibly brought before the Committee

131

where he was tried and convicted "by the evidence of Miss Goddard" and ordered to give security bond "for his future good behavior." [62]

One display of emotion by Miss Goddard remains enigmatic. She quarreled with her peripatetic brother; in 1785 they issued rival almanacs. Too gentlemanly to call names, William referred obliquely to his sister as a "certain *hypocritical character*" who is publishing an almanac "for the dirty and mean purpose of Fraud and Deception." She in turn brought five lawsuits against him, trying to collect money she believed he owed her. When accused of treating his sister badly, William, obviously deeply hurt, replied that she "caused five Suits in *one* day, to be commenced against her *only* brother, to perplex, harass, and, if in her power, destroy his fairest hopes in life." [63]

Miss Goddard's fourteen years as postmistress of Baltimore (a position possibly acquired through her brother's influence) culminated in an unfortunate incident. Dismissed from her job in 1789, she appealed for reinstatement, even writing to President Washington, and to the Senate. A petition to the Postmaster General signed by over 230 citizens of Baltimore was unsuccessful. Because the job now entailed "more travelling . . . than a woman could undertake," a *man* was appointed.[64] He died less than a year later, but a second attempt to reinstate Miss Goddard was also unsuccessful. She remained resentful and bitter.

Mary Katharine gradually relinquished her many duties. Having returned the newspaper business to her brother (about the time of the mysterious quarrel), she operated her bookstore for a few years, and then simply lived as "Mary K. Goddard, gentlewoman" until her death in 1816, at age 79. She willed her property to a Negro woman who had served her during her last years.[65] William, who inherited nothing from his sister's estate, lived until December 1817.

Part Two

The
ALMANAC
as Literature

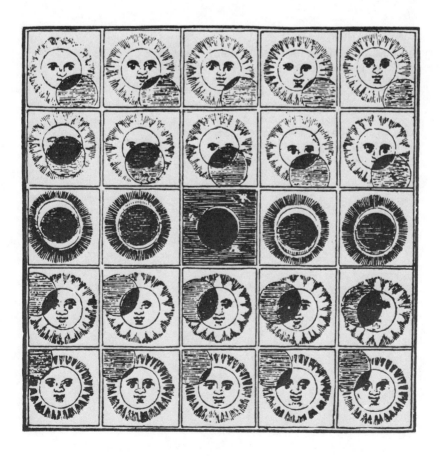

As we have seen, the early American almanac gradually developed a flexible format appropriate to its twin purposes of enlightenment and entertainment. It accomplished these purposes mainly through the use of established literary forms—the epistolary preface, the essay, the receipt (or procedure), the anecdote, the narrative, the maxim, the prediction, and—in poetry—the heroic couplet, the rhymed quatrain, and blank verse.

As almanacs became less astronomical and Puritanical, their prose and verse grew pervasively satiric, within conventions that largely echoed British exemplars, even to the perpetration of such hoaxes as false announcements of the deaths of rival almanac-makers, after the fashion of Dean Swift's reporting the death of a certain Partridge. The predominantly biographical and autobiographical narratives intended for the delectation of colonial farmers were typically couched in terms of lords and ladies, squires, and descriptions of the English countryside. And the epistolary prefaces were as a rule flatteringly addressed in the English manner to the "kind," "courteous," "ingenious," or "benevolent" reader, and written in the tone of a visiting parson. Nathanael Low tells the "Courteous Reader" (in 1765) "That a man had as good be out of the World as out of the Fashion; and since Epistles to all Kinds of Books are highly in Fashion, I shall ask leave to trouble you with a short Account of what I have designed for your Entertainment."

Almanac prose rarely presented pure fiction. An existing English literary convention of "factual" narrative was reinforced initially by a Puritan insistence on truth. Even the most bizarre tales were carefully documented to give the illusion of reality. Interest in exotic places and persons was manifest in travel accounts, biographical anecdotes, and stories of people in high places or of those with unusual accomplishments and personal characteristics. The almost Gothic character of some narrative accounts of captivities and of wondrous events and personages attests the typical reader's desire for other than pedestrian literature.

A Puritan preoccupation with death, time, and the ephemerality of man's existence permeates much of the early New England almanac verse, especially that on title pages and last pages. Occasionally, this gloom ties in with the seasonal verse, the change of seasons being taken as an analogy for man's mortality. Eighteenth-century American almanac poets, in mimicry of their British contemporaries, often used classical themes, ostentatious imagery, and pompous rhetoric. An epitaph in Low's almanac for 1767 imitates Pope:

On a Lap Dog.

Here Shock, the Pride of all his Kind is laid,
Who fawn's like Man, but ne'er like Man betray'd.

The colonial almanac-makers were not writing for sophisticates, but for a clientele comparable to that cultivated by English almanackers. Evaluation of literary quality must proceed from this circumstance. If the literary works of seventeenth-century Boston, for example, are compared with those of a contemporaneous provincial city in England, it can be seen that the colonials were well aware of the mother country's culture. When England hanged witches, New England hanged witches; when England accepted Copernican science, New England accepted it; and when English almanac-makers infused their compilations with "belles lettres" often worthy of Quince and Bottom, American almanac-makers followed suit. A comparison of seventeenth-century English and American almanacs shows that the American ones actually contain more verse than the English, with less repetition of the same verses from year to year. But the verse themes are similar, as are their mechanics.

The evaluation of almanac literature is complicated by the extent to which almanac-makers borrowed material from other writers. Borrowing, of course, was universal. J. A. Leo Lemay estimates that "over half of the poetry published in the colonial periodicals was reprinted—usually without acknowledgment—from English periodicals." Although Lemay tries to distinguish American from English verse, he concludes that "probably twenty percent of the poetry" included in his *Calendar of American Poetry* is English.[1] His estimate that "half" of this poetry came from English periodicals is probably a conservative one—for almanacs. Sometimes credit was given to the original author, and sometimes quotations were used without acknowledgment; the common practice was frank piracy. For example, on the September page of Ames's almanac for 1752, this verse appears:

> '*When Vice prevails, and impious Men bear sway*',
> Rather than be as meanly great as they.

Ames, more conscientious than other almanac-makers, notes: "This line from Addison's *Cato*." The unacknowledged title page verse for Low's almanac for 1772 begins: "Hope springs eternal in the human Breast." Low is not so honest here as in his almanac for 1764 (January page):

> I Wou'd inform my Readers, that the Poetry of the Almanack this Year, is chiefly my own: What I have borrowed from other Authors, is either subscrib'd with it's Authors Name, or distinguish'd with the Mark used for Quotations.—The Resolves which you will find in the Vacuum, is the Sentiments of several of the most worthy amongst the Antients, as well as our own.

Poor Job's unsigned calendar verse for July 1753 begins:

> *A* Little Learning *is a dangerous Thing;*
> *Drink* deep, *or* taste not *the Pierian Spring.*

In Titan Leeds's *American Almanack* for 1728:

> *Good Name's the immediate Jewel of our Souls.*
> *Who steals my purse, steals Trash: 'Tis something,*
>   *nothing.*

137

DECEMBER. *XII Month.*

'Here live enjoying Life, ſee Plenty, Peace ;
'Their Lands encreaſing as their Sons increaſe !
'As Nature yet is found in leafy Glades
'To intermix the Walks with Lights and Shades ;
'Or as with Good and Ill, in chequer'd Strife,
'Various the Goddeſs colours human Life ;
'So in this fertile Clime if yet are ſeen
'Moors, Marſhes, Cliffs, by Turns to intervene :

[*See Bottom of next Page.*] 'Where

		Remark. days, &c.	☉ riſ	☉ ſet	☽ pl.	Aſpects, &c.
1	6		7 19	4 41	♎ 23	
2	7	Day 9 22 long.	7 19	4 41	♏ 6	♀ ſets 6 25
3	A	Advent Sunday.	7 20	4 40	18	☽ with ♂ *Suc-*
4	2		7 20	4 40	♐ 0	☌ ♄ ☿ *ceſs has*
5	3	*Now more*	7 21	4 39	12	7 *s ſou. 10 44
6	4	Days dec. 5 34.	7 22	4 38	24	☌ ☽ ♄ ☿
7	5	*moderate,*	7 22	4 38	♑ 6	♂ riſe 5 13
8	6	Concep. V. M.	7 23	4 37	18	☽ with ♀ *ruin'd*
9	7	*now*	7 23	4 37	♒ 0	Sirius riſe 8 25
10	A	2d in Advent.	7 24	4 36	12	*many a*
11	2	*cold,*	7 24	4 36	24	*Man.*
12	3	*cloudy and*	7 24	4 36	♓ 7	♀ ſets 6 40
13	4	St. Lucy.	7 24	4 36	19	Sirius riſe 8 7
14	5	Days decr. 5 40	7 25	4 35	♈ 2	7 *s ſou. 10 4
15	6	*rain or*	7 25	4 35	15	☍ ♃ ☿ *Great*
16	7	*ſnow, with*	7 25	4 35	28	♃ riſe 5 51
17	A	3d in Advent.	7 25	4 35	♉ 11	⚹ ♂ ♀ *Pride*
18	2	*wind;*	7 25	4 35	25	☌ ☉ ♄ *and*
19	3	*then*	7 25	4 35	♊ 10	*Meanneſs ſure*
20	4	*more mo-*	7 25	4 35	25	*are near ally'd;*
21	5	St. Thomas.	7 25	4 35	♋ 10	☉ in ♑ ☌ ☽ ♃
22	6	Shorteſt day 9 9	7 25	4 35	25	♂ riſe 5 0
23	7	*derate.*	7 25	4 35	♌ 10	Sirius riſes 7 23
24	A	4th in Advent.	7 25	4 35	25	*Or thin Parti-*
25	2	CHRIST born.	7 25	4 35	♍ 9	*tions do their*
26	3	St. Stephen.	7 25	4 35	23	*Bounds divide.*
27	4	St. John.	7 25	4 35	♎ 7	♀ ſet 7 11
28	5	Innocents.	7 25	4 35	20	7 *s ſou. 9 0
29	6	*windy and*	7 25	4 35	♏ 3	
30	7	Days incr. 2 m.	7 24	4 36	16	Sirius riſe 6 52
31	A	*cold.*	7 24	4 36	29	☍ ☉ ♃

Ben Franklin quotes borrowed verse . . .

December hath xxxi Days.

D. H.			Planets Places							
New ☽	5	4 aft.	D.	☉	♄	♃	♂	♀	☿	☽'s L.
First Q.	13	6 aft		♐	♐	♋	♏	♑	♐	
Full ●	20	7 aft.	2	11	26	13	16	8	22	S. 1
Laſt Q.	27	10 mor	7	16	26	13	20	14	♑0	N. 4
☊ { 2 ♏ 15 Deg			12	21	27	13	23	20	7	5
12 15			17	26	27	12	27	27	14	0
22 14			22	♑1	28	12	0	♒3	20	S. 5
			27	6	28	11	4	9	24	3

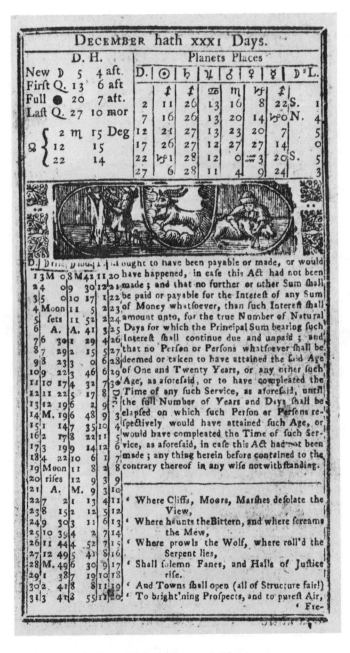

...ought to have been payable or made, or would have happened, in caſe this Act had not been made; and that no further or other Sum ſhall be paid or payable for the Intereſt of any Sum of Money whatſoever, than ſuch Intereſt ſhall amount unto, for the true Number of Natural Days for which the Principal Sum bearing ſuch Intereſt ſhall continue due and unpaid; and that no Perſon or Perſons whatſoever ſhall be deemed or taken to have attained the ſaid Age of One and Twenty Years, or any other ſuch Age, as aforeſaid, or to have compleated the Time of any ſuch Service, as aforeſaid, until the full Number of Years and Days ſhall be elapſed on which ſuch Perſon or Perſons reſpectively would have attained ſuch Age, or would have compleated the Time of ſuch Service, as aforeſaid, in caſe this Act had not been made; any thing herein before contained to the contrary thereof in any wiſe notwithſtanding.

' Where Cliffs, Moors, Marſhes deſolate the View,
' Where haunts the Bittern, and where ſcreams the Mew,
' Where prowls the Wolf, where roll'd the Serpent lies,
' Shall ſolemn Fanes, and Halls of Juſtice riſe.
' And Towns ſhall open (all of Structure fair!)
' To bright'ning Proſpects, and to pureſt Air,
' Fre-

in *Poor Richard Improved* for 1752.

The first line is a condensation of verse by Shakespeare; the others are unaltered (no credits). *Poor Job* in 1752 cites the same passage —no quotation marks, no acknowledgment—but omits the unwanted cue "Dear, my Lord." More than likely, available editions of Shakespeare were as variable as the quotations. In this same almanac, *Poor Job* paraphrases:

> *To-morrow, To-morrow, and To-morrow,*
> *Creep in a stealing Pace from Day to Day.*

Ellicott in 1781, giving no credit, quotes:

> *There is a Tide in the affairs of Men,*
> *Which, Taken at the flood, leads on to fortune.*

Although they make value judgments difficult, unacknowledged borrowings from British writers—together with credited excerpts from them—support a claim that almanacs exerted considerable influence on the literary tastes of the American people. They incidentally controvert the contentions expressed by Elizabeth C. Cook, early in this century, that "all the secular literature of the period with one or two exceptions, may be found in these early newspapers" and that "certainly the newspapers were the centers of all the literary influences in the colonies before 1740." [2] In fact, verse of a sort was published in the earliest extant almanacs, and the philomaths frequently authored many good essays, years before the first colonial newspaper appeared. As early as 1719, Titan Leeds included Bacon's essays, rather than verses, at the top of the calendar pages. In 1722 the Leeds almanac (printed at Philadelphia) included a satirical verse of Dryden's about the law and lawyers; and, in 1724, a Dryden stanza on "Reason." The 1739 Leeds almanac (A. Bradford, printer) quoted a stanza by Herrick, beginning "All Things decay with Time." Many other Leeds verses and essays may be borrowed British originals. Although unsigned, they appear to be a little too professional for Leeds.

The almanac-maker felt no embarrassment about this accepted practice of his time, nor was he averse to admitting an occasional originality. Ames in 1741 indulges his "Courteous Reader" with the explication:

The Verses over each monthly Page I have again this Year transcribed from several ingenious Authors; but what follows in this Page, and the Essay on the Microscope I offer you as something of my own, not borrowed nor stolen: since nothing that I can say will recommend my own Performances to you, I desire you would be pleased to take them as some Men take their Wives, *for better or for Worse:* some Men, I say for other some there are, who take them for *Better* and they prove altogether *Worse;* but this is a Digression, and if as beautiful, as true, I hope you will forgive your humble Servant,

N. AMES

Benjamin Franklin, as Poor Richard, tersely comes to the point in the 1748 almanac:

I need not tell thee that not many of them are of My Own Making. If thou hast any Judgment in Poetry, thou wilt easily discern the Workman from the Bungler. I know as well as thee, that I am not *Poet Born;* and it is a Trade I never learnt, nor indeed could learn . . . Why then should I give my Readers *bad Lines* of my own, when *good Ones* of other People's are so plenty?

Wreg's *Virginia Almanack* in 1758 quotes Pope shamelessly, without credit:

Know then thyself, presume not God to scan,
The proper study of Mankind, is Man.

Perhaps inspired by Pope's couplet, the original owner (perhaps a judge or other official) of one copy of Wreg's 1758 almanac left a record on an interleaved page of the following somewhat harsh datum for the poet's "proper Study":

Martha Eliot makes oath that on Thursday the 26th of Octr. she was Delivered of a Woman Child which she declares was begot on her Body by Wm Thompson a Pedlar, & that she never had any carnal fornication with John Wilson or any other Man since she & [Mr?] * Thompson was criminal and that the Child came exactly to the Proper Time of their being Criminal & that [Mr? said?] * Thomson before he Debauched the [said?] * Elliot Promised to marry her.

The prevalence of British literature in American almanacs is not surprising. Technically Englishmen, colonial Americans felt

* illegible

141

at home with British settings and expressions. At a time when importing British goods was considered almost treasonous, colonial almanac-makers continued to borrow narratives, anecdotes, and verse from British publications. The most non-British themes in almanac literature were found in essays. Verse themes, also, were occasionally indigenous. But even when the subject matter was American, literary forms usually followed the British patterns.

5 Epistolary Prefaces

The epistolary preface, or address to the reader, was a standard part of the American almanac from the seventeenth century on. Inconsistently located within the almanac, the preface varied its position from first page to last page and, on occasion, was even placed on the calendar pages, as in *Poor Robin* for 1732.

In keeping with British practice, the author of the preface assumed one or more of five general attitudes: 1) apologist for his humble efforts, 2) benefactor of the common man, 3) grateful recipient of the reader's indulgence and encouragement, 4) defender of his reputation, and 5) critic of his rivals. Excerpts illustrating the first three roles have been quoted previously *; the last two are best exemplified in the public feuds between rival almanac-makers.

Frequently the preface introduced the material contained in the almanac and explained how to read the calendar. Cotton Mather's preface in 1683 explained in detail each column of his calendar pages, from column 1 ("The *Day* of the *Month*") through column 7 ("The Moons Place"). Daniel Leeds, in his preface for 1708, told the "Friendly Reader" how to calculate the "High-

* Samuel Atkins, p. viii. Isaac Briggs, p. xii.

Traitor (Gov. Thomas Hutchinson) *at the Hour of Death.*
Cover illustration, Gleason's *Massachusetts Calendar* for 1774.

The Virtuous Patriot at the Hour of Death.
Cover illustration, Low's *Astronomical Diary for 1775.*

Water" for New York from the computations given for Philadelphia in the columns on the calendar pages. John Jerman's 1721 preface explained how and where he was treating the motions and aspects of the planets. In 1726 Ames used his address to the reader to explain the calendar columns and to give the "Names and Characters of the Planets, Signs, Aspects, and Nodes." As late as 1793, Father Tammany's preface explained how to understand the sun's, planets' and moon's places on his calendar pages.

Prefaces during the later eighteenth century were often appeals to the patriot. In 1766 the second Dr. Ames reminded the "Generous Reader" that, although the King had tried to enforce unbearable taxation laws, including the detested Stamp Act, American colonists were not yet ready to "think of independency." The following year he wrote about "that noble spirit of *Freedom.*" He admonished the reader to profit from the history of the Roman Empire, cautioning him against extravagance and encouraging home industries, such as the raising of silkworms for the home manufacture of raw silk. Other almanac-makers at this time were also imbued with the spirit of liberty. Abraham Weatherwise for 1769 told the "Courteous Reader" that his almanac was "printed on Paper manufactured in this Colony" and requested that he "encourage its Sale in Preference to *others*" not utilizing paper made in America. Dr. Nathanael Low frequently exhorted his readers to resist oppression. Nothing can compensate for the loss of liberty, wrote Low in 1769. In 1771 he justified rebellion and concluded with confidence that, with God's help, "we shall work out our political Salvation." He addressed the inhabitants of Boston in 1775 in four full pages of patriotic sentiment, reviewing in detail the causes of the conflict and again reminding them that the "cause of God in these Colonies" is at stake "and the religion of the gospel in danger of being wrested from our hands." The title page carried a full-page illustration captioned "The virtuous PATRIOT at the Hour of Death."

Sometimes the preface incorporated verse, particularly criticism of predictions and competitors. Clough concluded his preface for 1702 with a typically banal effort:

> *Reader, Expect not from me such Predictions,*
> *As I shall maintain true without restrictions;*
> *For with my predecessors, I promise*
> *T'will hap as there set down, or otherwise.*

In 1703 he continued with more of the same: "Should I foretel that this will Sell / Pray make it true, and so farewel." In 1704: "As I foretold, Even so it Sold." Jacob Taylor's almanac for 1705 put his competitor Daniel Leeds in his place. First he assessed his own abilities in "Our skillful Author by Experience Wise, / His sublime Muse so Nimbly scales the Skies." Then, abruptly changing his rhythm and tone, he launched into a brief ballad:

> *But Leeds exerts a Thumping Wit*
> *Above all Vulgar Measure:*
> *Moves Nature in a jumping fit*
> *According to his pleasure.*

The most enjoyable addresses are the least derivative. Touches of original style occasionally suggest a man behind the almanac. Nathaniel Ames, II, was a scholar and probably a gentleman, but human enough to indulge, with circumspection, in some remarks about rivals and personal problems. His son was not at all of such benign disposition, and his vituperative expression of pet peeves lacked his father's detachment and kindly amusement. The Franklin family was playful, creative, good-humored, and completely irrepressible. Mary Katharine Goddard was sincere, polite, conscientious, persevering, and literary. In the feud between Taylor and Daniel Leeds, and in the more famous feud between Titan Leeds and Ben Franklin, the quite different personalities of the Leedses are revealed. Daniel was outspoken, vindictive, and perhaps hypersensitive; yet—despite the vigor with which he entered into a dispute with his foremost rival—he had a sense of humor. On the other hand, his son Titan was a serious, self-righteous, gullible, practical man who appeared to take things at face value.

Although the prefaces of the Ames almanacs were usually given to instructive essay-like prose on astronomy, astrology, philosophy, and religion, the good Dr. Ames, II, on more than one occasion let his emotions partially govern his expression. In 1746 Ames was concerned about his personal difficulties:

I may say this Year past has been truly *Annus tenebrosus* with me. I have been violently assaulted; my Enemies in a private Way endeavour to blacken my Name and Reputation . . . They would have caused *Urania* to have quitted her friendly Visits, in Consequence of which you would have had no Almanack of mine this Year; but the Reproach and Scandal of the Base instamps the Character of Glory, and leaves on the Head of him they smite a Monument of Worth and Honour.

In 1752 he mentioned his personal problems, saying, "The Affairs of my House are of a publick Nature, and therefore I hope may be mentioned here without Offence . . . ."

In 1765 the second Dr. Ames expressed his feelings vehemently. His antipathies this year were three kinds of pseudo-professionals: quacks, "another Herd of these Drones . . . called *Pettyfoggers*," and some other "Clogs on our growing Wealth . . . who under the specious Pretence of Religion, and an alarming Conscience, walk to and fro, up and down the Earth, sowing Sedition among Churches . . . ." This misanthropic Dr. Ames disliked people in general, and printers in particular. In 1772 he told the "Benevolent Reader":

> The harmony and union which, in my Father's day subsisted among the Gentlemen of the TYPE, being now unhappily destroyed, renders it necessary for me to delay the publication of my Almanack. . . .

Perhaps there were Franklin family traits of sprightly wit and bantering humor. The prefaces in *Poor Robin, Poor Richard,* and *Poor Job* have these common characteristics. Although the two James Franklins did not fully create personae, as Ben Franklin did, their pseudonymous characters display distinctive personality traits. "Robin" emerges as an unwilling, though affable, slave to the stars; "Job" is every bit as clever and playful, but a little more independent.

James Franklin's *The Rhode Island Almanack* (or *Poor Robin*) was initiated in 1728 with an address "To my loving Countrymen in the Colony of Rhode Island, &c." He first explained the contents of his almanac, which included the Saints' Days and other Holy Days:

for the sake of some who keep Days holy, and others who keep Holy-Days. . . .

Tho' I have not given you my proper Name, yet I assure you I have had one the greatest part of half an hundred Years; and I know of no Necessity for parting with it at this Time, since I presume my Almanack will answer all the Ends design'd without that Expence. So, wishing you a happy new Year; bid you adieu.

In 1732 he confided:

There is not a more dishonest Business in the World than an Almanack Maker's. Some of us pretend to be *Students in Physick and Astrology*, others in *Physick* and *Astronomy*. Some are *Lovers of the Mathematicks*, &c. But when we would discover all our Stock of Learning in the Title Page only, we call our Selves *Philomat*.

To be plain with my Reader, I never could make an Almanack (like a Son of Art) but when I was distracted. I have sometimes indeed endeavour'd to write one when in my Senses. But as soon as I became distracted again, and perus'd my tedious Performance, I found my Calculations all wrong. The last Year I happened to be in my right Mind, which was the only Reason that I did not publish to my Country-Men what the Stars told me when I did not understand them. [Samuel Maxwell had compiled the 1731 edition.]

Poor Robin justified his omission of the Signs with "Is not a Man's own Head and Shoulders better than the Sign of his Head and Shoulders? For my Part, I like the former best, and so do all my Brethren; tho' they pretend to the Contrary, on purpose to deceive the Vulgar." He is confident that the reader can trust this year's almanac, "for I can assure him, I am, with the utmost Respect, His distracted Friend, and very Humble Servant, Poor ROBIN. P.S. If my Performance is approv'd of this Year, perhaps I may be out of my Head for the Year 1733."

The performance was undoubtedly approved, and Poor Robin was again out of his head for three more years, until his death in 1735. In 1734:

Many there are who ascribe to the Stars a binding and inevitable Necessity of Fate, affirming, That they compel Men to certain Actions. Of this Opinion are the *Chaldeans, Stoicks,*

Pharisees, and a multitude of *Farriers*. . . . Aristotle gives his Opinion in *Latin* and *English: Sapiens et omina Sapientis Medica Dominabunter Astris.* A wise Man, and the ominous Art of a wise Physician, shall prevail against the Stars. I am a wise Man, and have the ominous Art of a wise Physician; yet the stars will rule me so far as to oblige me to make an ALMANACK against my Will.

He hopes that the reader "will kindly accept what the Stars by main Strength have forced into the Head of Their Humble Servant . . . ."

In his last preface, for 1735, Poor Robin wrote that some astronomers say that the best almanac-makers are those who first have Love in the heart and convey that Love to the brain. He was "violently seiz'd with this Passion" but could not figure out how to get the Love from his heart to his head. But while gathering plums for his true love he toppled out of the tree, hitting his head on a stone. He fell into a swoon that lasted five days, three hours, and twenty-eight minutes, during which he visited notable astronomers (Bicho-Brachi, Erra Pater, Partridge, Dr. Whaley, and others) who helped him with his calculations for this year. He concludes with "I hope my Charming Beauty will not be offended at my Passion's flying aloft for a few Days, when I assure her that it is now dropp'd into its proper Seat, and that I am Her's and the Reader's . . . ." In a postcript he says that, in his swoon, he met Albertus Magnus who advised him to study "the Sciences of Astrology, Astronomy, Palmistry, Physiognomy, Omens, Dreams, &c. because, said he, it teaches us to consider the Causation of Causes in the Causes of Things."

In 1739 the Widow Franklin published *The Rhode Island Almanack* by "Poor Robin." Poor Robin, in this almanac, tells the reader that he has "receiv'd a Quietus from the Stars" and did not have to make almanacs for a while; but "like an angry Town-Council" they have revoked his "*Quietus,*" and he is forced back into business.

The Franklins had nothing to do with Poor Robin's almanac for 1744, but the preface was written in the spirit of James Franklin, Sr.[1] Scattered throughout the almanac, the "preface" satirically castigated rivals William Ball, John Jerman, and Titan Leeds. Titan had spread a "Caliginous Fog" over the land; the other two were a "strange Cloud" and a "strange Vapour . . . of such a Pestiferous Nature" that they had caused the planets to have fits and had driven the moon and stars "almost out of their Wits." The author corrected Ball's "wild Meanders" and ridiculed Jerman's prognostications.

Poor Richard's early prefaces contain some of Ben Franklin's best writing. Maintaining the bemused objectivity of the British "Mr. Spectator," he is often impish, but not petulant; delicately satirical, not sarcastic. And his development of two realistic characters, Richard and Bridget Saunders, is unique in early American literature. In 1736, Poor Richard says that some people believe there is no such person as he:

> But so long as I know my self to walk about, eat, drink and sleep, I am satisfied that there is really such a Man as I am, whatever they may say to the contrary. . . . I make this publick and serious declaration, which I desire may be believed, to wit: That *what I have written heretofore, and do now write, neither was, nor is written by any other man or men, person or persons whatsoever.* Those who are not satisfied with this must needs be very unreasonable.

In 1737, Poor Richard defends almanac-makers. They may miss a few things here and there, but they hit the day of the month, and, after all, that is one of the most practical things in an almanac. He criticizes John Jerman, who predicts weather with "Snow here or in New England" and "Warm to the Southward"; but Poor Richard claims to do better. If his predictions fail, it is likely because the printer has rearranged them to make room for his holidays.

In 1738, his wife Bridget writes the preface. She says that, before setting out to meet an old Stargazer, Richard left the copy with her to send to the printer. Suspicious because of his past aspersions on her habits, she opened the package to see what he was up to. Sure enough, he was again telling the public their domestic secrets. Bad enough that she was proud and that she had bought a new petticoat, but now the public was to know she had taken to drinking tea. So she deleted this foolishness—and more. Glancing at the weather, she saw entirely too many inclement days. Out they came; and she substituted some good weather so that housewives might dry their clothes.

In 1739 Poor Richard needles John Jerman, claiming that John had consulted the stars about the kind of nourishment to give a sick horse. Richard then explains his business arrangement with the printer Ben Franklin:

> By Virtue of which he runs away with the greatest Part of the Profit.—However, much good may't do him; I do not grudge it him: he is a Man I have a great Regard for, and I wish his Profit ten times greater than it is.

James Franklin, Jr., seemingly inherited a double dose of his father's and uncle's humor and pragmatism. The preface in *Poor Job* for 1750 explains, as many first prefaces do, why he has decided to write an almanac. The third reason is

> (to tell you the plain Truth) that my Almanack might sell well. For where is the Man, let him profess what he will, whose Undertakings are not with a View tending either to his Fame, Ease, or Profit?

If the reader should imagine that an almanac-maker is not interested in profit, he will be as deceived "as the Turks are in their Mahomet."

In 1751 Poor Job thinks it odd that some people believe there is no living person such as he. His method of proving his existence closely resembles that used by his Uncle Poor Richard several years before:

> But this I know, that I am living, and in good Health at this present Writing, and hope my Almanack may find my Readers in the same Condition . . . May their Bellies be always easy, by whose Bounty mine is daily fill'd with Beef and Pudding.

He offers additional proof of his existence. His mother, before he was born, dreamed she was "brought to-bed of a new Moon," and an astrologer interpreted this to mean that her son was to be an almanac-maker. Further, his nurse used to say that, when she laid fighting the Wind-Mills, has profelyted more to common Senfe, than fome undigefted Rubbifh I have feen, of a more ftarched Name; but my Modefty (for I have fome) checks me from affuming a Province not properly my own, therefore I fhall take myfelf away in as handfome a Manner as I can; and if fome condemn what is here wrote, as abundant Nonfenfe, I have this for my Confolation the World s a Scene of Folly, and it would be fomewhat ftrange, if an Almanack-maker had not his Share therein.

I remain,

Dear Reader,

Your Friend and Servant,

JOB SHEPHERD.

☞ *Such Readers as are inclin'd, are defired to erafe from the top of each Month, the Numbers XI, XII, I, &c. (which were printed off by miftake) as far as the Month of* September, *where that Trouble is fav'd them.*

Common Notes, 1752.

	Julian.			Gregor.
Dominical Letters	ED	-	-	BA
Golden Number	5	-	-	5
Epact	25	-	-	14
Cycle of the Sun	25	-	-	25
Number of Direction	8	-	-	5

Conclusion of *Poor Job's* preface for 1752.

him on his back in her lap, his eyes seemed to be fixed on the stars.
Poor Job asserts his independence in 1754:

> I have not been accustom'd to servile Fawning, and am deter-
> min'd not to begin now. I would always put myself on a Level
> with a Reader, and conceive myself under no great obligation:
> I have his Money, and he has my Almanack, and I am sure he
> may keep the one in his House, much longer than I shall the
> other in my Pockets. . . . I never pretended to give him any
> Thing more than an *Almanack*. . . .

As for critics, Poor Job says he can ignore them; yet he dauntlessly
attacks the ace almanac-maker of the day, while justifying an error, "lest *Nathaniel Ames* again commence Critic (in which his
Capacity is as extensive as that of *Physician* and *Conjuror*) and
vapour over a Mistake of a Press." Poor Job, with seeming seriousness, blames the printer (himself), and considers himself too mag-
nanimous to report the "multitude of Blunders" annually produced
in Nathaniel Ames's "shallow Composition."

A three-page preface in 1755 offers the reader something "more
solid and substantial" than Job's usual trivial preface. Poor Job discusses "True Philosophy" and "Virtue" in such terms as these: "To
think well, is only to dream well; but it is well-doing that perfects
the Work. As Virtue is the Lustre of Action, so Action is the Life of
Virtue." Learnedly, he alludes to "Lucurgus" and Aristotle, con-
cluding that man should study "NATURE." After two pages, Poor
Job can no longer suppress his humor. Begging indulgence for de-
viating from the serious, he presents a clever case for the almanac:

> . . . how contemptible must such Learning appear, when com-
> par'd with that beneficial Knowledge which constitutes an Al-
> manack-maker!

> History indeed informs us, That when *Alexander* had defeated
> the Army of Darius, amongst the Spoils, there was found his
> Cabinet, so rich, and of such Value, that a Dispute arose what
> to lay in it; *Alexander* said, *I'll soon end that Dispute, I'll lay*
> Homer's *Works* in it. Is it not probable, *kind Reader*, that
> were Almanacks as much in Vogue in *Alexander's* Time as at
> the present (notwithstanding the deserved Esteem *Homer* has
> met with amongst the Learned in every Age since) he would
> have prefer'd an Almanack to *Homer's* works.

154

Job reappears (1758) after a two-year absence. He explains, in a manner reminiscent of Bridget Saunders, why he has included both good and bad weather; the good, for housewives "to whiten their Linen and dry their clothes in, and for the careful diligent Husbandman, comfortably to attend his Farm"; the bad, for the good of shopkeepers, since female customers will tire of "tarrying at Home in foul Weather." Because of his absence, he feels it necessary to make another declaration of his existence:

> *I* Poor Job, *do hereby affirm, declare, and protest, that I am alive, and am no Spirit, but can speak without being spoken to which Spirits they say cannot, or will not do.*
> Now, if an hundred Critics should undertake to prove the contrary, by saying of me as a Person did once of a Brother Almanack maker, *that no Man alive ever wrote such Stuff,* I shall, so sure as I am alive, chastize the Rogues severely in my next Year's almanack.

There is no invective in the prefaces of Mary Katharine Goddard, nor is there humor. But the prefaces are noteworthy for three reasons: 1) they were written by an enterprising and accomplished woman; 2) they exhibit unusual sincerity, dignity, and learning; and 3) they are consistently written in third person, an uncommon style in preface writing. She introduced *Ellicott's Maryland, Delaware . . . Almanack* for 1781 with a Latin quotation followed by:

> He best succeeds, who blends the profitable with the entertaining.—This then will be the constant endeavour of the Publisher. . . . The Publisher will always be happy to have it in her power to contribute the least assistance to the advancement of true science and rational philosophy; she will therefore be extremely glad to receive any Essays, whether prose or poetical, from her literary friends, and will pay the highest deference to any Hints or Observations they may favour her with.

Her prefaces were always formal. A graceful style and a literary bent occasionally provided relief from the typical pomposity of the period. For example, in 1783:

> One year passeth away and another cometh—so likewise 'tis with ALMANACKS—they are annual productions. . . . In performances then of so transient a nature, it is no wonder,

when they become *old Almanacks*, that we frequently see them made use of by the pastry-cook, or flying in the tail of the school-boy's kite.—The works of greater authors meet with the same fate: Even Sir *Isaac Newton*'s *Principia*, together with *Quarles's Emblems, Pilgrim's Progress*, and many a system of metaphysics may be seen in the bottom of old trunks; but this militates nothing against the merits of any performance, neither does it discourage the Editor to proceed in her endeavours to please the Public.

From the beginning of the eighteenth century, some intense feuds were publicized. To what degree the rivalry was real is a matter for speculation. The two feuds involving the Leeds family reflect the interesting and diverse personalities of the participants.

A particularly abusive exchange is that between Jacob Taylor and Daniel Leeds. Taylor attacks Leeds in *Ephemeris Sideralis* for 1706, including in the preface a special section called "A Little (for the present) concerning D: Leeds." The "Little" was two and one-half pages long. Taylor accuses Leeds of being an "unreasonable Transcriber" who "filched matter out of other men's works to furnish his spurious Almanacks." In this diatribe against Daniel Leeds, Taylor perhaps surpasses all other almanac-makers in sustained vituperation. Though ostensibly religious, he obviously did not consider such spiteful invective incompatible with Christianity.

Daniel Leeds's preface for 1706 justifies the errors that had appeared in his 1704 edition:

> the Printer at that time (being sick) entrusted his Servant to print one or two of my former Almanacks. . . . At this Jacob Taylor in the *Quaker-Almanac*, 1705 crows like a Cock on his own Dung hill, and writes several pages to run me down [Leeds exaggerates] and set himself the wisest Astronomer in *English America.*

Then, almost petulantly, Leeds suggests that Taylor should "correct the Boston Almanack too," for it, too, differs from Taylor's. He contends that Taylor himself has different calculations for the same events in his Book of Eclipses and in his almanac for 1705, and adds that Taylor "could certainly have told us had it not been cloudy that day. This is no *Printers* fault but his Own. . . . He . . .

steals and or borrows . . . ." Leeds could say more, but he has accomplished his purpose. In a gay quatrain, he concludes that he has said enough to get a rise out of Taylor, "And so we shall have done I know not when . . . ."

Leeds really warms up for the contest in 1707, devoting a lengthy preface to Taylor:

> I am told that *Jacob Taylor*, the *Philadelphia*-almanac-maker (thinking himself great in Parts and Art) had 5000 of his Almanacks printed last year, but did not sell one quarter of them, notwithstanding his many pretty witty crabbed names he there bestows on me. But why should I complain, seeing he at last prefers me to be Rhodomanthus, i.e. Judge of Hell. . . . Well, but if I am Judge of Hell, let him take heed hereafter of abusing me, as he has done, lest when he comes there to be judged, I should Sentence him to be tormented according to his Deserts.

He cites specific errors in Taylor's calculations of the moon's southings:

> Whereas almost every Water-man, and every one that can but read knows the moon is ordinarily South a quarter of an hour later every night, as well at full as at any other time. Therefore *Jacob* is great indeed if he can flop the Moons Course to make it suit his Tables.

Leeds again concludes with verse, a rhymed triplet:

> *So now to his Quaker-Light I must leave him,*
> *And pray God by his Grace may undeceive him,*
> *And of his Pride and Confusion bereave him.*

The 1708 preface continued the attack on Taylor, pointing out particular errors. "Nay, behold how this wrangling *Taylor* hits himself a Box on the ear, by terming me a fool herein!" (Taylor had used the same method for the moon's southing as Leeds.) "But is not this *Taylor* a lump of deceipt" because he pretends to calculate "the Planets places himself, and has been vapouring and crowing against me . . . whenas he has all this while been lazily transcribing from a *German Ephemeris* . . . ." Leeds uses clever, though specious, rationale:

> This indeed is verylike him, especially considering his Monthly Rhymes last year, which are profane and Atheistical.

157

I'll give one instance thereof from two lines in *December*,
where he says,

> Created Forms Diffinitions, Orders, Rules,
> Bones of Religion make us fit for Fools.

Here he mocks at Religion; for I appeal to all judicious Men
whether any sect or Religion can . . . be preached without all
those, viz. *Forms, Diffinitions, Orders, and Rules.* And yet
those he says makes it fit for fools. So that none but Fools pro-
fess to be Religious.

I shall trace him no further, but must needs conclude, that
no Government else in Christendom would suffer such Atheis-
tical Scoffs at Religion to be published, without Just rebuke to
the Authors and Printers.

In his preface to 1710, Leeds accused Taylor of "multiferous
Lyes." Taylor had accused Leeds of attacking first, "which is another falsehood of his." Leeds claimed (justly, it seems) that he
wrote nothing against Taylor "till he fell foul on me for some errors of the Press." As was his custom, Leeds softened his blows
at the end with verse:

> No place but is of Errors rife,
> In Labours, Lectures, Leaves, Lines, Life,
> ` Then Taylor's Almanack, as ill as Mine,
> Has Errors in it. Yet he Contends,
> And so do I, whenas a Glass of Wine,
> If we should meet, and drink, might make us Friends.[2]

Subsequent almanacs signed "Jacob Taylor" may have been written by someone else, who capitalized on the successful name. Like
other imitators, the author carried on the same tradition as his
predecessor, railing sarcastically against competitors William Ball
and John Jerman for not knowing their astronomy.

Because he seems to have taken himself, and others, quite
seriously, Daniel's son Titan Leeds was the ideal butt for a joke.
With Leeds's (probably) unwitting help, Ben Franklin launched
his successful series of *Poor Richard* almanacs. Leeds rose to the
bait cast in Franklin's first preface. In 1733 Richard Saunders says
he is poor and his wife Bridget is proud. Furthermore, she has
threatened to burn his stargazing equipment if he does not turn
it to some gainful use. He would have written an almanac long
ago, were it not for his friend Titan Leeds, but Titan is soon to
die, so Richard can now publish an almanac in good conscience.

The famous prediction of the death of Titan Leeds follows: he will surely expire at 3:22 o'clock on October 17, 1733, "at the very instant of the ☌ of ☉ and ☿" (i.e., the conjunction of Sol and Mercury). Titan replies in 1734, in an almanac published by Andrew Bradford in Philadelphia, that Richard Saunders, "for want of other matter," has predicted his death, but that he has "by the Mercy of God lived to write a Diary for the Year 1734, and to publish the Folly and Ignorance of this presumptuous Author" who has "manifested himself a Fool and a Lyar." He concludes with "perhaps I may live to write when his Performances are Dead," and dates his preface "October 18, 1733.3 ho. 33 min. P.M." Richard replies in 1734 that Titan Leeds obviously had perished as predicted because 1) the Leeds preface for 1734 was written in an uncivil manner, completely unlike Leeds; 2) the stars could not have erred; 3) Leeds must die for the honor and glory of astrology as practiced by the Leeds family for two generations, and 4) the Leeds almanac for 1734 was so poorly constructed that it could not have been Titan's work. The wit was low; the hints, dull. The contents were totally unworthy. No living astrologer would have written such bad verse. Richard praises Leeds as a man and as an almanac-maker and bemoans his death. In 1735 Titan writes:

> [Richard] useth me with such good manners, I can hardly find what to say to him [except] to advise him not to be too Proud because by his Predicting my Death, and his writing an Almanack (I suppose at his Wife's Request) as he himself says, she has got a Pot of her own and not longer obliged to borrow one from a Neighbour, she has got also two new Shifts, a Pair of new Shoes and a new warm Petticoat; and for his own part he had bought a second-hand Coat so good that he is not ashamed to go to Town, or to be seen there (*Parturiant Montes!*). But if Falsehood and Inginuity be so rewarded, What may he expect if ever he be in a capacity to publish that that is either Just or according to Art?

Leeds advises Saunders never to "take upon him to praedict or ascribe any Persons Death, till he has learned to do it better than he did before."

The public was to be notified once more of the death of Titan

Leeds. In the *American Almanack* for 1739, in a preface signed "W. B." and "A. B.," the Bradford printers, under the pseudonym Titan Leeds, remind the reader of Poor Richard's false prediction, adding that they do not know who *Saunders* is (hardly true) but that he may be the British astrologer who has been dead for sixty years and is risen again "to try his Skill in Predictions here in America, but having been so long in the other World has forgot his Art of telling . . . Fortunes. . . ." They then announce that Titan, as of now, is indeed dead.

In his preface for 1740, Poor Richard inserts a letter purported to be by the ghost of Titan Leeds, in which the ghost makes three predictions: 1) a certain well-known person will astonish his friends by remaining sober for nine consecutive hours, 2) another Leeds almanac will be published by the Bradfords, and 3) John Jerman will turn papist on the 17th of September. The Bradfords retort with another letter from the ghost—in their Leeds almanac for 1740, the same year of Franklin's ghost-letter. The ghost claims to be surprised to read the letter in *Poor Richard,* "said to be writ by me with the Hand of *R. Saunders,* alias *B. Franklin.* I acknowledge I entered his nostril, but could not think he would change my Letter into such strange Language as he has done." The "real" letter:

> Dear Friend Saunders alias Franklin. . . . I expect to have you with us before many Years, where you will find your friend Titan waiting for you. I always wonder'd why you delay'd your Almanack so long, but since I have been free from my dark Prison of Flesh . . . I have found out the reason . . . which is, you wait till *Jacob Taylor*'s, Poor *Will*'s and mine are out, then . . . you patch up your Almanack. This is not doing justice to your Neighbours. . . . [Both almanacs were printed in 1739, for 1740. In this case, which one waited until the other came out? Or was there collusion?]

The ghost says he has told this to nobody, nor has he revealed that Saunders has two names, but if he is used *"ill any more,"* he will tell his friends to put the letter in the preface of their next almanac.

Poor Richard's stab at John Jerman (in the ghost's predictions) prompted the Quaker to deny that he had defected to the Roman

Church. Poor Richard countered in 1742 with proof that Jerman was indeed papist. Jerman had called November 1st All-Hallows Day. Obvious popery! He had also written:

> *When any trouble did me befall*
> *To my dear Mary then I would call.*

Richard argued:

> Did he think the whole world was so stupid as not to notice this? So ignorant as not to know that all Catholics paid the highest regard to the Virgin Mary? Ah, friend John, we must allow you to be a poet, but you certainly are no Protestant. I could heartily wish your religion were as good as your verses.

A few years later, Ben Franklin himself was printing John Jerman's almanac—for 1747 and 1748.

Almanac prefaces generally make good reading. The authors frequently took this opportunity to discuss their personal anxieties and preoccupations. In this respect, epistolary prefaces were forerunners of the modern journalist's editorial. Despite the heavy hand of stylistic convention, these prefaces often exhibit some blithe originality. As a literary form, they seem well suited for all purposes—instruction, entertainment, or a combination of both. Ranging from playfulness to sarcastic invective, the humor of the preface, unlike that in some other forms (for example, anecdotes and maxims) is rarely silly; for the most part, it is engagingly clever. The preface is perhaps the most felicitous literary form in the almanac for wit and humor. Max Savelle notes:

> There is no real study of early American wit, so far as I know, and no single place where it can be found. The most interesting way to find it is to get hold of copies of Ames's, Franklin's, Hutchins's, or some other almanac and read it in its natural setting. . . .
>
> Colonial newspapers . . . are interesting. . . . The almanacs are much more fun.[3]

6 Formal Essays

The subject matter of essays usually included astrology, astronomy, and general science; religion; health and medicine; manners and morality; and history and current events. Principally written for the purpose of instruction, they ranged in length from short essays of only one paragraph to many pages. Satire was rarely found in this genre, as compared to its prevalence in epistolary prefaces, verse, and maxims.

We have seen how the philomath essays of the seventeenth century stressed the science of astronomy. Applied science, unlike pure literature, found fertile soil in America. More academic than commercial, the Cambridge almanacs successfully counteracted astrological influences for a number of years. But as soon as readers had a choice of almanacs, the emphasis inevitably switched to giving readers what they wanted. The eighteenth-century almanac-makers were particularly competitive. Astrology intrigued the common man. The almanac-maker, to survive in the new world of free competition, could not ignore it: he could 1) embrace astrology wholeheartedly, 2) reject it, 3) reconcile it with astronomical science and religion, 4) ridicule it, or 5) double-talk so that the reader could believe whatever he wanted.

One of the most controversial questions of the century was whether the motions of the heavenly "bodies" affected the human body. Almanac-makers took sides; some even took both sides at once. Nathaniel Whittemore in 1719 stated categorically that "These Planets under God the Creator . . . have the Ruling of Animal, Vegetable and Mineral Kingdoms." Titan Leeds, in "Of Eclipses" for 1725 presented a crude bio-meteorological view:

> "As to the Effects of the Moons Eclipse . . . it presageth Tumults, Dissensions, Violence and Hatred; also, great Heats, Tempests, Lightning and Thunder, and causeth Dryness. He Bringeth upon Men Imprisonment, and causeth the Wrath of Great Men."

After he had finished his prediction, he said he would be silent on the effects of the eclipses, but

> if I was inclin'd to amuse my Readers with the Opinions of the Ancients, I could write many wonderful Things. . . . But now by the Improvement of Astronomy, the generality of the World are made sensible that Eclipses proceed from natural causes. . . .

In 1738 Ames confessed his belief that "Astrology has a rational and phylosophical Foundation" in so far as the heavenly bodies affect men's bodies. The seasons, he believes, are determined by the sun's rays, "Which fall under a mathematical Calculation. The Full Moon faces the World with so grand and serious a Look, that even Shepherds, and Plowmen, Old Women, &c, are not ignorant of its Effects." The influences of the planets are not so well known but they undoubtedly "act upon us." Ames then presents an argument based on observation, describing, first, the recent "Destruction of Fish and Water-Fowl" forecast by astrologers and, second, a comet seen in the sign *Pisces* ("which is of a watry nature"), and the floods it supposedly caused.

Nathanael Low in 1770 equivocated about the influences of comets:

But for my own Part I believe them to be capable of no such Mighty Feats, nor indeed of any other than that of a certain Panic into which great Numbers of People are generally thrown by such Appearances, *unless* [italics mine] some Alteration is produced in the Constitution of our Atmosphere by large Quantities of their Effluvia incorporating with it, then indeed we may be obnoxious to the Effects which such an Alteration must naturally produce. . . .

Poor Robin for 1742 termed prognostications of eclipses "rediculous":

It was a Custom among the *Romans* (as well as in the *East-Indies* at *Siam*, &c) to beat Pans and Basons of Brass to deliver the Eclipsed Moon, from her distress . . . But for us at this time o' day, who know what they [eclipses] are, and that they come of Course, as naturally (though not so frequently) as the Rising of the Sun in the Morning, to amuse feeble Readers with Prognostics on Eclipses, is more rediculous than the Old Pagans with their Brass Pans.

Dr. Ames, II, betrayed his fascination with astronomy in his rapturous description of the magnificence of the heavens and in his confession of a frustrated desire to explore personally these glories of God for himself. In 1728 he referred to one of his favorite dreams: habitation of the planets. Impressed by the magnitude of the solar system and the probability of other similar systems, he surmised, albeit theologically rather than statistically, "innumerable number of heavenly Bodies or Globes are without doubt, Worlds, or places of Habitation & Consequently stock'd with proper Inhabitants: for all the Multitude of Systems and Habitable Worlds are created of GOD." And God, of course, would not have created a whole system or world without people.

In 1737 Ames expanded these thoughts with originality. Beginning with Mercury, the nearest to the sun, he described the distance from the sun of six of the planets, the length of their days and years, and how the solar system must appear to the inhabitants of other planets. "The Inhabitants of VENUS," he wrote, "have much the same face of Things as those in MERCURY. The Sun appears by half larger in his Diameter to them than to us, and affords them above twice as much Light and Heat." After describing points of view of the inhabitants of Earth, Mars, Jupiter, and Saturn, he concluded with Earth's moon, leaving "the rest of our secondary Planets to the Astronomers of *Saturn* and *Jupiter* to which they properly belong." Uncertain whether the moon has inhabitants, mountains, rivers, or seas, Dr. Ames would like to see for himself:

> . . . if I had the Machine of the little Spaniard who flew thither with his *Ganses* [fabled bird who took a man to the moon], I could go and see; there if I found neither Atmosphere, Rivers, nor Seas, nor any living Animal: I should be sure to find the Earth's monthly Wane and Increase . . . I should see the Earth turn upon itself presenting me sometimes with a Prospect of *Europe* and *Africa*, and then of *Asia* and *America*.

Dr. Ames had not changed his mind about astrology in 1764, only a few months before his death:

> ASTROLOGY has a Philosophical Foundation: the caelestial Powers that can and do agitate and move the whole Ocean, have also Force and Ability to change and alter the Fluids and Solids of the humane Body; and that which can alter and change the Fluids and Solids of the Body, must also greatly affect and influence the Mind; and that which can and does affect the Mind, has a great Share and Influence in the Actions of Men.

In 1785 Samuel Ellsworth described the planets and their inhabitants with more detail but less restraint than Ames—and undoubtedly with one eye on the citizens of his home town. The inhabitants of Mercury were

> very sprightly, small in body, maintaining the upright posture of men, much given to talking, eloquent of speech, good lawyers and pettifoggers, and if they were a little more stored with a deep understanding would be very good attorneys. . . .

The people of Venus were "of a moderate make and slow of speech, are of a middling stature and moderate temper, and good genius, and much given to licentious love," whereas those who lived on Mars were "sprightly and quick of motion, strong in body, fierce in countenance, of a warlike disposition and very quarrelsome."

Nathaniel Ames often made cogent comments on scientific matters. None of his essays were pedestrian. In 1733 he inferred that the "worlds that dance their destin'd Ring around the Sun, (the Center of our System)" will someday disappear, as dictated by the word of God and by natural phenomena. The sun sends out millions of light and heat rays that it never gets back; therefore, the sun must be getting cooler. As the earth revolves, it gets nearer the sun every year, and "the Earth in Time would be joined to the very Body of that stupendous Luminary. Should Time continue," chaos would result. But this would take such a number of years as to be inconceivable, because

> We cant in reason think that this World will continue till it is worn out with Time; for it is easy to conceive how this Earth and all things in it, may be burnt up by the near approach of a vast Comet, as it comes red hot from the Sun.

Ames implied that it might be the same comet that caused Noah's Flood (by a "Vast Trail of Vapours") and that appeared in 1680 and will reappear in 2255. He cited Cotton Mather's calculations concerning the heat of this comet:

> What Horror & Consternation will this wicked World then be in, when they shall behold this vast Comet like a baneful torch, blaze & roll along the unmeasurable Aether, bending its course directly to this Earth with a Commission from Heaven to burn it up!

In 1739 Nathaniel Ames discussed the world's eternity, in terms of traditional theology. The world could not have existed from eternity because man is too industrious and wise to have lived for ages without "those Arts so advantageous for the Comfort and Benefit of human Life." The world could not have been "*ab eterno*" despite the opinions of "*Aristotle* and some other of the heathen Philosophers." He discussed the age of the world and the opinions of various philosophers on the subject, each taking up where the other left off, making improvements (such as the invention of the telescope in 1590) "till now in our Day, Astronomy is brought almost to the highest Pinnacle of perfection."

In 1740 Dr. Ames combined praise of God with praise of Newton by such rhetoric as "*who* before the Great Sir *Isaac Newton* did behold the Wisdom of the Creator, in that he has bestowed on

Ames's Almanack 1759.

The Solar Syftem.

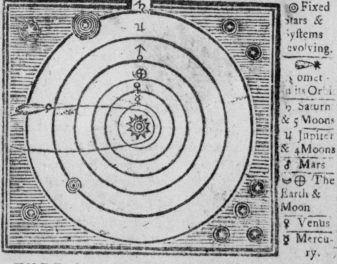

⊙ Fixed
ftars &
fyftems
evolving.

Comet
a its Orbit

♄ Saturn
& 5 Moons
♃ Jupiter
& 4 Moons
♂ Mars
♁ The
Earth &
Moon
♀ Venus
☿ Mercury.

☞ THE Explanation of the above Syftem is in the two Pages following the Month of *December*.
N. B. At the Writing this, it was not determined whether the COMET would appear or not, as expected.

DIRE Wars and mutual Rage are furely come,
E're any Comet blaz'd the threatned Doom!
Kingdoms and States impatiently attend,
The great Events now verging to an End;—
When three Times more the Sun has chear'd the Spring,
A new important Æra will begin:
From which young Date and fettled State of Things
A Train of ftrange Events and Wonder fprings.

BOSTON: Printed and Sold by
DRAPER, GREEN & RUSSELL, & FLEET.

Price Two Piftareens *per Dozen, and* Five Coppers *fingle*.

Title page illustration for Ames's 1759 essay on
"The Solar System."

167

Matter such a property as that every Particle thereof throughout the Creation, has a Tendency towards every other Particle."

In 1743 he wrote a lengthy technical essay called "Of Comets or Blazing Stars." He subdivided his material into Nature, Constitution, Head, Atmosphere, Tail, Magnitude, Appearance, Motion, and Number, and concluded with a detailed table of data. This scholarly paper is representative of the state of the astronomical art for the period.

An unusual essay style was used by Ames in 1746. In "A Dialogue Between a Scholar and a Clown," he gradually approached the serious presentation of astronomical data on eclipses and the stars by means of a rather coarse conversation with a rustic. The Clown inquires whether book-learning teaches what he has heard: that "the World turns round, and that the Sun and Stars stand stock still in the Skies." The Scholar replies that it does. The Clown says:

> I can tell you that a Cow is roundest when she is licking her ——; that a Goose hast more Feathers on her back when the Gander is on her; but you, to go a peg higher in your Pretences to Knowledge, tell us the World turns round, and because we han't Learning to conspute with you, you wou'd have us believe all you say is true?

The Scholar then presents the "consputation" that Ames intended to put across.

Other almanac-makers besides Ames were familiar with the latest development in the science of astronomy. Benjamin Franklin's *Poor Richard* for 1753 and 1754 carried a serial essay on the state of astronomy, which was practically definitive for the time.

Dr. Samuel Stearns, well known for his Tory leanings, began his 1772 almanac essay on the advantages of astronomy with the apologetic admission that "however cheap and contemptible a Thing an Almanack may seem to be," it cost him much effort to produce one. His essay, in contrast to the philomath essays, was jejune. In very general terms, he enumerates the advantages of astronomy: the navigator cannot navigate without it; it teaches us to "observe and discover the Motions of the Heavenly Bodies"; it foretells eclipses; it helps us to understand the "Harmony of Nature, and sheweth where with the whole Frame and Structure of all created Beings are linked and knit together, to constitute the great Machine of the Universe."

Briggs in 1798 began a two-part dissertation on astronomy, which he called "A little SKETCH of the WONDERS into the contemplation of which Astronomy leads its votaries. . . ." Through astronomy one can know more about God. Astronomy is "the most sublime, the most interesting, and the most useful" of all sciences. The student of astronomy, furthermore, has the opportunity to learn more about how the "SUPREME BEING" creates his "harmony." Briggs quotes the line "An undevout Astronomer is mad" from "Dr. Young's Night Thoughts." * Furthermore, Ames continued,

> Whoever imagines that [the brilliant stars] were created only to give a faint glimmering light to the inhabitants of this globe, must have a very superficial knowledge of Astronomy, and a mean opinion of the divine wisdom, since by an infinitely less exertion of creating power, the Deity could have given our earth much more light by one single additional moon.

It is important to realize, however, that most eighteenth-century almanac essays on science (except those of Ames and Franklin) were rarely as learned as those of the seventeenth-century philomaths. Fortunately, both Ames and Franklin were prolific. Despite the coupling of erudition in science with astrological naiveté, Copernican and Newtonian science was reaching the common man. The words printed on the title page of Joseph Browne's almanac for 1669 summed up the prevailing attitude of the teacher, student, or general reader more than a century later, at the end of the eighteenth century: "*Astra regunt mundum, sed astra regit Deus.*" [1]

Dr. Nathaniel Ames was something of a popular science omnivore. In 1736 a biology essay included a quotation from the "learned *Samuel Lee*," British Puritan divine and scholar, on the marvels of tiny creatures. Ames said that there was no "Equivocal

---

* Dr. Edward Young (1683–1765), royal chaplain. His *Night Thoughts* was one of the most important and popular blank verse poems of the eighteenth century.

169

Cover illustration, *Anderson's Improved Almanack*, 1774.

or spontaneous Generation of Animals" and that even "the most contemptible Insect" could not be generated without "Parents, Male and Female of the same kind." After explaining the roles of the male and female, he raised the question of "Worms bred in the Intestines of Man and Beast." Using such technical designations as "*Vermiculus*" and "*Pellicula*," he concluded that "There must be an *Ova* from the Female, impregnated with an *Animalcula* from the Male in the production of these Worms." Ames must have smiled as he added this last paragraph:

> Some Nurses are so Superstitious That they dare not give their Children Worm-Seed without pounding and sifting it, affirming that every Seed that escapes being bruised in the Mortar will become a live Worm in the Bowels of the Child. But, by-the-by, it is an excellent Medicine for the purpose, and they need not be afraid to use it; for, if they will prove that it will breed Worms in Children, I can as easily prove that it can breed Children in Women; and so those unhappy Persons who have had the ill Luck to have Children without Fathers need not lie under the Imputation of Scandal, if they can produce sufficient Evidence that they have taken Worm-Seed.

In the eighteenth century, Christopher Sauer was the greatest exponent of almanac religion. His almanac prose was permeated with theological arguments, enumerated point by point in the style of the early sermons. He discussed doctrine (baptism, communion, etc.), religious education, and morality. For example, in his almanac for 1757, he commented that "To some preachers who were exposed to the sinful life at the universities, drinking is not considered as sinful as it is by those who have been converted to God." Sometimes Sauer wrote essays with more fervor than accuracy. In 1754 the text for his discourse on wearing long hair and beards was: "Ye shall not round the corners of your heads; neither shalt thou mar the corners of thy beard" (Leviticus 19:27). The origin of beard-cutting, as Sauer explained it, had an interesting social basis: Frenchmen, to please the ladies, wanted smooth mouths to go with their smooth tongues.[2] Sauer concluded his sermon-essay with five specific reasons for the then-current popularity of beards in America, which ranged from a yearning to imitate the Divine Image to a distaste for frequent barbering.

Although generally confined to "receipts," the subject of health was occasionally treated in essays. In 1759 Ames was concerned about the "Cause of Sickness in the Camp and the Method to prevent the same." He believed (and who can doubt him?) that more men were dying of sickness in camp than were falling in battle. He explained why men at home could stay healthy on the very same diet that made them ill at camp.

> . . . Persons who live in single Families, besides a good Air, have the Advantages of Cookery and Cleanliness [whereas] Men come to encamp in any Army, their own foul Cloaths, the corrupt Air they Breath in, the rank putrescent Qualities of the Meat they feed on, besides which, their *Summum Bonum Rum* . . . and all this without any Wine, Lemmons, Cyder, Apples, or Acescent Substance to make a Balance between the Acid and Alkaline Salts of the Blood, it is not to be wondered, why so many are Sick and Die under these Circumstances; it is a meer Miracle that any, with these Errors, escape Death.

Some eighteenth-century Americans were concerned about drinking, smoking, and fresh, clean air. *Poor Will's Almanack* for 1774 printed an article "On Drunkenness," which revealed how some colonial Americans really felt about one biological necessity: "Drinking, in its natural state, is not only innocent, but absolutely necessary for the support of life." [3] Dr. Ames wrote "A Page for the Ladies" in 1762 on tea-drinking. He first presented the disadvantages of this practice, namely, its effects on the nerves; he then discussed the advantages, for he believed that "TEA is a Friend to the Muses, it brightens the Intellects and clears the Understanding." Somewhat facetiously, he added that, "next to Tea," the ladies' greatest concern "is their tender Offspring." The essay concluded with medical and cosmetic reasons why a woman should nurse her own infant.

In 1764 Ames, to be fair to both sexes, added a lighthearted essay called "A Page for the GENTLEMEN." First, he described the advantages and disadvantages of tobacco; "Secondly, Of SNUFF." The journeymen and apprentices of London were imitating "great Men" in taking snuff. But the ladies have criticized the gentlemen "for using it to Excess, because it makes them ap-

IN January, 1778, whilst the British troops were in possession of Philadelphia, some Americans, up the river Delaware, had formed a project of sending down by the ebb tide, a number of kegs charged with gunpowder, and furnished with machinery, so constructed, that on the least touch of any thing obstructing their passage, they would explode with great force. The design was to injure the shipping, which lay at an anchor opposite to the city, in such numbers that the kegs could not pass without encountering some of them. But the very evening in which those machines were sent down, the first hard frost came on, and the shipping hauled into the docks—so that the scheme failed. One of the kegs, however, happened to explode near the town: This gave a general alarm in the city—the wharves were manned with troops, and the greatest part of a day spent in firing at every chip or stick that was seen floating in the river: for the kegs were sunk under water, nothing appearing on the surface but a small buoy.

The fatal Consequences of LUXURY.

THERE is no greater calamity can befal any people than when luxury is introduced among them, especially where it becomes general, and is carried to so great an height that every individual is under some necessity of living beyond his fortune, or incurring the censure of being avaricious. A man once engaged in this extraordinary course of living, is seldom able to extricate himself in time, but is hurried on to the brink of ruin, reduces a helpless family to want and misery, and must at length sink under a weight of misfortunes: or, through necessity, be driven to what may sacrifice his honour, country, conscience, and every other consideration, to a present relief, which may—which must at last—end in his destruction. However amiable virtue and integrity may appear in our eyes, human nature will find it difficult to withstand the threatening misery of immediate want. A prison staring a man in the face, continual duns at his door, or a want of his accustomed pleasures, will drive him to extremities, which nothing but necessity could occasion. He is no longer master of himself, but, like a drowning man, catches at every thing, even his dearest friend, though he should perish with him. To what melancholy extremities will not this unhappy situation lead a man!—to poverty, shame, villainy, and disgrace; and at length, to sell one's
country,

5

Two essays from *Hodge's North-Carolina Almanack* for 1796 by William Thomas.

173

pear slovenly." The third subject of the essay was "Punch." At this point, Ames, who was an innkeeper as well as a physician, may have let the physician rule:

> . . . modern Punch bids fair to cheat the Drunkard into Temperance; for he may sooner hurt his Belly than his Brains by such Liquor . . . and the plentiful use of this Liquor is hurtful to such as have weak Bile, and are subject to Diseases arising from Acidity, as flatulent Cholics, Dysenteries and the Like.

Ames's second essay on health in this same issue was more serious. "The Doctrine of Perspiration" explained in detail a slightly questionable technical difference between perspiration and sweat: "the more a Person sweats the less he perspires; free Perspiration makes the Body light and chearful, but Sweat faint and dispirited . . . . He who has thro' any Error lessened Perspiration says he has catch'd Cold . . . ."

Addressed "To the GENTLEMEN SMOAKERS, whether of Pipes or Segars," an essay in Banneker's almanac for 1797 compared smoking with the vices "whereby hell may be gained":

> 1st. It was smoak; so are all the vanities of this world.
> 2nd. It delighteth them who take it; so do all the pleasures of the world. . . .
> 3rd. It maketh men drunken, and light in the head; so do all the vanities. . . .
> 4th. He that taketh tobacco, saith he cannot leave it, it doth bewitch him; even so the pleasures of the world. . . .
> And farther, besides all this, it is like hell in the very substance of it, for it is a stinking loathsome thing; and so is hell.

The author, "Tom Whiff," wanted gentlemen to think on these things whenever they smoked.

The following short essay of 1775 is an excellent example of the younger Dr. Ames's florid and poetic prose style:

OF AIR

The Air which fills our raptur'd Breasts with Joy, supports all Natures Sons with Life, without whose Energy the Blood of Man and Beasts would soon become a drossy Tide, and all the Efforts of the active Heart, would be unable to propell the purple Currant thro' its secret mazy Channels. Sometimes the Planets dart their Influence down; or from the Earth's wide Womb strange Plagues arise and Contaminate the Aethereal

Tracts of Air, which stains the blue Serenity of Heaven with Death in various Shapes. Breathe not the air of *Cities*, where breathless winds imbibe Effluvia, from the Sick and Dying, from the Dead, from Docks and Dung-hills: where Thousands of Lungs with Exhalations foul, sate the Air with strange Corruption, and make that vital Element a nauseous Mass, enough to spoil and corrode that weak and tender Organ thro' whose flexible Tubes the putrid Salts of all obscene corrupt offensive Things are carried to the Blood.

The elder Dr. Ames was interested in the occult, at least interested enough to write a well-argued "Essay on Conjuration & Witchcraft" for his 1747 almanac. First he defines *conjuration* as "a personal dealing with the Devil, to know any secret, or compass any Design." The fact that some persons have learned nature's secrets so much better than "the Vulgar," he says, leads the ignorant to believe these persons are *"Necromancers, Magicians, &c."* According to Ames, novelties are attractive, and even mathematics pleases man most because his discoveries are new. Furthermore, man likes to believe "Articles that are most beyond all Belief," to the degree that some "heathen" have profited from "the Credulity of their Fellow-Creatures." According to Cornelius Agryppa, if one calls on Satan by certain titles at certain moments, he appears with "Flaming Eyes and Face as black as Soot,/ A Pair of mighty Horns and Cloven Foot." But Ames is dubious about conjuration and witchcraft. It is strange, he says, that the person called a witch is always the old woman in the neighborhood who is "prodigious ugly," has red, hollow eyes and her "Face shrivel'd up," and is bent double. The pretty girls are never suspected, as if Satan "would select the most neglected Creature in the humane Species to be his Privy-Counsellor."

Dr. Ames's enthusiasm for his country inspired one of his best essays in 1758. In thoughts upon "The past, present, and future State of *North America*," he foresaw the future development of natural resources. His final remarks have ironic appeal for our time:

O! Ye unborn Inhabitants of America! Should this Page escape its destin'd Conflagration at the Year's End, and these Alphabetical Letters remain legible,—when your Eyes behold the

Sun after he has rolled the Seasons round for two or three Centuries more, you will know that in Anno Domini 1758, we dream'd of your Times.

NATH. AMES.

Manners and marriage were dealt with in many eighteenth-century essays. In 1711 Daniel Leeds described the various ways in which different economic groups and nationalities choose their mates. The following excerpt on nationalities is particularly enlightening:

> The *Italians* are of one humor in their Amours, the *Spainards* of another, the lacivious *French-Man* of a different humour, and the *German* of a fourth. The *Frenchman* feigns his Love, The *German* dissembles his heat, The *Spaniard* hath a good opinion of himself and believes himself believed; But the *Italians* Love is never without Jealoue. The *Frenchman* loves a Witty tho unhansom Woman; The *Spaniard* prefers a fair Woman before a Witty; The *Italian* loves a fearful bashful Woman; and the *German*, one that is bold, &c.

Nathanael Low's *Astronomical Diary* for 1764 presented a sympathetic essay on the many virtues of women, which he listed. Low's first point is "That Man was made her Governour, and so above her, I believe, rather the Punishment of her Sin, than the Prerogative of his Worth." God gave her a more beautiful and wonderful body than man; "And can we think GOD would put a worser Soul into a better Body?" Furthermore, she was built in Paradise; man was not. Woman is more modest, hence more virtuous. She is more merciful and more temperate. After all this praise, Dr. Low tempered his adulation. Women are more irresolute; "they are not of so tumultuous a spirit, so not so fit for great Actions." Conceding that he finds virtue more often in women than in men ("though weaker and infirmly guarded"), he adds, "Though hitherto I confess I have not found more sweet and constant Goodness in Man, than I have in Women; and yet of these I have not found a Number."

An essay titled "Complaint of an Old Maid" appeared in *Ellicott's Maryland and Virginia Almanack* for 1790. The old maid says that old maids are generally sneered at. For the sake of argument, suppose that they are unmarried because they "could not

176

HANNAH SNELL, was born in *Fryer-Street* in the Parish of St. *Hellen's*, in the city of *Worcester*, in *England*, on the 23d day of *April*, 1723. When the Father and Mother of *Hannah* died, *Hannah* came to *London*, and contracted an acquaintance with one *James Summs*, a sailor, who was a *Dutchman*. In a little time *Summs*, made his addresses to her as a lover, and gained her consent, and was married to her at the *Fleet*, on the sixth day of *January*, 1743-4. But all his promises of friendship, proved instances of the highest perfidy, and he turned out the worst and most unnatural of husbands. When she was seven months gone with child, he, finding himself deeply involved in debt, made an elopement from her. Notwithstanding these her calamities, she patiently bore herself up under them, and two months after her husband's departure was delivered of a daughter which lived no more than seven months. As she was now free from all the ties arising from nature and consanguinity; she thought herself privileged to roam in quest of the man, who, without reason, had injured her so much; for there are no bounds to be set either to love, jealousy or hatred, in the female mind. That she might execute her designs with the better grace, and the more success, she boldly com-

The Life and Adventures of Hannah Snell, a female soldier.
From *Thomas's New-England Almanack for 1775.*

177

get husbands." This argument presupposes that marriage is a happy state; singleness, a miserable one. Men have slighted the old maid, causing her to suffer. The writer protests, "We are supposed to have desired husbands, to be miserable without them, and yet we are made a jest of for not having them. Is this a fair procedure?" She compares the old maid and the cuckold, saying "we are made ridiculous because of our unhappiness out of the marriage state; he is made so, because of his unhappiness in it."

Etiquette was Tobler's interest in "Concerning CIVILITY and Good Manners," in his *Pennsylvania Town and Country-Man's Almanack* for 1773:

> COUGH, belch, spit, sneeze, and yawn as little as thou canst in Sight of Company, and when inevitable, make as little sound as possible for Decency's sake.
> In addressing any Person, especially of Distinction, hold not thy Mouth so near his Face as to bedew him with thy Breath; for all Mens Breath is nauseous, and some Mens intolerable.

Illustration for essay on the King of Prussia.
From Weatherwise's *Father Abraham's Almanack* for 1759.

Although history was earlier presented mainly in chronological tables, historical essays became popular in the eighteenth century. In Hutchins' almanac for 1759 are two: one, a biographical sketch of Charles Frederick, King of Prussia; the other, a continuation of the "Historical account of Affairs, in North-America, begun in our last Almanack." An essay on the Prussian King Frederick was illustrated in Weatherwise's *Father Abraham's Almanack* for 1759.

Political essays in the years before and during the Revolution were popular propaganda media, not theoretical discussions on liberty for the reader versed in Locke. Almanac essayists reached their audience by speaking of the liberties for which "the embattled farmer stood." [4] However, many popular almanacs avoided political comment altogether, as if oblivious of any unrest.

Edes and Gill's almanacs for 1769 and 1770 referred obliquely to the unpopular Governor Bernard of Massachusetts.[5] In 1769 a satirical allegory, "An Extract from the History of Publius Clodius Britano Americanus," explains how Publius Clodius learned in his childhood to tell lies about his fellow students, causing them to be punished unjustly. When he emigrated to America from "one of the European Islands" as an "overseer" for "Lord Leo," he continued to lie and to cause trouble generally. In Edes's almanac for 1770, he mentions that "G. B. has now come to the End of his Tether."

Low's almanac for 1769 quoted from "Cato's Letters; or Essays on Liberty, Civil and Religious, and other Important Subjects." An essay in West's *New-England Almanack* for 1775, "A Brief View of the present Controversy between Great-Britain and America" (three pages), reiterated the theme of preparation for the defense of liberty. The author quoted "the great Earl of Chatham" as saying, "Taxation and representation . . . are inseparably united: God hath joined them: No British Parliament can separate them . . . ."

An interesting, though inaccurate, essay on linguistics is found in Titan Leeds's almanac for 1714. The subject is a lesson in Hebrew and consists primarily of questions and answers. The writer begins with "As Letters were invented before Syllables, and Syllables before Words . . . ." The first question asks, "Which were

March was thus named and conferated to the God Mars, by Remulus, who was f...

...poted to be his Son. This was the first month of their martial Year.

An Account of Florida.

FLorida is a large fruitful Country in North-America, call'd by the Inhabitants Jaquorsa. It is bounded on the North-East with Virginia, on the South and some Part of the West with New-Galica, and some Countries not yet discover'd. The Air of this Country is very temperate, and Soil extreamly fertile, and produces Grain, Herbs and Fruit in great Plenty. The Floridans are tall, well proportion'd Wariers, and go almost naked, and tho' naturally white, paint themselves of an Olive colour: Their Arms are Bows-and-Arrows, headed with the teeth of Fish, or sharp Stones. They are great Dissemblers and Lyers : Their chief Employment is Hawking and Fishing. Ferdinando Soto, after the Conquest of Peru, enter'd this Country May 25, 1538, and gave it the name of Florida, because the Flowers were then on the Ground ; but died of Grief, for being disappointed of the Treasures which he expected. The Women are very nimble, and will swim a great River, holding their Children above Water: They will also climb to the top of the highest tree with great swiftness. Charles V. of Spain, sent several Monks and Friars to try whether they cou'd tame these Savages, but the Infidels cut their throats. The Commodities here are few and costly, viz. gold and silver, pearls and furs.

On a WATCH. By Father Weatherwise.

COULD but our Tempers move like this Machine,
   Not urg'd by Passion, nor delay'd by Spleen ;
But true to Nature's regulating Pow'er,
By virtuous Acts distinguish'd every Hour ;
Then Health and Joy would follow as they ought,
The Laws of Motion, and the Laws of Thought :
Sweet Health, to pass the Laws of Moments o'er,
And everlasting Joy, when Time shall be no more.

Defraud no one by false Weights and Measures.

An essay and a poem for March, 1759. Weatherwise's *Father Abraham's Almanack.*

The Character of a PATRIOT.

HE feels a more generous principle reigning in his breast and governing all his actions : whose soul is unbiassed by sinister motives, unaffected by the allurements of riches and honors, and blind to all the charms of pleasure and grandeur : whom flattery with her syren tongue cannot fascinate, whom corruption with her powerful bait cannot lure from his duty, whom threats cannot deter nor frowns dismay ; whose love for the community is not extinguished, nay, nor even damped by the ingratitude of his countrymen, but still continues with an unabated glow. Notwithstanding all his discouragements, he still remains firmly attached to the constitution of the STATE, still invariably pursuing the good of the Whole. On this his whole attention is fix-

The Hon. JOHN HANCOCK, Esq; PRESIDENT of the HONOURABLE the CONTINENTAL CONGRESS.

ed, hither all his endeavors tend, here all his actions terminate.

View him in his most private retirement, where he is no less active than in his public conduct. Here the whole force of his understanding is exerted, and every thought directed to the glory and welfare of his Country.——When he has projected any plan for its advantage, and contemplates the various and complicated parts, all harmoniously conspiring to the production of the desired effect, his soul is filled with the most refined delight, the most permanent satisfaction : Neither *Milton* in painting his lovely paradise, nor the bishop of *Cloyne* in adjusting his immaterial scheme, no, nor *Newton* in discovering and establishing the grand laws of nature, felt pleasures more in tellectual, joys more sublime,

Illustrated essay from *Bickerstaff's Boston Almanack* for 1777.

the first Letters that were invented?" The answer refers sequentially to Abraham, the Chaldeans, Assyrians, Phoenicians, Moses, and the Israelites. The answers to questions on phonetics have a more authoritative ring: vowels and consonants are divided into guttural, lingual, "palatable," dental, and labial.

Although almanac essays in the eighteenth century embraced a variety of subjects, astronomy and astrology continued to be the primary concerns of some authors, notably Dr. Ames, II. Another outstanding group of essays were the patriotic writings during the Revolutionary Period by Nathanael Low, Benjamin West, Dr. Ames, III, and the printers, Edes and Gill. These major interests prompted some of the best essay writing of the century. In quantity, quality, and variety of subject matter, the two Ameses had no serious competition in America for first place as eighteenth-century almanac essayists.

7 Receipts

One of the most popular features of the eighteenth-century almanac was the receipt, or recipe, which had little in common with today's cookbook. Food preparation was discussed only in terms of the preservation and use of large quantities of homegrown staples. In the seventeenth century, the typical receipt dealt with husbandry; in the eighteenth, the typical receipt was a formula for concocting and administering a cure for a specific malady of man or beast—often generalized to include hints on health and well-being, with an occasional "cure-all."

The few receipts found in seventeenth-century almanacs are how-to articles, or practical counsel for farmers.[1] For example, Daniel Leeds's almanac for 1687 contained "Short Rules in Husbandry" (on grafting trees, gelding cattle, etc.). Notes at the top of the calendar pages in the 1695 Leeds almanac referred to the care of cattle. Through their knowledge of the zodiac and the moon's phases, almanac-makers were able to advise farmers when to bleed and geld cattle and when to plant crops.

Miscellaneous practical counsel in the eighteenth century considered almost all problems—how-to articles concerning the management of the home, family, and farm; personal care; and even including some gadgetry. Nathan Bowen's almanac for 1725 explained "How to Make a Sun Dial for a Blind Man"; in 1728 he had a table for computing the contents of liquor "in any Cask" (hogshead, barrel, etc.). The Titan Leeds almanac for 1729 contained many how-to articles: how to make cutting tools, how to make iron soft, how to kill fleas, and how "To take the Height of a Tree, &c. very useful for those who work in Timber." In 1742 the Leeds almanac explained how *"To kill Buggs,"* presenting such alternatives as "Take the Gall of an Ox, mixt it with Vinegar, and rub the Cracks and Joints of the Bedstead with it," or "take the Juice of full grown Cucumbers, and wash your Bedstead with it." An instructive piece on dairy-farming told how "Mr. Bradley" pastured his cows and how much milk they gave. Richard Bradley (1688–1737), essayist, Fellow of the Royal Society, and Professor of Botany at Cambridge, said: "Black Cows give less Milk at a Meal than red, but go not so long dry as the red Cows." Longer than the usual receipts, one article on husbandry might also be called an essay. John Bartram, the most famous botanist in America, wrote it especially for *Poor Richard's Almanack* for 1749. The subject was the red cedar, how it should be planted and tended, its characteristics, and its utility. Poor Richard in 1753 described his famous invention in "Securing Houses Against Lightening"; and John Anderson's *Anderson Improved* for 1773 told about "Building Chimnies that will not Smoke."

Husbandry and "domestic science" were of special importance in the years preceding and during the Revolution, when the utilization of native products was necessary and "American." A mixture of topical reference and home economy appeared in *Poor Richard Improved* for 1765. This counsel recommended that Americans avoid paying high import taxes by making their own products; for example, how to make Madeira wine in America by first importing the grapevine cuttings and "How to manage the Distilling a Spirit from Rye, or other Grain, that shall be preferable to common Rum." Poor Richard also advocated sugar made from honey, apples, the sugar beet, and the sugar maple. Dr. Ames, III, in 1775 offered a timely article for the patriot: "The Method of Making Gun-Powder. By following which Directions every Person may easily supply himself with a sufficiency of that Commodity." In Poor Richard's *Rhode-Island Almanack* for 1789, sugar maple was suggested as a source of sugar, molasses, beer, wine, and vinegar.

Occasionally, receipts catered to women's concern for their families and for their own persons. *Poor Thomas Improved— More's Country Almanack* for 1768 may help to explain the high rate of infant mortality. Poor Thomas published "A Method of dry-nursing Children" written "By a Lady of Quality": "One hour after the child is born, give it a little oil of sweet almond, a little juice of sea onion, with a little sugar candy." The child should be given nothing else for a whole day and night. This method was preferred to nursing "by a strange breast." The same almanac also contained a discourse "On the ill Practice of rocking Children."

An entertaining receipt, to our eyes, is in *The Lady's Almanack* for 1786: "Preserving the Hair and promoting its Growth," which recommends a mixture of powder and "pomatum" for nourishment. The hair should "be combed out two or three times every fortnight" and re-dressed. An application of Pomade de Grasse was applied to the roots and extremities of the hair, to aid split ends. Caution was advised about the selection of powder, since the common kind contained lime, an ingredient detrimental to the hair. A receipt in the same almanac on "preserving and Drying Gooseberries, Damsons, or Plumbs" proves that fruit preservation has changed less than hair "preservation." *Ellicott's Maryland and Virginia Almanack* for 1789 offered women who wanted to change (or, in this case, to subdue) their hair color an opportunity to save half a guinea:

How to change Red Hair into a beautiful Brown. Take black lead, and black ebony shavings, one ounce each, let these boil an hour in a pint of clear water; when fine bottle it for use. You are to wet a comb in the liquid, and comb your hair often therewith. To make the hair black, add two drams of

185

camphire to the ingredients. This is the liquid for changing hair, advertised at half a guinea a bottle.

Recipes dealing with health and medicine have an interesting significance. Folk medicine reflected an important aspect of colonial life. Many early Americans were dependent either upon the almanac or upon hearsay for instruction in healing themselves and their animals. Physicians were scarce, and liable to be quacks. A widespread dissatisfaction with quackery prompted Virginia in 1736 to pass "what was probably the first law against illegal and irresponsible medical practitioners." [2] Fairly representative of contemporary medical knowledge, almanac recipes were of the same quality as the medication ordered by the doctor. Some of the almanac-makers were actually physicians; for example, Dr. Nathaniel Ames (father and son), Dr. Nathanael Low (father and son), and Dr. Christian Lodowick. Writings on medicine were extremely popular. In the seventeenth century, phlebotomy and purging were especially emphasized, always in connection with astrology.[3] Later, cures were given for everything from a head cold to cancer. Harris' almanac for 1692 demonstrates the traditional reliance on astrology as a ruling factor in the treatment of illnesses. Harris admonished the patient to "Take a Vomit that it may work thoroughly, when the Moon is in Aries, Taurus, or Capricorn." Daniel Leeds's almanac for 1695 explained when to gather herbs. Dr. Christian Lodowick in 1695 advised the reader what to do for "cholick," "worms in children," "Pyles," and "itch."

The advertisement of patent medicine cure-alls in almanacs was not prevalent until the nineteenth and twentieth centuries. However, as early as Atkins' *Kalendarium Pennsilvaniense* for 1686, an advertisement appeared "Of some experienced medicines" sold by William Bradford, the printer. One was "Charles Marshall's Spiritus Mundus," a treatment for fevers. Leeds's almanac for 1746 printed, instead of verse on the calendar pages, a long abstract from "Dr Berkley's *Treatise on Tar Water, adapted to Diseases frequent in America*":

I chuse the following Method (says the Bishop) to make *Tar Water, viz.* Pour a Gallon of cold Water on a Quart of Tar, stir and mix them thoroughly with a Ladle or flat Stick for the

Printer's advertisement for a cure-all, from Atkin's *Kalendarium Pennsilvaniense,* 1686.

Space of three or four minutes, after which the vessel must
stand 48 hours, that the Tar may settle, when the clear Water
is to be poured off and kept for use, no more being made from
the same Tar, which may still serve for common purposes—

The "Dr" was the famous Bishop George Berkeley, 1685–1753, of
"New Theory of Vision" renown. His tar water either prevented or
cured distemper, smallpox, ulcers, consumptive cough, ulcer in
the lungs, pleurisy, peripneumony, erysipelas, asthma, gravel, drop-
sey, and the bloody flux. Toblers' *South-Carolina Almanack* for
1758 included "A Receipt for making a very useful Ointment of
Tobacco-Leaves to dry up moist Sores and Ulcers, heal Scabs,
Burnings, ease Pain, etc." The same almanac carried "a short Description of the Virtue and use of some known Garden-Herbs,
taken from Dr. SALMONS New London Dispensatory," one of the
most popular medical books of the eighteenth century. Hutchins
included this panacea in his 1769 almanac:

Boil four Ounces of pure Quicksilver in two Quarts of Water
in a glazed Pipkin, until Half is wasted; bottle it for Use. The
Quicksilver will serve again, as often as you want a fresh Supply of Liquor.
This Medicine is as insipid in Taste, and as safe in using
as so much simple Water.

187

FEBRUARY, Second Month, *hath* 28 *Days.*

D. H.		Planets Places.							
			☉	♄	♃	♂	♀	☿	Moon's
Laſt ☾	2 8 morn	D ♒		♄	♓	♓	♓	♑	Lati.
New ●	9 7 morn	1	13 21	28 12	3	24	27	S. 5
Firſt ☽	15 11 aftern	7	19 26	29 13	7	♈ 1	26	2
Full ○	23 10 aftern	13	25 29	♒ 15 12	8	29	N. 5
♋ { 1 22 } Deg. 11 ♒ 21 21 21	19 ♓ 1 32	0 16 16	15	♒ 5	3
		25	7 34	1 18 21	22	12	S. 3

The ſpoil-devoted city wirh ſurprize,
Sees high encircling trenches round her riſe ;
When all her num'rous children ſhe contain'd,
Who at a ſolemn feſtival remain'd ;
O'er all the land Rome's rav'ning eagle flies,
And to a deſert turns a paradiſe ;
Yet in her boſom fierceſt factions rage,
Which not the public danger can aſſⱴage.

D.	☽ riſe	☽ ſo.	T.
1	morn	4 41	7
2	12 27	5 27	8
3	1 33	6 17	9
4	2 38	7 12	9
5	3 44	8 11	10
6	4 43	9 12	11
7	5 34	10 14	12
8	6 14	11 13	1
9	Moon	aftern	2
10	ſets.	1 3	3
11	8 16	1 54	4
12	9 32	2 46	5
13	10 47	3 37	6
14	morn.	4 30	7
15	12 1	5 23	8
16	1 11	6 18	9
17	2 17	7 14	9
18	3 16	8 9	10
19	4 6	9 1	11
20	4 46	9 50	12
21	5 21	10 36	1
22	5 47	11 20	2
23	Moon	11 58	3
24	riſes.	morn.	3
25	7 14	12 38	4
26	8 16	1 19	4
27	9 15	1 59	5
28	10 18	2 40	5

Gum Plaſter.

TAKE of the common plaſter, four pounds ; gum ammoniac and galbanum, ſtrained, of each half a pound. Melt them together, and add, of Venice turpentine, ſix ounces.

This plaſter is uſed as a digeſtive, and likewiſe for diſcuſſing indolent tumours.

On the RIGHT EMPLOYMENT *of our* TIME.

TIME is precious, but its value is unknown to us. We ſhall attain this knowledge when we can no longer profit by it. Our friends require it of us, as if it was nothing ; and we give it to them in the ſame manner. It is often a burden to us ; we know not what to do with it, and are embarraſſed about it.

The day will come, when a quarter of an hour will appear of more value, and more deſireable, than all the riches of the univerſe. God, who is liberal and generous in all his other gifts, teaches us by the wiſe œconomy

my

Receipt for "Gum Plaster" in Mary K. Goddard's almanac for 1785.

Many and various are the Virtues of this single and simple Medicine, when both externally and internally tried: wherefore I recommend it to destroy Worms, to cure all Impurities of the Skin, to purify the Blood, heal Ulcers, open Obstructions, and scour the Glands. Drink of it freely as a Diet Drink, and as much and as often as you please.

Although advertisements for patent medicines were uncommon in the eighteenth century, *Mary K. Goddard's Pennsylvania, Delaware, Maryland, and Virginia Almanack* for 1785 contained several. The last page mentioned various categories of items for sale at Miss Goddard's general store. Among those listed were:

PATENT MEDICINES.

Turlington's Drops; Balsam of Honey; Anderson's, Keyser's and Hooper's Pills; Daffey's Elixir; Godfrey's Cordial; Harlem Oyl; Jesuit's and Bateman's Drops, with various other kinds. A Salt that takes Stains of all Sorts out of Linen, Lace, &c. &c. Court Plaster, Teeth Powder, &c.&c.&c.

The "Observations for Physick and Diet" given in *Poor Robin* for 1728 were typical of advice for general health and well-being:

[Sept.] Provide your Winter Garments, hang them on loosely, to prevent that you may after repent of. Good for Physick and Phlebotomy. Eat Good Butter with your *Tautaug* [black-fish] this month.

[Nov.] The best Physick in this month is good Exercise, warmth, and wholesome Meat and Drink. Kill your Swine in this Month, and after Pork and Pease be sure to break Wind.

Some ailments had a variety of remedies; others were mentioned infrequently. A careful study of almanac cures would doubtless indicate something of the general nature of diseases in early America. For example, corns were often discussed, as were earaches, headaches, stomach aches, and the "bloody flux." Cures were particularly common in the Titan Leeds (posthumous) almanacs of the 1740's. After Leeds's death, the Bradfords published the almanac, and as we have already seen, William Bradford kept medicinal preparations for sale at his printing shop. The Leeds almanac for 1742 told the reader that, *"To Stench a Bleeding Wound,"* one simply lays "Hogs Dung (hot from the hog) to the Bleeding Wound." The 1742 almanac was full of cures: for "Hardness of Hearing," a sore mouth, canker, the "Teeth-Ach," "Bleeding at the Nose," sore eyes, the "Head-Ach," and the itch. "A good Water for Sore Eyes" required a little advance preparation:

> Take an Egg hard sodden, cut it in the middle, and take out the Yolk, and put thereto as much white Copper as a small Nut, then close it together, and wrap it in red Flannel, and lay it to sleep 24 Hours in Rose-water; then strain it hard through a Cloath, and drop two or three Drops into the Eyes Morning and Evening; it hath cured a great number of sore Eyes.

But, if he preferred, the reader could mix up a batch of an alternate sore-eyes cure and have enough left over to share with his neighbors: "Take Loaf Sugar 3 Ounces, Valerian Roots (or Setwall) and Fennel, each 2 pounds, mixt them well together, take Morning and Evening the quantity of three Knife Points full, chew it well and then swallow it." The "itch" patient was advised to "Take sweet Butter, unwrought Wax, and Brimstone, Rose water and red clove water, boil them till they be like a Salve, and anoint your Body, Arms and Legs three times by the Fire." After eleven calendar pages of such receipts, an unsigned Dryden couplet in December suggested the very best:

> *The Wise for* Cure *on Exercise depend;*
> *God never* made *his Work, for Man to* mend.

Leeds's almanac for 1743 continued treatment for the afflicted:

> *For the Spleen.* Let the Person grieved accustom himself to drink the Water wherein hot Iron has been often squenched, and eat Capers: White Wine wherein hot Iron has been several Times quenched is also good. *Or,* Boil the Rind of Ash in Wine and drink thereof 6 or 7 Mornings fasting. The Spleen is a great Pain in the left Side, under the short Ribs, and is generaly worst after Meat. It is good to annoint the grieved Place with Ointment of Marsh-Mallows.

The poor sufferer who had "a *Scald or Scabby Head*" could

> Take fresh butter and boil it with the Soot of a chimney, wherein no Sea-Coal is burn'd, till it be black, and therewith anoint the Head. Or, Take oil-Olives (sweet oil) and put it in a dish with fair water, beat or stir them well together, then take it up and put it in another vessel, and put Powder of Brimstone, and *May* Butter thereto, then make an ointment

thereof by setting it on a few coals, wherewith anoint the Fore-head.

The central ingredient of the 1743 receipt "For *Kibes or Chil-blains*" was turnips. For corns, "Cut them close and lay on a Plaister of burnt Allom, the Heart of an Oyster dry'd and powder'd, and a little Venice-Turpentine. Or tye on bruised Housleck." The au-thor concluded very detailed instructions for the cure of stomach pains with "Some for want of other Things, have swallowed Pep-per Grains." For "the Stone and Gravel," he said, "Egg-shells dried and beaten to Powder and drank with White-wine is also good." To cure warts, the reader could "Put the Feet of a Hen in hot Em-bers till the Skin thereof be seperated or shrunk from the Legs, and with that Skin warm rub Warts three or four times or more." The following cure for "Worms in Children" from Leeds's 1743 almanac was similar to one in Poor Tom's (Thomas More) alma-nac for 1750:

> There is not a faster or surer Remedy to kill *Worms* in Chil-dren, than to take 6, 8, or 10 red Earth-Worms, and let them purge in Bay Salt, then slit them open and wash them in fair Water, then dry them in an Earthern Dish and beat them to a Powder, and give them to the Child in the Morning fasting, for 3 or 4 Mornings, but let them eat nothing for an hour after.

"To purge the Head," he said, "Rub a green Marigold Leaf be-tween your Fingers and put it up your Nose, and it will draw away the Humours and Rheum annoying the Head." Formulae for "drenches" were not uncommon, but the one in this 1743 almanac seems a little more drastic than some:

> Take white Dogs-Turd in Powder, and a handful of Rue beat small, boil them in Sallet-oil till thick, then spread it on a Cloath Plaster-wise and apply it to the Sore from Ear to Ear.

All twelve calendar pages of Leeds's 1745 almanac were de-voted to "*A full Discovery of the Medicines given by me* Joanna Stephens, *for the Cure of the Stone and Gravel; and a particular Account of my Method of preparing and giving the same.*" Joanna explained, "My medicines are a Powder, a Decoction, and Pills."

191

She described in detail how and when to prepare each of the three medicines and how they should be administered. The powder, for example, "consists of Egg-Shells and Snails, both calcined."

A highlight of Thomas More's 1750 almanac ("Poor Tom") was a "recipe" for curing deafness:

> Cut a white loaf in the middle, just come out of the Oven, and lay it to the Ear, and if any live Thing be in the Head, it will bring it out, shifting it with hot Bread, until all be come forth.

West's 1763 *New England Almanack* inserted a treatment for the bloody flux which may have made many readers prefer to keep the "flux":

> A Choice Receipt for the BLOODY-FLUX, as it
> has been successfully try'd

> Take a large Tea-spoonful of Cochineal, bruise it fine, Half an Ounce or more of Cinnamon, and three Ounces of Loaf Sugar; put them into two Quarts of Spring Water, boil them over a slow Fire, and keep stirring till it comes to about three Pints: The Patient to drink Half a Pint of it Milk-warm; and the Rest a Gill at a Time, warm as their common Drink: Let them drink nothing else whilst it lasts. If the Above do not quite cure the Person, repeat the same again, which scarce ever failed. When the Flux is stopt, and the Patient finds a Pain about the Stomach, give a Spoonful or two of Daffy's Elixer, as their Stomach will bear it: The Food for the Afflicted is to be Rice and Milk, Flour and Milk, Bread and Milk, or poach'd Eggs; but no Broth or Flesh. If there be no Elixer to be had, the Patient must take a Spoonful of Syrrup of Rhubarb.

Tobler's *Pennsylvania Town and Country-man's Almanack* for 1768 gave the patient several alternatives for curing the "Ear-Ach":

> Rub the Ear hard for a Quarter of an Hour:
> Or, apply to it a hot Roll:
> Or, put in a roasted Fig, as hot as may be:
> Or, blow the Smoke of Tobacco strongly into it:
> Or, drop in Juice of Goose-Grease.

Prescriptions were available for all disorders; none was too trivial or too serious. West's 1769 *Bickerstaff's Boston Almanack* printed this cure for baldness: "Rub the part morning and evening, with onions, 'till it is red and rub afterwards with honey." A cure

The North-American's
ALMANACK

Being, The GENTLEMENS and LADIES DIARY
For the Year of Christian Æra,

I 7 7 I.

Being the 3d Year after BISSEXTILE or LEAP YEAR.
And the 11th Year of the Reign of King GEORGE the III.
Calculated for the Latitude 42 Deg. 25 Min. North,
And fitted to BOSTON's Meridian.

C O N T A I N I N G,

The Lunations, Eclipses of the Luminaries, Aspects, spring-
Tides, Judgment of the Weather, Feasts and Fasts of the
Church, Quakers Meetings, Courts in the four *New*
England Governments, Sun and Moon's Rising and Setting,
Moon's Place, Time of High Water. Morning and Evening,
Clock Equations, Interest Table, Publick Roads, with the
Stages to put up at ; also, a Variety of Excellent Medicines,
extracted from Authors, shewing an easy Way of curing
Diseases, with an account of the wonderful Operations
of the Bite of a Mad Dog, on the Human Body, and
Directions for working the Cure of the same, &c. &c. &c.

By *SAMUEL STEARNS,*
A Student in the MATHEMATICKS

BOSTON : Printed and Sold by R. DRAPER,
T. & J. FLEET, and EDES & GILL.

Rare title-page illustration for a receipt—
a cure for the "Bite of a Mad Dog."

193

Locked Jaw, on the 4th day of the diforder. He had been taking liquid laudanum in great dofes without effect. The Phyfician who had prefcribed this remedy, gave him over. The Phyfician who fucceeded him, bled the patient plentifully, and afterwards gave him large quantities of wine and bark. He likewife applied blifters to the outfide of each of his jaws. By the ufe of thefe remedies, he was relieved in twenty-fix hours. It is to be hoped this communication of a cure of a diforder, fo often fatal, and by remedies which have fucceeded in many fimilar cafes, will prove ufeful to the citizens of the United States, and lead them to reject a dependence upon a remedy (laudanum) which has feldom done fervice when ufed alone, and which is prefcribed only in complaifance to great names.

An infallible remedy for the dangerous wound occafioned by a nail running into the foot or hand.

Mix as much foap, chalk, and water as will give it the confiftency of a falve; and apply it to the wound in a quantity that may not foon harden.

One application generally proves fufficient, if foon applied; but if any degree of inflamation has already taken place, a fecond may be neceffary, in which cafe let it be fpread upon the fkin or fat of boiled bacon.

An infallible cure for the bite of a mad Dog.

Take of the leaves of Rue picked from the ftalks and bruifed 6 ounces; Garlick picked from the ftalk and bruifed, Venice Treacle or Mithridate, and fcrapings of Pewter, each 4 ounces—boil all thefe together over a flow fire in two quarts of ale till one pint is confumed—keep it in a bottle clofe ftopt, and give of it 9 fpoonfuls, a little warm, to the perfon bitten 7 mornings fucceffively, and fix to a dog to be given 9 days after the bite—apply fome of the ingredients to the part bitten.

N. B. This receipt was taken out of Cathorp Church in Lincolnfhire, the whole town almoft being bitten, and not one perfon who took this medicine but what was cured.

An infallible remedy for a mortal diforder in Hogs, which prevails very much at this time, called a Swelling in the Throat.

Under the jowl, there is a fmall knob or fwelling, which being fplit and rubbed well with fine falt, removes the diforder and gives immediate relief.

SUBSTITUTION FOR SOAP.

Peal and grind, or grate, 20 horfe chefnuts. Pour on them ten quarts of hot water. In this infufion, either linen or woolen may be wafhed, without any foap, and it will be found to take out all kinds of fpots.

"Infallible remedies"
from *Hodge's North-Carolina Almanac* for 1797.

for "a cold in the head" was "Pare very thin . . . [the] rind of an orange. Roll it up inside out, and thrust a roll into each nostril." The same year, Weatherwise's almanac presented one of the most popular remedies of the century—a live toad used to suck out cancer. Weatherwise's version:

> An extraordinary and surprizing cure for a Cancer, communicated by a Lady, whose Veracity may be depended on, to the Authors of the London Magazine. November 1767.
> A Poor distressed Woman, near Hungerford, had laboured many Years under a most inveterate Cancer in her Breast. A Gentleman in the Neighbourhood told her, if she would use Toads as directed, they would cure her. Agreeable to his Order, she applied eight Toads, tied up in Muffin Bags, to eight Holes in her Breast, which sucked amazingly.—The Toads fattened eagerly, like Leeches.—When they had sucked themselves full, they dropped off in Agonies, terrible to behold. I do not hear they gave any Pain, but, on the contrary, her Pains abated from the first Application. She repeated this till she had demolished 120 Toads, by which Time the Wounds were healed, and her Breast was of the usual Size. She has been well ever since.
> The Toads were applied every Night. The better she grew, the longer they lived, and the longer they sucked.

The grateful lady attended two other patients in the neighborhood until their cancers were cured—apparently by using "Toads as directed."

Tobler's *Town and Country-man's Almanack* for 1770 included, among its many cures:

> One of the best Ways of leaving off the bad Habit of drinking Drams is, by Degrees to mix Water with the Drams, to lessen the Quantity of the Drams every Day, and keep to the same quantity of Water, till in about the Course of a Week, nothing of the Dram kind be used along with the Water.

For the "HIC-COUGH" Ellicott in 1787 suggested: "A single drop of chymical oil of cinnamon dropt on a piece of treble refined sugar, let it dissolve in the mouth leisurely." And for "Bleeding at the NOSE": "RUB your Nostrils with the juice of nettles, or young nettles bruised."

Rivington's *New Almanack and Ephemeris* for 1774 (written by "Copernicus") anticipated a supposedly modern remedy:

195

mouth-to-mouth resuscitation for drowning persons. Fourteen years earlier, *Poor Richard Improved* for 1760 appended to "A Finlander's Method of Artificial Respiration" a note that "blowing in the mouth and distending the chest" might be more effective than rolling the body to and fro on a cask. Ben Franklin himself may have made this comment, although he disclaimed direct association with the almanac after 1758. Almanac-makers not only borrowed receipts from previous almanacs but also quoted popular medical journals and books. In 1756 Poor Richard had acknowledged the fifth volume of *Edinburgh Medical Essays* as a source for "a *Specific* for the Dysentery or bloody Flux." But acknowledgments were rare, even for Franklin.

Poor Richard Improved (1774) had a wide range of receipts for cleaning teeth and gums, toothache, corns, scurvy, and consumption. In this version, corns could be removed by heating a clove of garlic and tying it on the corn before going to bed, for three or four consecutive nights.

Although not nearly so common as cures for disease in humans, cures for animal diseases were printed often enough to warrant consideration. The Leeds almanac for 1744 (published by I. Warner and Cornelia Bradford) contained "A few useful and necessary Receipts for the Cure of Horses and other Cattle" which filled the extra space on all the calendar pages. Cures for at least fourteen different ailments were discussed, as well as one remedy good "for all fresh Wounds, cut Sinews, Shot-wound, Lime-burning, Dogs-bite, Foundering, Frettizing [weak feet], surbating [sore] Hoofs, casting of the Hoof, and Hoof-bound." The following examples are typical:

> *For a Pinch or Gall in the Withers.* First cut out the dead Flesh and make a Tent with the white of an Egg; then wash the part with warm White-wine, and afterwards anoint the sore Place with sweet Sewet.

> *For the Staggers.* When you find your Horse distemper'd in his Head, take a Piece of Woollen Cloth and bind it fast to the end of a Stick, being well rubb'd with good black Sope, and then put it into both his Nostrils with as much ease as you can, and

Excellent REMEDIES *for the* DISEASES *of* HORSES.

A never-failing cure for a cough in either horse or cow.

TAKE a quart of fresh ale, or good strong beer, warm it, and put thereto a pound of treacle, and a quarter of a pint of distilled anniseed water; stir it well together, and give it to the horse, or cow, after their ordinary meat; next morning give a pail of warm water, with a handful of oat-meal in it; with a small mash of malt, and a handful of beans for a horse.

An excellent ball for broken-winded horses.

MYRRH, elicampane, and liquorice root, in fine powder, three ounces each; saffron three drachms; assa-fœtida one ounce; sulphur, squills, and cinnabar of antimony, of each two ounces; aurum mosaicum one ounce and a half; oil of anniseeds eighty drops.——You may make it into paste with either treacle or honey, and give the horse the quantity of a hen's egg every morning for a week; and afterwards, every other morning 'till the disorder is removed.

For a swelling in a horse's back.

BOIL soap in strong beer grounds, when off the fire, mix some spirits of wine with it, and bathe the part as hot as possible, and it will reduce a swelling in an hour's time. If you have not the spirits, make use of brandy or gin; dip a rag in it, and apply it to the tumour, afterwards chamber or make a hollow place in the saddle.

For the cankered tongue of a horse.

BEAT blue vitriol to powder, and mix it with old verjuice, and apply it by means of a rag tied to the end of a stick. This never fails of curing at two or three times using.

For killing of worms in horses.

BEST roll tobacco, shred very fine; of which give the horse every day one ounce at a time amongst his wetted corn, &c. This may be given every morning and night, but not to a horse that goes to grafs.——If his case is desperate, you may give him more, even for some time.——It is a certain cure.

Remedies for Disease in Horses from
Weatherwise's *Father Abraham's Almanack,* 1774.

197

draw it forth very gently again. This is a present and perfect Remedy.

For the Cough in Horses. Take Garlick and Gun-Powder, pound them well together with Vinegar, and pour it down his Throat: Or use sharp Vinegar alone.

Tobler's *The South-Carolina Almanack* for 1756 included several suggestions for curing such common problems in horses as botflies and foundering. The following cure is perhaps still effective:

For a foundered Horse.
If a Horse is so foundered that he scarce can walk, clean the under side of his Hoofs, pour boiling Pitch or Tar in them and tye them up with Horse Dung; he will be able in the Morning to go on his Journey.

Humor and satire are noticeably absent from receipt-writing. Matters of health were serious business. The above examples of almanac receipts for cures tell us three things: 1) the early American obviously could take his medicine "like a man," 2) his cure was often as bad as his ailment, and 3) he dosed his animals as humanely as he did himself.

8 Narratives

Almanac narratives included short moralistic and humorous pieces, or jokes; much longer stories of the same type, labeled "anecdotes" by the almanac-maker; stories of Indian captivities; scientific instruction made more pleasing in narrative form; and firsthand accounts of unusual events and people.

The practice of dressing up moralistic fiction as fact has already been alluded to. The technique of "documentation" with the names of famous historical personages and real places enhanced credibility. Occasionally, the tales were allegorical. Thus the almanacker, at his least sophisticated, assumed the mantle of morality playwright.

The *South Carolina and Georgia Almanack* for 1767 printed three anecdotes relating to "God's vindictive justice, as publish'd in the English papers." All three were "documented" as truth. A gambler "uttered the dreadful wish *that his flesh might rot and his eyes never shut,* if he did not win the next game." He lost the game: his flesh rotted, and his eyes never shut. The second incident was that of a woman who had been called into court because she had reneged on the payment for some corn she had bought. She told the court "that she had paid her money, and prayed that if she did not speak the truth, *God would immediately strike her dead.*" These were the woman's last words. The third story was of a cockfight, where "one of the cockers said, with an imprecation, that if the cock was killed he would die also. It so happened that the cock was killed, and the man did not survive many minutes. This happened June 14, 1765."

In 1765 *Poor Roger* related an "An Affecting Story" of an English Lord's relationship with a curate, revealing the nobleman to be truly noble and kind. *Hutchins' Improved Almanack* for 1766 offered the "Story of Ortogrul" as proof that money does not buy happiness. The moral was explicitly stated by Ortogrul: "How long . . . have I been labouring in vain to amass wealth, which at last is useless. Let no man hereafter wish to be rich, who is already too wise to be flattered." The same almanac described "The Farmer's Dream," which moralized that "an honest industrious man may always find a pot of gold, whether from a pear tree, or the open fields, is no matter." Anecdotes in *Hutchins' Improved* for 1768 were told of Theodoric, Cambyses, and Louis XI, showing that each man suffers the consequences, or reaps the rewards, of his actions. *Poor Richard* in 1768 used a Roman Senator as the central character in "An Instance of True Magnanimity."

"A remarkable Instance of Humanity" in Low's 1774 almanac told of a benign ecclesiastic who gave to a deserving widow a note in which he instructed his steward to give her the five crowns she had requested to pay her rent. The steward gave her fifty crowns instead, which she refused. Both went to the patron, who said that he had indeed made a mistake, changed the sum to 500 crowns, and advised her to save some of the money for her daughter's dowry.

In "The Cruel Officer Punished," from Rittenhouse's *Virginia Almanack* for 1775, moral justice was dramatically meted out. An officer during Queen Anne's reign ordered that a man be executed by his own brother. The brother chose to shoot the officer instead. Interpreting this drastic action as due vengeance, Queen Anne rewarded virtue by pardoning both brothers. A "Jest" in the same almanac was called "The Reward of Avarice." A miser in France hid himself and his wealth but starved to death. It was found that "He had gnawed the flesh off both his arms, as is supposed, for subsistence." This almanac contains twenty-four pages of literary material. A longer story related a "Remarkable instance of female CREDULITY and FORTITUDE." A young girl killed a French officer who had seduced her sister. The moral ambiguity posed by this plot was cautiously evaded: "we would therefore recommend to our fair readers, whose interest and happiness we have most sincerely at heart, rather to guard against the cause of her rash conduct, than to imitate her example."

Ellicott's Maryland and Virginia Almanack for 1787 printed "An instructive story," an anecdote about a tailor and a conjurer. The moral is stated at the outset: "To know one profession only, is enough for one man to know; be content, therefore, with one good employment; for if you understand two at a time, people will give you business in neither." The tailor moaned that, if ever people should do without clothes, he would suffer. Pitying the tailor, the conjurer was happy that he could do many different tricks. Yet during a famine, people still had to have clothes, and the tailor was able to earn a living; as for the conjurer, "it was in vain, that he promised to eat fire, or to vomit pins." The conjurer was finally forced to beg from the tailor.

Not all didactic fables were so naive. In *Ellicott's Maryland and Virginia Almanack* for 1791, the principal character was the Marquis of Halifax, grandfather to the Earl of Chesterfield. In this tale, some men who had been zealous revolutionaries requested, as rewards, positions exceeding their abilities. The Marquis replied,

The prevalence of fashion, or the cobler turn'd bankrupt.

A NOTED cobler in the city of London took it into his head to be as *fashionable* as his neighbours, which was, as he himself explained it, to become a *bankrupt.* Accordingly he shut himself up in his stall, where, ere long, his reverie was interrupted by a gentleman's servant, who came for his master's boots. Solitary Crispin gave no answer for a considerable time ; till having reason to fear rough proceedings from without, he bid the servant go and tell his master that, like many of his brother cits, he had made himself a bankrupt. The servant was highly diverted at the oddity of the whim ; but, nevertheless, cried aloud for the boots, which were refused by the cobler. " I tell you," says he, " you cannot have them, for I am broke." At length, however, Robert beginning to be apprehensive of his master's displeasure at his long absence, was proceeding in earnest to help himself by violence ; when the irritated cobler threw open the door of his habitation, and thus exclaimed : " You are an impertinent blockhead to keep dunning me in this manner, when I told you, over and over again, I am a bankrupt ; however, since you will force me to a *dividend* so soon, I will be honest ; I shall pay *ten shillings* in the pound, and so (hurling it at his head) there is *one* of the boots for you."

An ANECDOTE.

A LACEDÆMONIAN, whose affairs obliged him to go out of Greece, fell into some company, who were very inquisitive about the constitution of Sparta. One of them, among other particulars, desired to know what was the punishment for adulterers ? The Spartan readily replied, That they had no adulterers in Lacedæmon : But upon the querist persisting to know in what manner he believed an adulterer would be punished, that should happen to be detected, " I believe (says the Spartan) our senate would order the criminal to give the person he had injured a bull, with a neck long enough to stand upon the continent of Greece, and drink out of a river in Peloponnesus." Upon the inquisitive gentleman's seeming to apprehend, that it was absolutely impossible to find such a bull, " Sir, (says the Spartan) give me leave to tell you, that 'tis full as impossible to find an adulterer in Lacedæmon."

Anecdotes from Weatherwise's *Father Abraham's Almanack,*
1774.

"I remember to have read in history that Rome was saved by geese, but I do not remember that these geese were made Consuls."

In an anecdote in Briggs's almanac for 1798, a Quaker who found that his neighbor was stealing his wood had a cord of wood delivered to the neighbor so he would "have no occasion for stealing."

Biographical and allegorical stories also served as morality lessons. Tobler's *Pennsylvania Town and Country-man's Almanack* for 1769 presented "An Extract of the Life and Death of the Lady Elizabeth Hastings." The author paid loving tribute to the Lady's spiritual goodness, her neighborliness, and her fortitude. Suffering for eighteen months with cancer, the Lady Elizabeth gloried that she was worthy to be chosen to suffer. An allegory in Rind's *Virginia Almanack* for 1774 was a tale of an old man who entertained some young people at table with three separate courses. The fare ranged from plain to sumptuous. Explaining that the first course represented the simplicity and frugality of their forefathers, the host cautioned the youths against extravagance. We are not told whether flatulence followed the second course. *The Kentucky Almanac* for 1794 contained "The Origin of GAMING, and her two children DUELING and SUICIDE. An ALLEGORY." The goddess of Fortune and the god of War begot "a misfeatured child" called Gaming, who, as an infant, "despised the rattle, and was quieted only by cards and dice."

In 1767 *Hutchin's Improved* commented satirically and allegorically on celibacy. "The Batchelor's Will" is a fanciful description of the disposition of an estate, narrated by the bachelor. He leaves his "Manor of Long-Delay," his "farms and messuages" of doubts, fears, irresolution, fickleness, and obstinacy. He disposes of his house of "*Vain-Hopes* lying in *High-Street,* in the town of *Castle Building,* in the County of *Imagination.*" Property to be auctioned includes a woodland of "Ambiguity" planted with "pun-trees," quirks, and "thickets of *incomprehensibility.*" The bachelor, realizing the folly of his ways, admonishes his heirs regarding their new possessions. He sincerely desires that they do not hoard them up . . . but that they should endeavour to put them off as soon as possible; to the end, and that they may be the better fitted, and disposed to follow me, into that happy state, into which I am now about to enter.

Hutchin's Improved for 1768 contained an allegorical reproach of contemporary society. "A Description of the Land of Promise" deals primarily with the inhabitants of this fantastic country where "mountains seemed to be covered with gold, the vales to glisten with precious stones, the trees to be laden with the richest fruit, and the rivers to flow with milk and honey." The citizens are "running to and fro, regardless of everybody but themselves, and wearing the face of care and importance." The main gate to the land is "Favour," guarded by a stronger gate called "Interest," and "nobody was allowed to go in by any other way." A nearby fortress called "Hope" is a shelter for those who are unable to get through the gates. Of the many "air-castles" scattered throughout the land, the "castle of vanity" is the greatest. "Pride" shows those who are interested the way to the castle. Most of the populace are concerned with getting to "The Grand Treasury," where "Some small portions of the Wealth . . . are dealt out in the form of bribes, pensions, and secret service. The rest is divided among the chief keepers."

The great "palace of Preferment" is located in "the heart of the country," where "Ambition" is the ruling factor. When aspiring candidates fail to reach this palace, they crash on the "rocks of Disappointment." But there are several methods of entering: "Some indeed, who took the high road of Dependency, got *Places* therein, and others stole into it through the bye-paths of Patriotism."

Religion in this land is that of "dissimulation and hypocricy." Nobody really has any opinions of his own; the custom is for the inferior social and intellectual classes to borrow their "sentiments from the superiour." The people are extraordinarily polite "and complaisant":

You are sure to receive a smile, a squeeze of the hand, a nod, or a bow, from everybody you address yourself to. They are

always mighty glad to see you, are your very humble servants.
. . . But their memory is unhappily very short, and sometimes
they forget they ever knew their most intimate acquaintance.

Their industry is deplorable, for "They are particularly fond of
procrastination; and *to-morrow* is a word continually in their
mouths." The "River of Attendance" is well-traveled. Those who
row down this river are often "overwhelmed in the gulph of
Despondency or swallowed up in the quicksands of despair."

Humorous anecdotes frequently contained social satire directed against marriage and the middle-class professions. Stories
of encounters between the rustic and the city dweller ended with
the rustic's outsmarting his smart friends (of course!). It is difficult to categorize the subject matter of some stories told simply to
entertain. Frequently, they have the character of "the perfect
squelch," a type of joke still popular in the twentieth century. Just
as frequent are the purely scatalogical.

An anecdote in Hutchins' almanac for 1753 referred to infidelity, a theme also quite popular in almanac verse. The time and
place of this story was Market Day. An archer placed an arrow in
his bow and loudly cried, "*Now, have at a Cuckold.*" One of the
women in the crowd, thinking the archer was aiming toward her
and her husband, quickly said, "*Stand away Husband, stand away
Husband;* why, you silly Jade, quoth he, *I am no Cuckold, am I?*
No, no, quoth she; but you don't know how a *Plaguy Arrow may
glance.*"

Rivington's *New Almanack and Ephemeris* for 1774 (written
by "Copernicus") contained a good example of the rustic's superior
wit. The countryman was sowing in the field when "two smart Fel-
lows riding that Way" approached him. One of them insolently
remarked, "Well, Honest Fellow . . . 'tis your Business to sow, but
we reap the Fruits of your labour." The countryman aptly re-
sponded, " 'Tis very likely you may, truly; for I am sowing Hemp."

The readers of Rittenhouse's *Virginia Almanack* for 1775 were
regaled with a three-and-one-half-page episode called "A WAGE
whimsically won." Jemmy Spiller, a comedian, wagered with a
friend that he could get lodgings in Epsom, already overcrowded.

Jemmy pretended not to hear the hostler, or the host and hostess, or anyone else. Through this ruse he blandly sat down to supper with a private party, followed a chambermaid into someone else's room, bolted and barred the door when she ran out to see her mistress, and, in every way, pulled off a smart job. On leaving next morning, he ordered a glass of brandy after he was on his horse. The hostess brought it. He thanked her for her hospitality, but,

> During this short space, the lady having occasion to break wind, and not dreaming that he should be informed of the report, she stood not upon ceremony, but let fly with the voice of a cannon. At this salute Spiller cries out, "Well said, madam, by Heaven it was a rouzer; I hope you are better, madam; I think I never heard such a banging f—t in my life."

The lady was amazed and enraged. Spiller's punch line, however, was tamed by contemporary moralistic requirements: "None, madam, so deaf as those who will not hear."

Ellicott's *Maryland and Virginia Almanack* for 1789 had two anecdotes of varying literary merit. The first was superior to the second. While in disguise, the father of the late King of Prussia found a young village woman who was seven feet tall. He wrote to the Colonel of the Royal Regiment of Grenadier Guards in Berlin that the bearer of the letter should be married to the tallest man in the Guards. He then instructed the girl to deliver the letter personally. The girl, not wishing to make the trip, arranged for an old neighbor woman to deliver the letter. Later, when the King requested to see "his handsome new married couple," the old woman made a speech thanking Providence for its blessings.

The second anecdote is long-winded, and its point is obscure to modern readers. A bachelor clergyman, friend of a nobleman, was known for making jokes, often at his friend's expense. The vengeful nobleman invited the clergyman to visit, dropped his guest's clothes in the tub while the clergyman was taking a bath, gave him a blanket to wrap around himself, and insisted that he come to dinner. The nobleman then slowly removed the "skewer" holding the blanket together, exposing "the picture of Adam in his primitive purity, to the full view of a dozen ladies." Can we detect a double hit here—at hypocritical divines and at resistance to the social injunction "Marry and multiply?" ·

"A Laughable Anecdote" in *Ellicott's Maryland and Virginia Almanack* for 1790 will hardly raise a weary smile today, but combines typical colonial humor with one of the most horrifying horse-cures of eighteenth-century medicine.

DOCTOR DOVER, an eminent physician, published some years ago a book, entitled *Doctor Dover's Last Legacy to his Country*, in which he strongly recommended the use of quick-silver, insomuch that it became the medicine of high and low, till a lady of distinction, dancing at a public assembly, the quick-silver she had taken that morning dropt plentifully from her, and all bespangled the floor, which, by the glaring light of many candles, the gentleman took to be brilliants, and stooped down to take them up accordingly; but finding it was only quick-silver, and judging from whence it came, they cried out, *that somebody had scattered her diamonds*, which occasioned a horse laugh among the gentlemen, and put all the ladies to the blush. This whimsical accident discredited the prescription.

The following anecdotes from Elisha Thornton's almanac for 1792 exemplify the taste of the printer, Peter Edes:

Two country Attornies riding home from the term, overtook an honest carter, and begun to jeer him, asked him why his fore horse was so fat, and the rest so lean, the carter (knowing them to be Lawyers) reply'd, know you not that? I will tell you, my fore-horse is a Lawyer, and those that follow him are his Clients.

An Oxford scholar having been very extravagant, and having writ to his father to supply him with money, and used all means, but nothing would do, he very ingeniously wrote to his Father that he was dead, and desired to send him up Money to pay for his burial.

Banneker's almanac for 1797 offered "A Burlesque on Genealogy." Two men argued about their pedigree. In an effort to outdo the other, one said that his ancestry went back to Adam. The other claimed that his origin was even earlier—before Adam. The first man conceded defeat, because at that time "there were no animals but Brutes, and it is very certain you are descended from them."

Two final examples will suffice to show the typical range of almanac humor, from childlike punning to labored subtlety. Polished verbal wit was hardly the proper medium for the almanacker or his clients, neither of whom had yet experienced a culture overloaded with words. The first is found in Poor Roger's (Roger More) *American Country Almanack* for 1768. The kindly family physician told a concerned lady "that her husband must get him an *Appetite*, she thinking he said an *Ape tied,* got an Ape, and tied it to his Bed." The second, from Briggs's almanac for 1798, satirized the scholar:

> A SCHOLAR, a bald man, and a barber, were traveling together, agreed each to watch four hours at night, in turn, for the sake of security; the barber's lot came first, who shaved the scholar's head when asleep, then waked him when his turn came. The scholar scratching his head, and feeling it bald, exclaimed, you "wretch of a barber, you have waked the bald man instead of me!"

Some narrative accounts were reports of historical events. Low's *Astronomical Almanack* for 1772 told of the "Boston massacre." Another battle report—of Concord and Lexington written by Rev. William Gordon of Roxbury—happens to be one of the earliest descriptions of this battle, and a valuable historical source. The author described in detail the line of march of the opposing troops to the field, as well as the battle itself. In 1776 the account was published simultaneously in the almanacs of Nathanael Low, Samuel Stearns, and Daniel George.

Published in repeated editions, narratives of Indian captivities were probably the most fascinating of all kinds of reading matter to the early American. Occasionally, such a narrative appeared in an almanac. More's *Poor Roger* for 1765 contained "A True Relation of the unheard of Suffering of *David Menzies*, Surgeon, among the *Cherokees;* and of his Surprising Deliverance in South-Carolina." As was the custom in stories of captivities, the account was carefully documented; the hero was providentially saved from starvation; and the ordeal, in the final analysis, was beneficial. The descriptions of torture, exquisitely excruciating, must have delighted many a supposedly squeamish reader. The captive's scientific detachment regarding his physical sufferings further titillates the reader. It seems that these Indians, in their travels, had eaten some larded venison which was very much to their liking. Having stolen some bacon and some larding pins, they were all set to try this process for themselves. The captive was handy. Menzies described the experiment:

It was evening, and these barbarians brought me stark-naked before a large fire. . . . After these cooks of Hell had larded all my left side, they turned it close to the fire, and proceeded on the other; but as this performance took up much time, on account of the unskillfulness of the operators and of my struggling; and as I afforded infinite entertainment and laughter . . . for I own that, being one of Sancho's disciples who can't suffer in silence, I squalled and roared most abominably (larding being in reality a very painful process to a live creature, the pin not merely going through the insensible epidermis, or scarf-skin, but lacerating also the pyramidal papillae of the true skin which anatomists agree to be the seat of feeling) and as the savages the mean while plied their rum impatiently . . . my executioners grew languid and drowsy. . . . I did not let this providential opportunity slip, you'll believe, but instantly disengaged my right arm (at the expense of the greater part of the belly of the palmaris brevis muscle, and with the dislocation of the eighth bone of the carpus) and fell to untying myself with expedition; I then escaped. . . .

And the providential provision of food? "the bacon that was saturated by the juices of my own body"! Resignation and thanksgiving were expressed in Menzies' report that he had been mercifully "rid entirely of a paralytic complaint I had been afflicted with for years in that left side of mine which was roasted."

Not all accounts were of this nature. Some presented the humane side of the "salvage." The "Adventure of a young English Officer among the Abenakee Savages," in West's *Bickerstaff's Boston Almanack* for 1769, concerns a soldier, who, as an adopted member of the tribe, has a tender parting with an Indian of noble sentiment. The Indian asks, "Hast thou a father?" The young man replies that he has. The Indian says that he too "was once a father." He saw his son "fall in battle" and "die like a man."

As he pronounced these words with the most pathetic emphasis, he shuddered; he seemed to breathe with pain, choked with inward groans, which he was endeavouring to stifle. His

eyes looked wild, but no tears came from them. Little by little
the violence of his agitations ceased. He grew calm. . . .

The Indian no more enjoys the beauties of nature, which, since
the death of his son, leave him "without delight." Hurriedly, he
adds, "Depart,—haste,—fly to yon camp of thy friends. Get home,
that thy father may still see with pleasure, the rising of the sun,
and the flowers of the spring."

Another narrative that showed the Indian in the role of a man
of feeling was "An Indian Story" in the second Dr. Ames's almanac for 1769. He wrote a better essay than story. In this narrative,
it is sometimes difficult to distinguish the speakers, for the story is
told from three points of view: that of the Indian, *"du-Pratz,"* and
Ames. Based on a history of Louisiana by "Monsieur *du-Pratz,"* the
story relates the treachery of the French in a false peace treaty
with the Natchez nation. Beguiling the Indian nation into a feeling of security, the French attacked and slew a large number of
the tribe. The author (*du-Pratz*) records his conversation with a
chieftain, who explains that his tribe, generous to the French, had
received nothing but ill treatment in return. The tale concludes
with "Whereupon the French massacred the bigger Part, and
at length extirpated every Soul of this sensible Nation."

An instructional piece of writing on astronomy, in the guise of
a conversational narrative, appeared in *The New Jersey Almanack* for 1768 (by Copernicus Weather-Guesser). "Copernicus Alone" is eleven pages long. Copernicus and a young lady
meet in a garden, as if for a clandestine romantic rendezvous, but
the sole purpose of the meeting is to instruct the lady regarding a
specific scientific concept. Copernicus explains, "The appointed
Hour is just at Hand, that I am to meet that beautiful young Lady,
I am under no doubt about answering all her Objections that she
has made against the diurnal Motion of the Earth." The lady's objections prove to be based on scripture, and no doubt represent
the conventional arguments of her more tender-minded contemporaries against the Copernican theory. She says, "Sir, I have only
produced two Proofs of the scriptural Authority to prove the Sta-

210

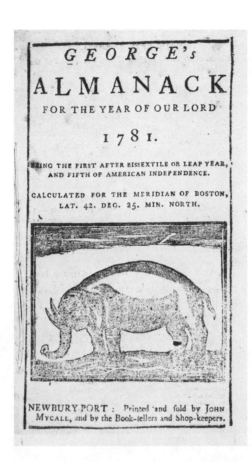

FOR THE YEAR OF OUR LORD

1 7 8 1.

BEING THE FIRST AFTER BISSEXTILE OR LEAP YEAR,
AND FIFTH OF AMERICAN INDEPENDENCE.

CALCULATED FOR THE MERIDIAN OF BOSTON,
LAT. 42. DEG. 25. MIN. NORTH.

NEWBURY PORT : Printed and fold by JOHN
MYCALL, and by the Book-fellers and Shop-keepers.

Illustration for "An Account of an Elephant."

bility of the Earth, and the Sun's Motion, but I can produce many
more . . . ." Copernicus replies:

> Madam, I grant that you can; but this may be said in general,
> to all the Proofs you can bring against the Copernican system;
> that since the Design of the holy writings, is not to instruct
> Mankind in Philosophical Things, but in divine Matters,
> therefore it is not necessary to restrain the Sense of Those
> Texts, to the strict Propriety of the Words. . . .

The popularity of "true" accounts that deal with the bizarre attests a provincial fascination for this kind of literature. Colonial
credulity seems to have been infinite. These tales, which purported
to be instructive, were entertaining and, often, titillating. Many

211

Illustration for an essay about Patagonian Giants.

were borrowed from British publications. For example, Freeman's *New York Almanack* for 1767 included an "Account of the Gallies, and Galley Slaves, in Italy. From Dr. Smollett's Travels." Another example, a satirical story directed against Catholicism, appeared in Low's Almanac for 1776. "Extracted from Don Antonio Gavin's Master Key to Popery," the account described the attempts of the Spanish Inquisition of Zaragoza to arrest a horse. Some borrowed narratives may have been altered to give them "authentic" American settings. A few were original.

Vicarious travel to strange lands was a frequent entertainment, and provided a primitive and slightly inaccurate foretaste of *The National Geographic Magazine*. Daniel Leeds, as early as 1712, included "A Page of Curiosities." These "curiosities" were paragraphs describing customs among the Tartars and among other groups of people. Tobler's *Pennsylvania Town and Country-man's Almanack* for 1768 published "An Account of some peculiar Customs of the Lacedaemonians." West's *Bickerstaff's Boston Almanack* (1768) inserted "A faithful and compleat account of the Giants called Patagonians lately discovered in South America by the Hon. Commodore Byron." An article on the "Orang Outang" appeared in the edition of the following year. Rittenhouse's *Virginia Almanack* for 1775 told a short story about "The Two Negro Friends." Two slaves on the isle of St. Christopher loved a beautiful slave girl, but the two men were devoted friends. Their rather ruthless solution was to kill her and then themselves. An anecdote was also told of Mahomet, who slew his mistress before a large assembly to prove that he was still master of himself. *Bickerstaff's Boston Almanack* for 1780 (by Ezra Gleason) printed an article on Russian weddings; and in 1786, a story of Bengal marriage customs.

Natural phenomena continued to intrigue the average reader. However, his attention, during the latter part of the century, was diverted from astronomical to geophysical wonders. Gleason's *The Massachusetts Calendar* for 1774 carried "An Account of a Woman's being killed by an Eruption from the Earth, in 1755 (Ventimiglia, Italy)." The eruption was not an earthquake, but a sort of vapour. Although some of the victim's flesh disappeared,

The ORANG OUTANG.

From *Bickerstaff's Boston Almanack* for 1769, illustrating
an account of the "Orang Outang".

214

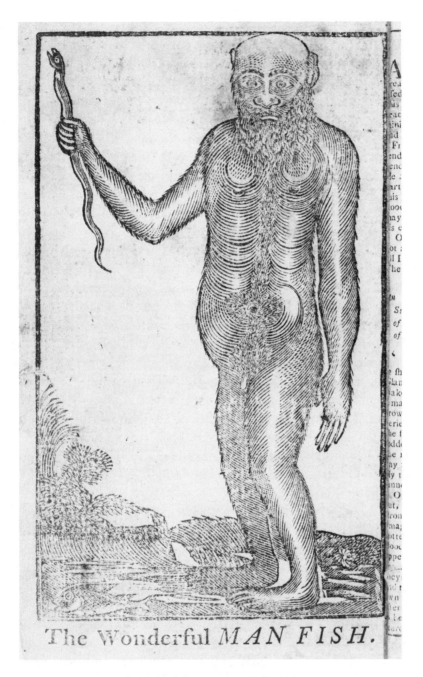

The Wonderful *MAN FISH.*

Illustration for the story of the "Man Fish" from *Bickerstaff's Boston Almanack* for 1772.

there was no trace of blood. This event was reported, it is said, to the Royal Academy of Sciences in Paris. Daniel George's "An Account of some extraordinary Rarities of Nature" in his 1778 almanac reported strange flames from the earth and unexplainable boiling waters.

Descriptions of freaks of nature were especially pleasurable to the almanac audience. The Ames almanac for 1772 described "the extraordinary Person who lately made her appearance in this town," somewhat incompletely, "as she would not admit of an accurate examination." Miss Emma Leach was a twenty-two-inch deformed dwarf, so twisted in shape that she was unable to walk. Her deformities were detailed. The writer (probably the printer, Ezekiel Russell, who advertised an entire publication about a number of "remarkable small persons") concluded, "She now enjoys herself very agreeably in her native place."

"A strange Phenomenon in the natural history of Man, from Father Fryjoo" was recounted as fact in West's *Bickerstaff's Boston Almanack* for 1768. A small boy, presumedly drowned in Italy, is seen five years later swimming in the river like a fish. He remains at home—as an idiot—for nine years, when he disappears again. Names, dates, and places are mentioned with authority. The same almanac, for 1772, describes a "Man-Fish" caught in England. No relationship between the two stories is specified, but the implications are certainly clear: the Italian child-fish, now fully grown, has obviously swum to England.

A unique variation on the traveler's-tale theme appeared in Stearns's *Universal Calendar* for 1788, elaborately illustrated with a full page showing a fantastic monster whose highly symbolic anatomy was accurately described in the text. It is "The MAJESTIC MERMAID A SEA MONSTER. Lately seen on the Coast of BARBARY, by the People on board the AMERICAN Brigantine COLUMBIA, Captain HARDY." According to the log, "On the 4th of July, at nine o'clock A.M. being in lat. 25, lon. 33, sailing with a pleasant breeze and smooth sea, we suddenly descried a surprising agitation on the water . . . ." The monster appears. Perceiving it to be non-violent, the beholders are able to describe

Illustration accompanying an account of the dwarf Emma Leach.

accurately its shape and size. The upper body is longitudinally divided between the sexes. It has four faces, each betraying a different human emotion and ethnic complexion, and the lower body tails off into a fish. Suddenly, the seamen are petrified to hear "a voice like thunder, issueing from the mouth of DEFORMITY, articulating in tremendous accents." The voice forebodes dire events caused by tyranny and decay in Europe and Asia. But Americans, though "highly favored" with sages, generals, artists, philosophers, poets, historians, and a religion "that will stand the test of AGES," are currently in danger of a like disintegration unless they pull themselves together. The voice continues:

> You need only RESOLUTION to be A PECULIARLY HAPPY PEOPLE; exert yourselves in promoting the USEFUL ARTS, MANUFACTURES and AGRICULTURE, be UNITED, repose Confidence in your RULERS, and keep at all times an EYE towards HEAVEN. Then shall all nations, kindreds & complexions yield to America the palm of PRAISE, and animated by so sublime an example, shall study the arts of PEACE and HARMONY and LEARN WAR NO MORE.

Evidently Stearns's warning *ex machina* was unheeded. But it is hard to guess what kind of reader was moved or amused by his quaint symbolism.

It was primarily in the latter half of the eighteenth century that the narrative became a popular, distinctive literary form in American almanacs. The selection of this material was usually left to the commercially oriented printer, the author being more often only the hired calculator of the astronomical and calendar information. This form is perhaps found more consistently in almanacs by "Bickerstaff," whether compiled by Benjamin West or another "Bickerstaff." A relatively late development, the personal narratives, exotic adventure stories, allegories, and accounts of the supernatural provided a main source of literary entertainment during a period when almanac publications were most prolific. Despite occasional satire, these narratives gave the appearance, for the most part, of being factual.

9 Maxims, Predictions, and Fillers

The maxim, perhaps the briefest of formal compositions, was ideally suited to the twofold purpose of the almanac, which might be paraphrased as *per trivia ad gravitatem*. Because one of the principal functions of instruction was to inculcate morality, the maxim was especially appropriate. It adapted well to Puritan philosophy, and it cleverly expressed the emerging emphasis in the eighteenth century on those virtues best propounded by Benjamin Franklin. These concise bits of sententious wisdom were especially designed to be slipped into extra spaces on the calendar pages.

Special prominence was sometimes given to maxims by placing them on pages other than those reserved for the calendar. At times they ceased to be maxims and grew into brief homiletic essays; yet the almanacker, unconscious of his inaccuracy, continued to designate these overgrown sayings as "maxims."

JANUARY begins on *Thurſday*, hath XXXI Days.

LO ! my fair, the morning lazy,
Peeps abroad from yonder hill ;
Phœbus riſes red and hazy,
Froſt has ſtopt the village mill.

SOLAR CALCULATIONS, &c.

Days.	☉	H	♄	♃	♂	♀	☿
1	♑ 11 50	♍ 23	♓ 17	♋ 21	♑ 10	♐ 6	♐ 29
7	17 56	23	17	22	12	13	♑ 9
13	24 4	24	17	24	15	21	20
19	♒ 0 11	24	16	26	17	♑ 0	♒ 0
25	6 16	24	16	28	20	7	10

M. D.	W. D.	Calender, remarkable Days, Obſervations, &c.	☉ riſe.	☉ ſets.	L. D. H. M.	☉ S.
1	5	Circumciſion.	7 33	4 27	8 54	4
2	6	King of Denmark born 1749.	7 33	4 27	8 54	5
3	7	Night's len. 15 h. 4 m.	7 32	4 28	8 56	5
4	D	Sunday paſt Circumciſion.	7 32	4 28	8 56	6
5	2	Night's length 15 h. 2 m.	7 31	4 29	8 58	6
6	3	EPIPHANY, or twelfth Day.	7 31	4 29	8 58	6
7	4	*The epicure*	7 30	4 30	9 0	7
8	5	St. Lucian, Mart. *puts*	7 30	4 30	9 0	7
9	6	*his purſe into his*	7 29	4 31	9 2	8
10	7	Vir. Mary b. year of the world,	7 28	4 32	9 4	8
11	D	Sunday paſt Epiph. (3985.	7 27	4 33	9 6	9
12	2	*belly, and the*	7 26	4 34	9 8	9
13	3	*miſer his belly*	7 25	4 35	9 10	9
14	4	Peace Ratified by Congreſs 1784	7 25	4 35	9 10	10
15	5	*into his*	7 24	4 36	9 12	10
16	6	*purſe.*	7 23	4 37	9 14	10
17	7	King of Poland born 1732.	7 22	4 38	9 16	11
18	D	2d paſt Epiph. Q. Charlotte of	7 21	4 39	9 18	11
19	2	(England, birth day kept.	7 21	4 39	9 18	11
20	3	King of Spain born 1716.	7 20	4 40	9 20	12
21	4	*Keep dry your feet, your body*	7 19	4 41	9 22	12
22	5	*warm,*	7 18	4 42	9 24	12
23	6	*And exerciſe will ſhield from*	7 17	4 43	9 26	12
24	7	*harm.*	7 16	4 44	9 28	13
25	D	Converſion of St. Paul. A.D. 34.	7 15	4 45	9 30	13
26	2	*It is deſire only*	7 14	4 46	9 32	13
27	3	*that makes us*	7 13	4 47	9 34	13
28	4	Peter the Great died 1725.	7 12	4 48	9 36	13
29	5	*either poor, or rich.*	7 11	4 49	9 38	14
30	6	K. Charles I. Martyr. 1648.	7 10	4 50	9 40	14
31	7	*Waſte no time.*	7 9	4 51	9 42	14

Interspersed aphorisms on calendar page of *Thomas's Massachusetts, Connecticut, Rhode-Island . . . Almanack* for 1789.

The unique character of the American pioneering experience lent itself well to pragmatic philosophy. The guiding principle of functionalism was second nature to Americans. If something worked, they wanted to know about it. The proverb and the maxim, natural outgrowths from earlier advice on weather and farming, began to appear in the latter part of the seventeenth century. Proverbs were by no means common to all almanacs, despite their association in the mind of the modern reader. Daniel and Titan Leeds were among the first to include this literary form, but Ames and particularly Franklin made it a relatively frequent almanac feature.

Although they were of inconsistent quality, the Leeds maxims were passable one-liners of the period. The best of them can hold their own with the more famous proverbs of Benjamin Franklin, published a quarter of a century later; for example, in the Leeds almanac for 1713: "Women are fitter to conceive Children than to conceal secrets." In the 1718 almanac were several worthy sayings: "He is sober who is never Drunk with any thing but Wine"; "The Old Woman would not seek her Daughter in the Oven had she not been there her self"; "Passion runs through all languages"; and "Hungry Dogs will eat dirty Pudding." And in 1728: "He danceth well, to whom Fortune pipeth."

Dr. Ames, II, liked to write verse; consequently, many of his comments on the calendar pages were rhymed couplets. He could, however, compose (or borrow) proverbs of average pithiness. His almanac for 1735, on the May page, had "Three Things breed Jealousy. A mighty State, a rich Treasure and a fair Wife." In April 1747 he said, "A Look that's cross and a tongue that raves, spoils a Beauty." Examples from his 1758 almanac prove that he had a facility for phrasing cracker-barrel philosophy in the manner of Poor Richard:

> February: If you fall into Misfortunes, creep thro' those Bushes which have the least Briars.
>
> April: Industry and Frugality makes a poor Man rich.
>
> June: They who have Nothing to trouble them, will Themselves, be a Trouble to Others.

All human Skill can't Natures Art devife
From different Mixtures, different Forms arife ;
Hence Different Men and different Matters flow
Which mans inhumane Actions daily fhow,
Thus Fools turn Poets, and great blufters make
Yet buy or Steal Verfe for each Almanack. *Remus*

1	6	Day 10 ho, 26 m.	3 h	♓ 6		46	Sun rife at 6 4 7
2	7	Purifi. V. Mary.	4	21 7		48	Sets at 5 13
3	F	4 Sun. p. Epiph.	5	♈ 8		51	*the beft fide out-*
4	2	*Wether's never ill*	6	17 9		53	*wards*
5	3	*If the Wind lye ftill.*	6 h	♉ 10	After-noon	57	Firft Quar 7 da.
6	4	7 ftars fo. at 5 30	7	14 12		7	
7	5	☊ 16 ♎ Warm for	8	27 13		10	*Zeal has fill'd the*
8	6	▢ ☉ ♂ the Seafon	9	♊ 14		10	*World with blood-*
9	7	✳ ♂ ♀ but wet.	10	25 14		4	*fhed.*
10	F	5 Sun. p. Epiph.	10	♋ 15		59	*Not very fecure.*
11	2	7 ftars fo. at 5. 9.	11	24 16		45	*A pleafant meeting*
12	3	Tides Rife.	0	♌ 17		30	Full ● 14 day
13	4	☽ near Cor ♌	1	24 Moons			at 10 morn.
14	5	Valentine Mart.	2	♍ rifing.			Sun rife at 6 30
15	6	Days 11 hours.	3	23 7		4	Sets at 5 30
16	7	Tydes fall.	3 h	♎ 8		12	*Weep and laugh*
17	F	Septuagefima.	4	20 9		15	*together*
18	2	SS ♀ ♀ Rain or	5	♏ 10		16	*Cold entertain-*
19	3	♂ ☉ ♀ fnow,	6	16 11		16	*ment.*
20	4	♂ near Cor ♏	7	28 12	After-noon	12	Laft Quar. 22 d
21	5		7 h	♐ 13		3	*hard to be trufted*
22	6	7 ftars fet 11, 40	8	22 13		54	
23	7	foul weather,	9	♑ 14		36	*For better for*
24	F	St. Matthias.	10	15 15		16	*Worfe:*
25	2	△ ♃ ♀ dirty Febr.	11	27 15		54	
26	3	Day 11 h. 30 m.	0	♒ 16		31	*He miftakes Zeal*
27	4	☊ 15 ♎	0 h	22 17		5	*for either Pride ro*
28	5	Spring Tydes.	1	♓ 17		35	*Intereft.*

Bright fhining Venus is our morning Star till the
8th of *June*, and from thence our Morning ftar
till the years end.

Calendar page from Titan Leeds' almanac for 1717, showing
interfperfed aphorisms and comments.

July: He can't speak well, who always Talks.

October: There are three faithful Friends: an old Wife, an old Dog, and ready Cash.

November: Were things done twice, many would be wise.

In 1763 Ames voiced a *bon mot* which is apt in any period: "To some men their country is their shame; and some are the shame of their country."

The most expert proverbialist in America was Benjamin Franklin, who, as Poor Richard, brought proverbs into the homes of countless Americans. Franklin's reputation "as the 'quintessential ethical capitalist'" was based largely on his almanacs, and especially on the aphorisms printed in them.[1] But Lemay points out that the aphorisms constitute only a small percentage of total almanac content. In his almanacs, Franklin encouraged industry and frugality "as the means of procuring wealth and thereby securing virtue," but the remainder of *Poor Richard* had little to do with "ethical capitalism." Franklin should not be remembered in American almanac history primarily for his aphorisms: his greatest contribution to American literature is found in his almanac prefaces, in the creation of his characters, Richard and Bridget Saunders.

Franklin's borrowed proverbs from earlier English and European writers were probably much more popular in eighteenth-century America than they had ever been in their own country at the time of their writing. Because today's reader is familiar with Poor Richard's sayings, a few examples should suffice:

1733: After three days men grow weary of a wench, a guest and weather rainy.

1734: Onions can make ev'n heirs and widows weep.

1735: A ship under sail and a big bellied woman are the handsomest things that can be seen common.

Three things are men most likely to be cheated in, a horse, a wig and a wife.

Deny self, for self's sake.

1758: (Father Abraham's Speech)

The Sleeping Fox catches no Poultry.

He that lives upon Hope will die fasting.

223

A small leak will sink a great ship.

Fools make Feasts and wise Men eat them.

Lying rides upon Debt's Back.

Experience keeps a dear School, but Fools will learn in
no other, and scarce in that.

The maxim was not limited to the proverb. In 1753 Poor Job
wrote, "Since, *Reader*, the Time past cannot be recall'd . . . for the
Improvement of the Time present, I have added some short MAX-
IMS." These "short maxims" were actually paragraphs on Religion,
Discourse, Silence and Secrecy, Reputation, Vain-Glory, Virtue,
Riches, Suits of Law, and Marriage. The subject of one of Low's
maxims for 1764 was women. "Some," he said, "are so uncharitable,
as to think all Women are bad: And others are so credulous as to
believe they are all good." But the author believes that women, like
men, partake of both qualities.

Another opinion was expressed in Rittenhouse's *Virginia Almanack* for 1775: "INDOLENCE deprives men of all that activity
which should call forth their virtues, and make them illustrious.
An indolent man is scarce a man; he is half a woman."

Dr. Ames, III, added this sage comment in 1773: "As the
Reformation is said to have begun in *Harry the 8th's* breeches, so
in our times some notable reformations begin there . . . and there-
abouts is often the spring of noble deeds imputed to virtuous
resolutions."

Under "Rules and MAXIMS for promoting MATRIMONIAL
HAPPINESS," *The Virginia Almanack* for 1775 warned all men,
"As the woman is deemed the weaker vessel, the man should give
grains of allowance for frailties," and counseled him "to *love* and
cherish her," despite her shortcomings, so that "she will cheerfully
obey so endearing a husband."

The Vermont almanac for 1795 (by "Adam Astrologist") included "Moral PRECEPTS and MAXIMS for the Conduct of Life"
from Plutarch. "Marriage," he said, "enlarges the scene of our happiness or misery; the marriage in love is pleasant, the marriage of
interest easy, and a marriage where both meet, happy." In "The
Art of getting riches," a rich grandduke of Tuscany advised a Ve-

224

MAY. *V Month.*

And when too populous at length confeſs'd,
From confluent Strangers refug'd and redreſs'd:
When War ſo long withdraws his barb'rous Train,
That Peace o'erſtocks us with the Sons of Men:
So long Health breathes thro' the pure ambient Air,
That Want muſt prey on thoſe Diſeaſe would ſpare;
Then will be all the *gen'rous Goddeſs* ſeen,
Then moſt diffus'd ſhe ſhines, and moſt benign.

Her

		Remark, days, &c	☉ riſ	☉ ſet	☽ pl.	Aſpects, &c.
1	6	PHILIP & JACOB.	4 56	7 4	♉ 8	♀ riſe 3 51
2	7	☉ eclipſed, viſible	4 55	7 5	22	*'Tis more noble*
3	D	Rogation Sunday.	4 54	7 6	♊ 7	☽ w. ☿ *to for-*
4	2	*Clouds, and*	4 53	7 7	22	☽ with ♃ *give,*
5	3	Day inc. 5 6	4 52	7 8	♋ 7	☽ with ♂ *and*
6	4	*thunder*	4 51	7 9	22	♂ ſets 10 25
7	5	Aſcenſion Day.	4 50	7 10	♌ 6	♃ ſets 8 44
8	6	*with*	4 49	7 11	20	♄ ri. 9 7 *more*
9	7	*rain, then*	4 48	7 12	♍ 4	☉ in ♊ *manly*
10	D	6 paſt Eaſter.	4 47	7 13	17	☌ ☉ ☿ *to deſ-*
11	2	Day 14 28 long.	4 46	7 14	♎ 0	*piſe, than to*
12	3	*fair*	4 45	7 15	13	*revenge an In-*
13	4	*and*	4 44	7 16	26	*jury.*
14	5	*pleaſant,*	4 44	7 16	♏ 8	*A Brother*
15	6	*ſomething*	4 43	7 17	20	*may not be*
16	7	*colder,*	4 42	7 18	♐ 2	♀ riſe 3 34 *a*
17	D	Whitſunday.	4 42	7 18	14	⚹ ♂ ♀ *Friend,*
18	2	Days inc. 5 28	4 41	7 19	26	☽ with ♄ *but*
19	3	*then*	4 41	7 19	♑ 8	*a Friend will*
20	4	Ember Week.	4 40	7 20	20	*always be a*
21	5	*ſhowers*	4 40	7 20	♒ 2	♂ ſet 10 16
22	6	*and*	4 39	7 21	14	♃ ſet 8 3
23	7	*fine ſea-*	4 39	7 21	26	♄ riſe 8 4
24	D	Trinity Sunday.	4 39	7 21	♓ 8	*Brother.*
25	2	Days 14 44 long.	4 38	7 22	21	*Mean-*
26	3	*ſonable*	4 38	7 22	♈ 4	☍ ♄ ♃ *neſs*
27	4	*weather.*	4 38	7 22	18	☌ ♀ ☿ *is the*
28	5	Corp. Chriſt.	4 37	7 23	♉ 2	*Parent of*
29	6	K. Cha. reſto.	4 37	7 23	16	*Inſolence.*
30	7	Pr. Ame. b. 1711	4 37	7 23	♊ 1	☽ with ♀
31	D	1 paſt Trinity.	4 36	7 24	16	☽ with ♃

Interspersed aphorisms from *Poor Richard Improved* for 1752.

netian nobleman: "I never ask another to do that which I can do myself: I never put off till to-morrow what may be done to-day; nor do I ever think any gain so trivial as to despise it."

The precepts or maxims are Franklin philosophy in longer form. Whether short proverb or long maxim, the message is the same: how to improve yourself so that you can obtain wealth, "thereby securing virtue."

Predictions (or prognostications) had been a major feature of European almanacs from the beginning, and of most American almanacs since John Tulley, in the late seventeenth century. Although predictions were sometimes presented in standard verse, as were almost all kinds of almanac subject matter, they never achieved a set form in prose.

As official interpreters of astrological signs and portents, the almanac-makers were expected to comment on the eclipses and the movements of the planets. Samuel Clough, in his almanac for 1706, quoted one of the most famous interpreters of the age—John Partridge. In 1702 a conjunction occurred of Saturn and Jupiter in Aries. Partridge had explained its meaning: the "perfect Day" would arrive on earth by the year 1778.

Predictions of wars, the fall of people in high places, floods, earthquakes, and plagues were common astrological fare. The most interesting predictions, at least to the modern reader, are satires such as those written by James Franklin, Sr., in *Poor Robin* for 1729. Concerning February:

> This Month is propitious to Lovers. And because many fooling Things have been wrote by Pretenders to Astrology, relating to Love and speedy Marriage, I shall mention one Sign only, which is infallible. In the Evening of *Valentine's Day*, do you take two White Oak Leaves, and lay them across your Pillow, when you go to bed, putting on a clean Shift or Shirt, and turning it the wrong Side outwards, lay down and say these Words out aloud, Good Valentine *be kind to me, In Dreams let me my true Love see.*
> So carefully drawing your right Leg behind you, put it over your left Shoulder. In like manner put your left Leg behind you, laying it across your right Shoulder; and be sure take Care that the Soles of your Feet meet under your Chin. Then go to Sleep as soon as you can: And if you dream you see two

226

Moons touching each other, you will certainly be marry'd very speedily, whether you be a young Man, Maid or Widow.

In his June prediction, which attacked lawyers, he said that, as "A Student in Physick and Astrology," he learned things from the stars, "which were they made known to the common People, would terrify and surprize them." For example,

they tell me, that at a certain Court, which will be held some Time in this Month, a *Strange Lawyer*, will, in the face of the Court, and not having the *Fear of his brethren before his Eyes*, prove himself an *honest Man*.

Predicting that tattling would be the favorite vice of the planets during the whole month of August, Poor Robin offered a solution:

The only Remedy the Sons of Art prescribe in this Case is, for the *Tattler* to go to a Brook which is govern'd by Luna, which is vulgarly called the *Moon*, or in Cases of Necessity to any other Brook, under no Government at all; and there let him or her take a mouthful of Water, on the first Day of the Month, when the Moon is in Aries, (id est, in the *Head*) and hold it in his or her Mouth until the End of the Month. This is an approved Remedy, and never failed Of Success.

December is the month when evil spirits have no luck at all; "And therefore if Goody Stiffendorff, who now lies Bed-rid, should be suspected by her Neighbours of killing their Goose, they will do her much Wrong." Poor Robin realizes that some astrologers believe that these evil spirits have power only on Christmas Eve, but he knows "the whole Month has as much Power as any Eve in it." He has no fear of "wandering Spirits here and there"; for they can accomplish nothing, "nor can they be seen without a Tellescope."

Poor Robin's "Predictions" at the bottom of the calendar pages for 1734 were perhaps facetious. Based on the movements of the planets, he foresaw "contagious Airs, and unwholesome Dews, Blasts, and such like extravagant Errors of Nature," which "may occasion the Diseases of Cattel." Bloodletting was recommended. He justified his concentration on such matters with "We write not these things as if we were either Farrier or Cowleech, but out of Civility to the *Yeomanry* of *New England*, and those industrious *Farmers*. . . ."

Poor Richard in 1738 took no chances that his predictions would fail: "This Year the Stone-blind shall see but very little; the Deaf shall hear but poorly; and the Dumb shan't speak very plain. As to old age, it will be incurable, this year, because of the years past." Ben Franklin was doubtless aware of Rabelais' sixteenth-century "Pantagruelian Prognostication"—or of others like it:

> No matter what these crazy astrologers . . . tell you, do not be-
> lieve that in this year there will be any other governor of the
> universe than God the creator. . . . This year the blind will see
> only a very little; the deaf will not hear well; the dumb will not
> have much to say; the rich will fare better than the poor and
> the well than the sick; several sheep, oxen, pigs, birds, chick-
> ens, and geese will die.

Although Ames believed in astrology and wrote serious prognostications, he omitted the Man of Signs after 1734, and he added short humorous predictions in the extra space on the calendar pages. Calculated devices such as this helped to ensure the success of his almanac with all kinds of readers. These samples of Dr. Ames's humor are from his 1743 almanac:

> May: There will be a vast Quantity of Bread and Wine
> rain'd down not many days hence.
>
> June: A great Politician comes off harmless by a cunning
> Artifice, contrary to all Expectation.
>
> October: A great Struggle between a great Man & a little
> Woman for the Mastery. She gets the Day.

Rittenhouse's *Maryland, Virginia, and Pennsylvania Almanack* for 1780 contained some predictions that—to use Poor Robin's word—were more "Ass-trological" than astrological:

> June: A member of assembly shall be found in bed with his
> neighbor's wife—both dead.
>
> October: Tantapaulin shall receive a mauling.
>
> November: A cow shall be heard to speak Latin.

Others were political:

> February: The Cock (i.e. the French) shall strike his spur
> in the bull-dog of England; and the thirteen stripes shall
> be seen in the harbour of New-York.

April: The man whose name begins with the word Wash,
         shall wash the wounds of the army in a piece of good
         news to be read in the general orders.

Weather predictions were an integral part of almost all almanacs. Samuel Clough's for 1707 quoted "Prognostics" from John
Foster's almanac for 1676. These prognostics explained the signs of
rain, wind, storms, and hot, cold, and fair weather. *Poor Robin* for
1728, in a fairly serious tone, also explained the weather signs. For
example: "If sheep do bleat, play or skip wantonly, it is a sign of
wet weather. If the Bees fly far from their Hives, it is a sign of foul
weather."

More specific comments on weather were usually found on the
calendar pages opposite the dates of the month. Some are serious,
and some, ridiculous. Many suggest that the writer was hard put
to find anything to say. Nathan Bowen wrote in his almanac for
1722 opposite August 18th, "Cool Showers"; and, for the 19th and
20th, "Refreshes the Weary Earth." In Leeds's almanac for 1733,
published by William Bradford in New York, occurred "It's an ill
Wind that blows Nobody no good" (November 28–30). Ames, in
1735, said for December, "Now warming Pans are better than
Fans." He must have liked this one, for he paraphrased it in 1744
for January. "If it don't rain, I shall wonder" was placed opposite
November 9–11 in Leeds for 1738, published by Andrew Bradford
in Philadelphia. The poetic Dr. Ames became more metaphorical
for September 1742 with "A Spell of glorious Weather, but *Boreas*
will soon commit a Rape on *Flora*." For March 1744: "Very dirty
wet miry bad travelling except for the Geese overhead." The second Dr. Ames, or his printer, chose a different literary device when
in 1774 he used a terse personification: "Puffing, belching, f*****g
Weather." Ordinarily a fact sheet, *Gaine's New York Pocket Almanack* for 1775, by Thomas Moore, interspersed "If it rains about
this time it ant my fault."

Isaiah Thomas mixed predictions with weather in his 1779
almanac. He informed readers in October: "A Man may take his
female bed-fellow in his arms without danger of over-heating his

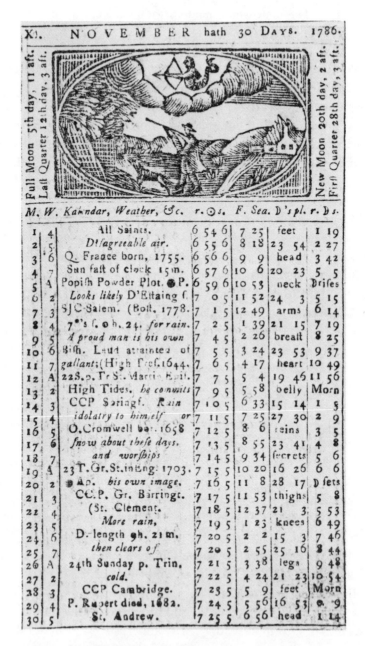

Full Moon 5th day, 11 aft.
Laſt Quarter 12th day, 3 aft.

New Moon 20th day, 2 aft.
Firſt Quarter 28th day, 3 aft.

M.	W.	Kalendar, Weather, &c.	r. ☉ s.	F. Sea.	D's pl.	r. D s.
1	4	All Saints.	6 54 6	7 25	feet	1 19
2	5	Diſagreeable air.	6 55 6	8 18	23 54	2 27
3	6	Q. France born, 1755.	6 56 6	9 9	head	3 42
4	7	Sun faſt of clock 15 m.	6 57 6	10 6	20 23	5 5
5	A	Popiſh Powder Plot. ☉ P.	6 59 6	10 53	neck	D riſes
6	2	Looks likely D'Eſtaing ſ.	7 0 5	11 52	24 3	5 15
7	3	SJC Salem. (Boſt. 1778.	7 1 5	12 49	arms	6 14
8	4	7 ☉'s ſ. o h. 24. for rain.	7 2 5	1 39	21 15	7 19
9	5	A proud man is his own	7 4 5	2 26	breaſt	8 25
10	6	Biſh. Laud attainted of	7 5 5	3 24	23 53	9 37
11	7	gallant; (High Tref.1644.	7 6 5	4 17	heart	10 49
12	A	22 S. p. Tr S. Martin Epit.	7 7 5	5 4	19 46	11 56
13	2	High Tides. he commits	7 9 5	5 58	belly	Morn
14	3	CCP Springf. Rain	7 10 5	6 33	15 14	1 5
15	4	idolatry to himſelf or	7 11 5	7 25	27 30	2 9
16	5	O. Cromwell ber. 1658	7 12 5	8 6	reins	3 5
17	6	ſnow about theſe days,	7 13 5	8 55	23 41	4 8
18	7	and worſhips	7 14 5	9 34	ſecrets	5 6
19	A	23 T. Gr. St. in Eng. 1703.	7 15 5	10 20	16 26	6 6
20	2	☽ Ap. his own image.	7 16 5	11 8	28 17	D ſets
21	3	CCP. Gr. Barringt.	7 17 5	11 53	thighs	5 8
22	4	(St. Clement.	7 18 5	12 37	21 3	5 53
23	5	More rain,	7 19 5	1 25	knees	6 49
24	6	D. length 9h. 21 m.	7 20 5	2 2	15 3	7 46
25	7	then clears of	7 20 5	2 55	25 16	8 44
26	A	24th Sunday p. Trin.	7 21 5	3 38	legs	9 48
27	2	cold.	7 22 5	4 24	21 23	10 54
28	3	CCP Cambridge.	7 23 5	5 9	feet	Morn
29	4	P. Rupert died, 1682.	7 24 5	5 56	16 53	☉ 9
30	5	St. Andrew.	7 25 5	6 56	head	1 14

Seasonal calendar art and interspersed aphorisms in *Bicker-staff's Boston Almanack* for 1786.

reins, and of which a good account may be given some nine months after." And in the same jocular mood for November: ". . . him that then goes with his gloves in his pocket, the weather may invite to put them on; and him that is in bed with another man's wife, her husband may invite to come out."

The Virginia Almanack for 1770 combined weather and wisdom:

> Now the nights beginning to grow cold shall cause some young bachelors to think that a good wife, with a great deal of money, will do well. . . . Women while they are maidens wish wantonly, while they are wives they will willingly, while they are widows they would willingly.

The author reminded the young bachelors that "love without lands is like a fire without fuel" and "They are ill horsed, and worse wived, that ride on colts, and marry young giglets."

Fragments other than predictions appear in all shapes and sizes, and deal with a limitless variety of subject matter. As filler material, these comments are conveniently dispersed in whatever space is available. Some are as long as paragraphs; others are lists; and some brief observations in the calendar-page columns are so esoteric and enigmatic that communication fails completely, if, indeed, any was ever intended.

An item of humorous filler from the Leeds almanac for 1734 listed "The properties of a good Horse necessary to be know'd and observed by the Buyer." "Properties" are itemized, sequentially, that a horse should have of a man, lion, hare, fox, and ass. The last category is:

> The 10 Properties a Horse hath of a Woman are 1. to be merry at Meat, 2. Well paced, 3. broad Forehead, 4. broad Buttocks, 5. hard of Ward, 6. easy to be leapt upon, 7. good at a long Journey, 8. ever busy with the Tongue, 9. to be shewing the Bridle, and 10. to be active and stirring under a Man.

Stearns Universal Calendar for 1791 described "a woman of pleasure" in a catalog of metaphors: "a syren's voice—a crocodile's tears—a peacock's pride . . . . Like the insidious spider, she extends her net—sucks to death unwary fugitives . . . She resembles a light, painted frigate, without helm or ballast, with colours streaming, and a rotten bottom . . . ."

Satirical calendar comments on medicine, lawyers, and marriage brightened the pages of many eighteenth-century almanacs. Poor Robin in 1728:

> January: The best Physick in this Month, is warm Cloathes, good Fires, and a merry housewife. But beware of Counterfeits.
>
> March: Now advise with a learned, honest and able Astrological or Hydrogebihipnotitharneupismanecedichical Physician; but in Cases of Necessity, you may make use of a Seventh Son.

Ames hit his favorite target in September for 1742 with "Now if a Lawyer should be charg'd with a Lie, He would say he had it from his Client," and again in 1750 with "I should predict good Weather this Week, but there's so many Courts, the Lawyers may raise a Storm . . . ." The *Virginia Almanack* for 1771 (Purdie & Dixon, printers) continued the attack on its October page with "The summer's gone, the Court begins, Whoever lose, the lawyer wins."

Another favorite subject for almanac satire was expressed in Ames's almanac for 1740. In September: "Cuckold, thou so ingrateful art! / as not to thank thy Maker."

The Daniel Leeds almanac for 1706 was one of the first to fill in blank calendar spaces with inanities such as "In a Hurly-burly" and "Be sure to please the Old one." Nathan Bowen in 1724 inserted "Good Weather for Hoop-Petty-Coat Lady's" for May 29–30. Interspersed on Poor Robin's January page for 1730 is this strange remark:

> January 24 *I got a Wife! Yes;*
>   25 St. Paul Convert.
>   26 Inclining to Snow or
>   27 Sup. C. Charlstown
>   28   Rain
>   29 *And my Child is dead*
>   30 K. Charles I Beheaded
>   31   *of the Meazles too.*

Lſt Q 4 D. a 8 Morn. N. ● 10 D at 12 Night.
Frſt Q 17 D a 11 Night. Ful ○ 26 D a 5 Morn.

M|W|C Spr. T Sr D. aſ. W ☿c ●Pl. ⦿S. R ⊙S. F Sea

1	3	All Saints.		reaſ	09	03	7	09	5	11	54
2	4	All Souls.		rea	09	58	7	10	5	12	26
3	5	7 Stars ſouth 12 20		heart	11	07	7	11	5	01	26
4	6			heart	12	06	7	12	5	02	18
5	7	POWDER-Plot.		bowel	mor		7	13	5	03	07
6	8	Falling Weather.		bowe	02	24	7	14	5	03	59
7	2	N. E. Wind &		reins	03	41	7	15	5	04	46
8	3	Snow		reins	04	53	7	15	5	05	3
9	4	or Rain for		ſecret	06	05	7	16	5	06	49
10	5	ſome Time.		ſecret	he		7	17	5	07	54
11	6	Snow or		thigh	●		7	18	5	08	52
12	7	Rain with		thigh	Ser		7	19	5	09	53
13	8	ſtormy Weather.		knees	07	21	7	20	5	10	49
14	2			knees	08	24	7	20	5	11	49
15	3	Inf. C. Newp. & Fairſ.		legs	09	32	7	21	5	12	30
16	4	S. E. Winds		legs	10	38	7	22	5	01	18
17	5	Rain or Snow		feet	11	44	7	23	5	02	04
18	6	with cll Weather.		feet	12	52	7	24	5	02	52
19	7	She told him that Hole		feet	Morn	7	25	5	03	52
20	8	was there 'fore.		head	02	46	7	25	5	04	12
21	2	7 Stars ſouth 11.		head	03	48	7	26	5	04	56
22	3	Inf. C. N Lon. Snow		neck	04	41	7	27	5	05	34
23	4	or Rain.		neck	05	48	7	27	5	06	17
24	5	S. W. Winds		neck	06	38	7	28	5	06	40
25	6	and rainy Weath		arms	th		7	29	5	07	23
26	7	If it won't roaſt let it		arms	●		7	30	5	08	05
27	B	Advent Sunday (burn		breaſ	Ris	7	31	5	09	02
28	2	Snow or Rain.		br aſ	06	49	7	31	5	09	46
29	3	Days 9 h. long.		breaſ	07	45	7	32	5	10	54
30	4	St. Andrew's Day.		heart	08	45	7	32	5	11	22

Now the Summer's paſt,
the Winter's drawing nigh,
And we are haſtning all
unto Eternity

Curious filler from calendar page of Stafford's *Rhode Island Almanack* for 1737, printed by Ann Franklin.

Titan Leeds had some silly sayings in a 1731 edition printed by William Bradford in New York: for August 26–28, "Peaches begin to come. O dear!"

Some of the Widow Ann Franklin's blank-space filler is now unintelligible at first sight and may have been then. Although many almanackers "filled" with trivia rather than maxims, in the manner of Poor Richard, Ann's 1737 and 1738 *Rhode-Island Almanacks,* compiled by Joseph Stafford, contained filler both intriguing and provocative by what it omitted. In the space for February 26 is "Moll, don't curse Folks." In March, "Dickie trips up's Heels." In May, "She kicks up her Heels and shows her fine legs." June 5, following a weather warning of thunder and lightning, carries the enigmatic query, "Who cut the Rag," while June 16 explicitly tells the reader, "Now beware of Thieves." On July 8 we are told "Ronald's drunk to-day." On July 14, "Moll runs after him." (Whom? Ronald? Surely not!) But by July 23, and 24, the plot has reversed: "A Match making between Tom & old Moll." Only three days later, "Tom & Moll's marri'd," and by the end of the month, "They live a poor Life." There is a quite shocking revelation during four days of December 1737, which, we hope, was not meant directly for the reader: "ly aff the Tail o' my Sark [Shift] ye Lousie Dog / Your A-s's been frozen this twa years."

Equally intimate fillers in the 1738 almanac hint at personal problems: "The Old Woman's Dater's [daughter's] Teeth's all rotten / it isn't with eating hot / Po-ta-to, I think not" (April 26–29); "I am quite sick of it" (September 17); and "I wish he'd let me alone" (September 23).

The fillers in Ann's 1739 almanac are more intelligible. For example, for April 17 and 18, we find "Better not be led at all than misled." And scattered through the first week of May: "Poor Doll's Petition / humbly shewing, the Beer she drinks was / Roger's brewing." Did the judge, we wonder, order a wedding? There are indications, two years later, that the dull machinery of printing was occasionally oiled, even when Puritan women were on the job: "Had not my muse drank Ale in plenty / This Vacancy must have been empty."

Filler material was frequently the province of the printer. The Ameses probably wrote their own. In the case of the Widow Ann Franklin and Joseph Stafford, we cannot be sure; but the content, in some instances, permits the conjecture that the Widow Ann be given the credit—or the blame.

The Right Honourable
WILLIAM PITT,
Earl of CHATHAM.

10 Verse

The second extant American almanac, Samuel Danforth's for 1647, contained verse. The Cambridge philomaths, the first American almanac-makers, frequently filled their extra space with appropriate pastoral-type verses of their own, a practice which prompted Samuel Eliot Morison to call the Cambridge almanac "the annual poetry magazine of Harvard College." [1] Gradually, verse became a popular vehicle for expressing almost every kind of subject matter in the almanac: seasons and weather, astronomy and general science, history, husbandry, fashion, manners and morality, health and medicine, philosophy and religion, religious and political propaganda, predictions, and personal and prefatory comments.

Humor and satire pervade well over half of almanac verse, if we except the Spenserian seasonal verse on the calendar pages. Prime targets were astrology, lawyers, religion (Catholicism), and the foibles of men and women (manners, marriage and infidelity).

The most prevalent verse form is a narrative stanza or verse essay composed of couplets. Couplets were also used for such thematic variations as elegies, epitaphs, and dialogues. Distinctive metrical forms are represented in the heroic couplet, the ballad, stanza, other rhymed quatrains, and blank verse. Ames, II, occasionally invented rather intricate metrics that defy classification. An interesting (but uncommon) linguistic feature of some early almanac verse is the use of various dialects.

More than one commentator has listed "bad verse" among the characteristics of an almanac. Franklin has Richard Saunders say in 1737 that an almanac-maker "shou'd not be a finish'd Poet, but a Piece of one, and qualify'd to write, what we vulgarly call Doggerel." The mediocrity of American almanac verse is a rule only rarely infringed by shining exceptions. The selections included in this chapter are representative of the range of almanac verse, which is as wide as that of verse itself.

Danforth's first calendar verse in 1647 was an enigmatic mixture of seasonal and topical allusions:

> March: *A Coal-white Bird appeares this spring*
> *That neither cares to sigh or sing.*
> *This when the merry Birds espy,*
> *They take her for some enemy.*

> August: *Many this month I doe fore-see*
> *Together by the eares [corn] will bee:*
> *Indian and English in the field*
> *To one another will not yield.*
> *Some weeks continue wil this fray,*
> *Till they be carted all away.*

Danforth's poetical abilities improved by the following year. The four-couplet stanzas represent an allegorical account of the founding of America, using the metaphor of a plant. These stanzas typify a quality of much early American verse: a deliberate striving after Ancient Greek and Roman virtues, clothed in an appropriately Anglo-Saxon, rustic dress:

> *Awake yee westerne Nymphs, arise and sing:*
> *And with fresh tunes salute your welcome spring,*
> *Behold a choyce, a rare and pleasant plant*

237

> *. . . . .*
>
> *T'was but a tender slip a while agoe,*
> *About twice ten years or a little moe*
>
> *. . . . .*
>
> *At this tree's roots Astraea sits and sings*
> *And waters it, whence upright JUSTICE springs,*
>
> *. . . . .*
>
> *PEACE is another fruit; which this tree bears,*
> *The cheifest garland that this Country wears.*

Danforth's 1649 almanac contained verse in the same form and theme, but this time America was an "Orphan." Perhaps Samuel Danforth was the first versifier to smooth American Indian sonorities into iambics—a less felicitous choice of rhythm, however, than Longfellow's meter in *Hiawatha* proved to be. Danforth used the prevailing rhythm of his day:

> *But by & by, grave Monanattock rose,*
> *Grim Sasacus with swarms of Pequottoes.*

In Daniel Russell's verses for 1671, we can almost hear the poet counting out his measure on his fingers:

> April: *The Airy Choristers, they now begin*
>   *To warble forth their Native Musick in*
>   *The new-leaf'd Boughs. . . .*
>
> September: *The* Indian *Stalks, now richly fraught with store*
>   *Of golden-colour'd Ears, seem to implore*
>   *By humble bowing of their lofty Head,*
>   *From this their load to be delivered.*

In 1706 Daniel Leeds wrote for August: "Now Phebus and the furious Lion treats / Us with those faint and suffocating Heats . . . ." For January 1726, Ames said: "Our Northern Climes in shiv'ring Cold remain / Till Glorious Phoebus shall return again." And for November: "Terra doth Mourn because she must Entomb / The seed she bore, again within her Womb."

Dr. Ames could do a little better than this. In April 1748, spring was announced imaginatively:

> *Consuming Winter's gone, the Earth hath lost*
> *Her snow-white Robes, and now no more the Frost*
> *Candies the Grass, or casts an icy Cream*
> *Upon the silver Lake and chrystal Stream.*

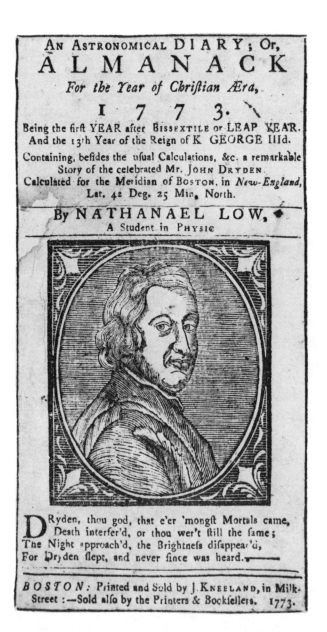

An Astronomical DIARY; Or,

ALMANACK

For the Year of Christian Æra,

I 7 7 3.

Being the firft YEAR after Bissextile or LEAP YEAR.
And the 13th Year of the Reign of K. GEORGE IIId.

Containing, befides the ufual Calculations, &c. a remarkable
Story of the celebrated Mr. John Dryden.
Calculated for the Meridian of Boston, in *New-England,*
Lat. 42 Deg. 25 Min, North.

By NATHANAEL LOW,
A Student in Physic

Dryden, thou god, that e'er 'mongft Mortals came,
Death interfer'd, or thou wer't ftill the fame;
The Night approach'd, the Brightnefs difappea'd,
For Dryden flept, and never fince was heard.——

BOSTON: Printed and Sold by J. Kneeland, in Milk-
Street :—Sold alfo by the Printers & Bookfellers. 1773.

Illustrated verse on title page of Low's *Astronomical Diary,*
1773.

239

Dr. Ames's verse is undoubtedly original. But *Poor Robin* for 1733 had carried a similar January verse beginning:

> *Now* Hyem *binds the Floods in Silver Chains,*
> *And hoary Frost doth candy all the Plains;*
> *The Trees and Fields do now more lovely show,*
> *Whilst they do penance in white Sheets of Snow.*

If this was original James Franklin, then his skill must have had catastrophic lapses:

> *If thou hast store of Worldly Pelf,*
> *Think 'twas not given thee for thy self.*

Ames's imagery in December 1748 may have almost sparkled:

> *Now every hoary-headed Twig*
> *Doth wear a snowy Perriwig.*

But it descended into mud-caked boots in June 1749:

> *The Indian corn sprung up begins to grow,*
> *And Husbandmen whet up their Scythes to mow:*
> *The Country Maids with Sauce to Market come,*
> *And carry Loads of tatter'd Money Home.*

In March 1749, after a bit of trouble with his poetic footage, Ames achieves a mock-Vergilian bucolicism:

> *As* Ori'n's *Bands dissolve, the Farmer now*
> *With Wounding Steel gives Earth a furrow'd Brow,*
> *And as he tugs the peaceful Plow along,*
> *Sweetens his Labour with some Rural Song.*

Even the colonial reader must have welcomed a change from this pedantic performance. Titan Leeds dared to inject some refreshing echoes of what was more probably on his readers' minds in August 1714:

> *The Weather's hot, days burning eye*
> *Doth make the earth in favour frye,*
> Dick *on the Hay doth tumble Nell,*
> *Whereby her Belly comes to swell.*
> *The Dog star now we hot do find,*
> *And some have Dog tricks in their mind.*

However, he did not dare to omit a timely moral:

> *June joys the heart and jocund makes the mind*
> *Yet see you learn to shun the female kind,*

Wine, Women, Baths, (by art or Nature warm)
Us'd or abus'd do men much good or harm.

Even more interesting, possibly quite original, was the genre
of technological/ scientific versifying. Dr. Ames in 1741 described
the marvelous microscope in eighty-four continuous lines of original metrical form:

—ARTIFICER go make a Watch,
  In which no seeming Imperfection lurks
Whose Wheels with Time exact do onward roll,
And one small Spring maintains the Motions of the whole,
  'Tis all an Artless homely Botch
Compared with the least of Natures Works
  If thro' an Optick Glass
  You view a spire of Grass
  That in the Road is trod
With Admiration you may gaze
On Veins that branch a thousand ways
  In nice proportion wrought.

Franklin's *Poor Richard Improved* for 1756 presents an ode
ostensibly to astronomy but which in fact eulogizes science and
scientists in general:

Astronomy, hail, Science heavenly born!
Thy Schemes, the Life assist, the Mind adorn.

. . . .

Cassini next, and Huygens, like renown'd
The moon *and wondrous Ring of* Saturn *found*
Sagacious Kepler, still advancing saw
The elliptic motion, Natures plainest Law,

. . . .

Newton! vast mind! whose piercing Pow'rs apply'd
The Secret Cause of Motion first decry'd.

Thus was popular science first digested in America, and the original art form persists today.

Readers sometimes submitted mathematical problems for other
readers to solve—perhaps an early example of reader participation,
in verse. George Eyres contributed clumsy, but technically far-
sighted, thoughts in verse to Titan Leeds's 1731 almanac:

In the year 1729,
On Candlemass Eve the Eclipse of the Moon
Made her talk't of much more than would else have been done;

Her vulgar Admirers all guess'd at her Nature,
By which it appear'd they knew nought of the Matter,
. . . .

So whatever one said, was opposed by another,
Which was likely to make a most Dam—ble Pother;
When a Plow-man starts up, and thus spoke t'her Honour,
And after this sort commented upon her,
Good Neighbours, the Moon is a World I dare swear,
. . . .

Then cease your dull Whimsies, and study with me,
How to settle a Trade betwixt they and we,
Should we lose Gibraltar and the Port of Mahon,
Pray judge the Advantage of a Trade to the Moon.
. . . .

Such Heads being a work we need not to fear,
But we shall soon have Ships sailing up in the air,
And the way without doubt must easy be made,
And the World of the Moon America's chief Trade.
. . . .

So for want of fit Words to Gurgle and Chime,
I'll Query in Prose, and cease my dull Rhime.

The question Eyres posed involved the weight of goods on the moon and the profits from their sales. Poor versification, perhaps, but certainly relevant for astronauts two centuries and a half later.

Daniel Leeds in 1709 discussed the portents of the year's eclipses:

Let fools rail on, let the Illiterate bark
At this Eclipse, although but partly dark,
. . . .

The effects afflict and gaul the Gallick *parts*
And forreign place; cheer up brave British hearts.

Dr. Ames occasionally appeared in defense of a benign astrology, purged of all taint of Satanism. In 1731:

There's some I know that presume to say,
The World was ne'er forewarned such a way,
But I unto such "fiery Zealots tell
"Astrology's from Heaven not from Hell.
"Tis no Black Art, no damned Necromancy
"No Witchcraft neither, as some please to Fancy."

But in 1739 Poor Robin had turned the tables on the astrol-

The FARMERS ALMANACK

[Corrected & Amended,]
For the Year 1 7 1 4.

By *N. W.* A Lover of the Truth.

Long Live Queen ANNE *in Peace and Glorious Reign,*
The World's Rare Wonder, and our Great Sov'raign.

From Heav'n above on Her Great Blessings flow,
That She may Reign, and on us Favour show.

A R

That She may be true Protestants Great Defender,
And of the True Religion She may be most Tender.

Beneath her Feet let all Her En'mies low'r,
And never rise against Her any more.

America Printed, Sold at the Bookseller's Shops at
Boston in *New-England.* 1714.

Superior illustration for a poor verse about Queen Anne.
Whittemore's *The Farmer's Almanack* for 1714.

ogers by using their own traditional Man of Signs and his accompanying verses for ridicule. The November stanza:

> *One tells you Aries rules my Head,*
> *With the same Truth, he might have said*
> *(Which Whimsy would as soon prevail,)*
> *That Aries rules as well my Tail;*
> *(Since Paper stain'd with such a Whim,*
> *May serve [not Head, but] Tail to clean;)*
> *That Taurus rules my Neck; I hope,*
> *He does not mean because, like Rope,*
> *Or Noose, it seems both Ends aslope;*
> *That Bowels are cajol'd by Virgo,*
> *That Libra weighs the Reins, a tergo;*
> *And Leo boldly plays his Part,*
> *And seeks for Prey upon my Heart;*
> *That Sagitarius hold my Thighs,*
> *While Scorpio at my Secrets plies;*
> *That Capricorn makes Knees to meet,*
> *And Pisces rules by turns my Feet,*
> *My Arms by Gemini, Breast by Cancer,*
> *Are rul'd.—All Lies, As I'm a Man, Sir.*

Poor Robin had more fun with astrology in his almanac for 1733. He concluded a long poem:

> *Strange Things this Year will come to pass,*
> *I'm told by Ass-trological Glass,*
> *The Birds will sing, and Sheep will bleat,*
> *And hungry Folks will want to eat.*

A 1690 *Poor Robin* had contained a burlesque horoscope called "the ass-trological scheme . . . By this Scheme, a man may foretel things that never will be, as well as those that never were; and is as proper for an Almanack as a Nose for a mans Face: for as a Face looks ill favouredly without a Nose, so doth an Almanack without a Scheme." [2]

Weather commentary sometimes appeared in couplets, to substitute for the usual longer calendar verse. Thus Ames's almanac for 1729:

February: *Boreas's chilly breath attacks our nature*
              And turns the Presbyterian to a Quaker. [3]

June: *SOL's scorching Ray puts Blood in Fermentation*
        And is stark naught to Acts of Procreation.

Although the receipt was the usual form for health hints, some writers could not restrain their muses, nor their qualms about "modern medicine." In 1708 Daniel Leeds had intoned:

The learned Physicians, *such as were of Old,*
Galen *and* Hippocrates *lie and mould,*
Now Paracelsus *claims the curing part*
And most men practice the spagyrick art,
Yet Herbs when gathered in their proper seasons
More harmless physick makes, for diverse reasons.

And Samuel Clough in 1701:

May: *Rise early now this month of May,*
           And walk the Fields that are so gay.

August: *With little Sleep be now content:*
           Purge not, nor Bleed, least thou repent.

September: *Raw Fruit though Ripe, may sickness bring:*
           Unripe much Eat, a dangerous thing.

In 1719, Daniel Leeds slipped the familiar slap at lawyers into his July verse on general health:

Use frequent exercise, with sparing Dyet,
Take Physick seldom, study to be quiet;
For he that (like Tobacco Physick takes,)
Feeling no need but what that taking makes,
Is greater fool than he (whom oft I Rate)
That in the Law, for Toys, spends his Estate.

Lawyers in the eighteenth century evidently played a scapegoat role akin to mothers-in-law in the early twentieth.

Almanac-makers referred frequently to the rules of drinking. Titan Leeds explained his position in the following lines published in his almanac for 1728 (printed by Keimer in Philadelphia):

Drink was ordain'd to help man's fainting breath,
And from that liquor Drunkards draw their Death;
. . . .
Good friendly drinking I account not evil,
But much carousing makes a man a devil.

But by 1776 the immoderates of both parties seemed to be gaining ground. Stearns's *North American Almanack and Gentleman's and Lady's Diary* for that year was emphatic:

I.   JANUARY, hath xxxi days.

NOW the declining Sun did downward bend
From higher Heavens, and from his looks did fend
A milder flame ; when near the Tyber's flow
A Lutanist allay'd his careful woe,
With founding charms, and in a greeny feat
Of fhady oak, took fhelter from the heat ;   **A**

Laſt Quar. 5 d. 0 h. 44 m. after. | Firſt Quar. 19 d. 10 h. 40 m. mor.
New Moon 12 d. 4 h 0 m mor. | Full Moon 27 d. 2 h. 7 m. aft.

Days M	w	CALENDAR, &c.	☉ riſes & ſets.	Full Seas. Morn	Even	☽'s place	☽ riſ. & ſets
1	7	N. year's d. Circum	7 32 5	1 4¹	2 3	22 46	8 32
2	B	Epiphany.	7 32 5	2 26	2 50	Belly	9 35
3	2	In Court Briſtol.	7 31 5	3 14	3 38	18 27	10 36
4	3	I C. Boſt.York & Am	7 31 5	4 2	4 26	Reins	11 42
5	4	Vacat. Harvard Col.	7 31 5	4 51	5 16	15 8	Morn.
6	5	7*'s 8 h. 36m. ſouth	7 30 5	5 41	6 8	28 58	0 50
7	6	*A good fire*	7 30 5	6 34	7 1	ſecrets	1 54
8	7	*and an indepen-*	7 29 5	7 28	7 56	27 39	3 0
9	B	1ſt paſt Epip. ☽ Perig	7 28 5	8 25	8 55	thighs	4 5
10	2	*dent guinea*	7 28 5	9 26	9 56	27 25	5 9
11	3	I.C Charl. & N.Ham	7 27 5	10 28	10 59	knees	6 10
12	4	*will now be of*	7 27 5	11 29	11 58	27 15	Sets.
13	5	*ſervice.*	7 26 5	0 0	0 26	legs	6 34
14	6	*Now expect a*	7 25 5	0 55	1 20	25 59	7 36
15	7	*ſpell of very*	7 24 5	1 45	2 10	feet	8 44
16	B	2d paſt Epiph. *cold*	7 24 5	2 35	2 58	22 54	9 51
17	2	I. Court Eaſt Green.	7 23 5	3 21	3 44	head	10 56
18	3	*weather.*	7 22 5	4 8	4 30	18 12	11 58
19	4	Snow, with wind.	7 21 5	4 53	5 15	neck	Morn.
20	5	Char I. bro't to trial	7 20 5	5 37	5 59	12 26	0 58
21	6	☽ ☉ ☌ *Moderate*	7 20 5	6 21	6 43	24 19	1 56
22	7	☽ Apog. *for theſea-*	7 19 5	7 5	7 29	arms	2 50
23	B	3d paſt Epiph. *ſon.*	7 18 5	7 51	8 15	18 5	3 41
24	2	K. of Pruſſia b 1712.	7 17 5	8 39	9 3	breaſt	4 30
25	3	Conver. of St. Paul	7 16 5	9 27	9 51	12 12	5 20
26	4	*Windy*	7 15 5	10 14	10 39	24 27	6 8
27	5	*Perhaps rain.*	7 14 5	11 4	11 28	heart	Riſes.
28	6	7's ſouth 6 h. 47 m	7 13 5	11 52	0 0	19 32	6 10
29	7	*Clear and cold.*	7 12 5	0 16	0 40	belly	7 12
30	B	K. Cha. I. beheaded.	7 11 5	1 3	1 28	15 24	8 14
31	2	*Take care of your fire*	7 10 5	1 52	2 16	28 17	9 20

Verse and interspersed weather predictions in Gleason's
Massachusetts Calendar for 1774.

246

> *The thirsty Earth soaks up the rain*
> *And drinks and gapes for rain again;*
> *The planets suck in the earth and are,*
> *With constant drinking, fresh and fair;*
> *The sea itself, which one would think*
> *Should have but little need of drink,*
> *Yet drinks ten thousand rivers up*
> *So fill'd that they o'erflow the cup:*
> *The busy sun—and one would guess*
> *By's drunken fiery face no less—*
> *Drinks up the sea, and when he's done,*
> *The moon and stars drink up the sun.*
> *They drink and dance by their own light;*
> *They drink and revel all the night:*
> *Nothing in nature's sober found.*
> *But an eternal health goes round:*
> *Fill up the bowl then! fill it high!*
> *Fill all the glasses there; for why*
> *Should every creature drink but I?*
> *Why? Man of Morals—tell me why!*

The almanackers had discovered that man is mortal and were uncertain what to do about it in an age when the establishment had lost the keys to heaven and hell—or had gotten them confused. Time, eternity, and death no longer chanted in paradisiac harmony in the eighteenth century: they suggested some unaccountable disturbance in the Newtonian clockwork. In 1705 Daniel Leeds mused:

> *Death is a Fisher-man, the World, we see*
> *His Fish-Pond is, and We the Fishes be:*
> *He sometimes, Angler-like, doth with us play,*
> *And slily takes us One by One away;*
> *At other times he brings his Net and then*
> *At once sweeps up whole Cities full of Men.*

And on his 1711 title page:

> *Time devours all, and doth all Waste,*
> *And we waste Time, and so we're even at last.*

Titan was comparably trite in December 1721:

> *Sleep, and his Brother Death, conspire our Fall,*
> *The one steals half our Lives; the other all.*

And Nathan Bowen, apparently depressed, in 1723:

247

The weary Pilgrim oft doth Ask & Know,
How far he's come, how far he has to go.

However, Ames expressed this theme in fair rhyme in 1727:

Swift winged Time Feather'd with Flying Hours,
Whose Hungry Jaws all Things on Earth Devours.

In 1737 his *tempus fugit* theme ventured into slightly less hackneyed metaphor:

January:　——— *Time is a short Parenthesis,*
Placed in between the two Eternities,
And joins the vast unlimited Abyss,
(Eternal Space) at its Extremities,
The Length whereof's but a contracted Span,
And one small Point includes the Age of Man.[4]

John Jerman's signed original verse on the astronomy page of his almanac for 1723 reiterated the *time* theme: Ben Franklin, as Saunders, had teasingly termed Jerman a poet but no Protestant. The opposite verdict, however, would seem to be more accurate.

Let all Mankind remember this,
That whilst on Earth we have no Bliss,
But Sorrow constantly attends,
Until at last our life it ends.

Titan Leeds restores our literary faith when in December 1716 he observes with moderate urbanity:

Our Life is nothing but a Winters Day,
Some only break their Fast, and go their way,
Others stay [to] Dinner, and depart full fed,
The greatest Age but sups and goes to bed.

Rationalist, skeptical stoicism was all very well for the elite, ensconced' in their comfortable studies. But the true Puritan had Bible and sword in hand, and both feet behind the plough. Josiah Flint in 1666 had discarded "Heathenish Language" and pagan symbols even for naming the months, so that his preference for the Hebraic produced this new version of an old story:

Jehova-Nisi *now his Banner spred,*
When's harness'd Host he out of Egypt *led.*
Now Pelah, *Wonderful, did's Wonders show,*
That th' unbelieving Israelites *might know*

248

He was El-shaddai, *mighty* Jah, *whose hand*
Must carry Israel to the blessed Land.[5]

Joseph Stafford (*Rhode Island Almanack,* 1738) favored a more conventional hymn style:

> March: *The Days and Nights are just*
> *now at an equal Length,*
> *So let Religion shine*
> *still with a greater strength.*
>
> June: *We must praise god and him*
> *forevermore adore,*
> *Who makes the Earth to yield*
> *to Mankind all her stores.*

Two couplets from Ames's February verse for 1731 angrily refuted a statistical interpretation of the universe:

> *Stupendous Atheistical Nonsense!*
> *That Atoms floating in a Space Immense,*
> *Should by the jumbling hand of Chance be hurl'd*
> *Into that order which compos'd the World!*

Ames continued his Creation account serially in 1733. Two couplets of the October verse are particularly British in rhyme and diction:

> *The Scaley Tribe amidst the Liquid Seas*
> *Nor Stormes, nor driftings fear, they Sail with ease*
> *O're all His Works that Sublinary be,*
> *He cast a Saphire Glittering Canopy.*

The theme of Ames's verse for 1734 was nothing less than that attempted years before, and with some success, by John Milton. The old story is charmingly and vividly described. Adam is created and given the command, "Go dress yon Charming Garden which I've made." All goes well until "Man receiv'd his fatal Fall." When he heard God's voice, "with shame abash'd the guilty Rebel fear'd." So far this is not bad for a homespun Milton. Ames was less happy when he tried to popularize the epic passages:

> *All nature groan'd, the Sun his Lustre shrouds*
> *In thick'ning Storms, in Tempests, and in Clouds.*

God talks to his Son about man's plight:

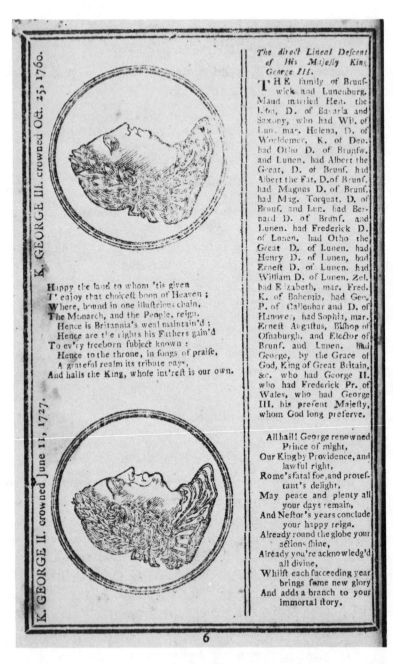

A favorable account of George III in West's *Bickerstaff's Boston Almanack* for 1774.

> *O Son! . . .*
> *He has my Hatred and is pinioned fast*
> *To horrid Flames that Ever! Ever! Last,*
> *But if his Ransom be Atchiev'd by Thee,*
> *Thereby great Glory shall derive to me.*

Son consents:

> *These Robes of Light, in which I am arrayed*
> *I'll leave with Thee, and go and be betrayed,*
> *And Crucified and Die for Sinner's sake.*
> *Their Flesh and Blood upon Me I will take*
> *Then let thy Wrath and Vengeance light on me*
> *I'll bare the Curse to set the Sinner free.*[6]

Ames's calendar verse for 1736 is a story of Judgment Day reminiscent of Michael Wigglesworth's "The Day of Doom." The long poem (three heroic couplets per page) begins in January with "The Muses tremble with a faultering Wing, / While Nature's great *Catastrophe* they sing." But Ames's muse was made of sturdy stuff and unfalteringly described horrors from which more timid muses would have turned their eyes. In February, the sun is dark; the moon is bloody. The following month, the stars fall. The situation is desperate: in March, "nature in darkness ends, / Except what light hell's horrid bosom sends," and the earth rolls in "trembling agonies." In May, the seas roar; the lakes and rivers murmur; the rocks explode; "the trembling mountains nod"; and the "valleys rise at the approaching God . . . ." June describes the fright of "impious Sons of Men" who cower before their "incensed Judge." By October, the throng is assembled. The judgment is made: in November, the damned go to hell; and, in December, "The Good are crown'd with joys that never cease, / With Realms of Light! and unmolested Peace!"

Dr. Nathaniel Ames, II, was the most versatile poet of all the almanac-makers. In the elegiac stanza in praise of his father (1737), he can touch us with a measure of quiet dignity:

> *His great Seraphick Genius now is fled, He's Dead!*
> *The melancholy news has reached your Ears*
> *Doubtless before this little Tract appears,*
> *But since his Labours first matur'd its Birth,*
> *It is but justice here to mourn his Death.*
> *I, in his Arms from Evening Dews preserv'd,*

251

The wandering Glories overhead observ'd:
Scare pip'd the shell, ere his too fond Desires
My Talent in this public way requires.
When puzzled, I could unto him repair,
Who knew the Heav'ns as if he had dwelt there:
Imbolden'd thus, I ventured on the stage
And run the risque of carping Critic's Rage.
But now he's gone! URANIA O, make
Me, me thy Son! For thy Beloved's sake.
Bear the Deceas'd upon thy Wings, O, Fame,
Among th' Astronomers give him a Name:
For if Pythagoras believ'd had been,
Men might have thought great Newton's soul in him
But hold: if him I've praised in what I've done
It may be called immodest in a son:
But Gratitude Extorts from me this due
And Envy owns that what I've writ is true.

This verse has integrity: form and diction are compatible with purpose and feeling. But when Ames forced the contents of a chronological table into heroic couplets, the result is less fortunate. Events were given on the left side of the table and "Years since" on the right. Thus in 1745 we have doggerel, albeit learned. For example,

Since Homer *liv'd, for Poets never die* *2594*
Since Daniel *wrote his wonderous Prophesie* *2227*

.   .   .   .

Since Harvard *did the College first provide* ⎫
Where great Apollo's *learned Sons reside.* ⎭ *106*

Blank verse was uncommon, but here are six of forty-two lines composed by Ames for his 1744 almanac:

Glory to the Father of endless Ages,
From endless long Eternity thou wer't
Though in thyself unchangeable and fixt:
At thy Command unwearied Revolutions,
Roll thro' thy Worlds, and tumble up and down,
The toss'd and fickle mortal Sons of Change.

Rhymed epitaphs were generally satirical. In 1750 Poor Job's May verse, "Tom's Epitaph," ends with "His darling Wife of him bereft, / Is only griev'd there's Nothing left." Poor Richard's "Epitaph on Another Clergyman" in *Poor Richard Improved* for 1755 shows the eighteenth-century versifier at his best:

252

Cornwallis turned Nurse, and his Mistress a Soldier. From
Sharp's *The Continental Almanac*, 1782.

> *Here lies, who need not here be nam'd,*
> *For Theologic Knowledge fam'd;*
> *Who all the Bible had by rote,*
> *With all the Comments Calvin wrote;*
> *Parsons and Jesuits could confute,*
> *Talk Infidels and Quakers mute,*
> *To every Heretick a Foe;*
> *Was he an honest Man? . . . So so.*

Satiric verse was perhaps the most genuine contribution of the era, certainly its happiest literary convention; and the almanac, an ideal vehicle. In this form, political and religious propaganda bit deep, always with a smile on the lips. Witness Felix Leeds in 1730:

> *No Jesuit e'er took in Hand,*
> *To plant a Church in barren Land,*
> *And where there is no Store of Wealth*
> *Souls are not worth the Change of health.*
> *Spain, in America, had two Designs,*
> *To sell their Gospel, get their Mines:*
> *For had the Mexicans been poor,*
> *No Jesuit twice had landed on their Shore.*

But even satire hobbled on lame feet, when an almanac had to leave the press. Poor Robin in 1730 could only mutter:

> *O Learning! O Learning! This Month I can see,*
> *That I'd been a Fool had it not been for thee:*
> *Or at best I had been but a Catholick Roman,*
> *Dispis'd by good Men, and respected by no Man.*

And in October he was merely abusive:

> *When* Harry *the Eighth left the Pope in the Lurch,*
> *The* Romish *Priests made him the Head of the Church,*
> *In hopes to enjoy their old Profits.*

The anonymous author of the following horror script appears to have had an anti-Papist bias, since the 1641 massacre alleged below (and elsewhere) was subsequently proved false. *Poor Robin* for 1740:

> *I'th* Irish Masacre *their Zeal was shown,*
> *Where all the Acts of cruelty were done,*
> *The Murd'red Bodies lay in heaps about,*
> *Woman ript up, and their Babes Brains dast out;*
> *Guts torn out alive, before them laid,*
> *And of their fat these Saints their candles made.*

When propaganda was paramount, the subtler skill of satire

An Aſtronomical Diary; Or, An

ALMANACK

For the Year of our LORD,

1 7 7 3.

Being the firſt Year after Biſſextile
or Leap Year.
Calculated for the Meridian of
BOSTON, NEW-ENGLAND,
Lat. 42 Deg. 25 Min. North.
Containing beſides what is common
in Almanacks,— A Method of
Planting Vineyards. — How a
Nation may be *ruined* and
reformed, &c.&c.

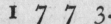

Our great Forefathers, fir'd with virtuousRage,
  Did all the Perils of the Deep engage,
To fly thoſe Realms where proud tyrannic Sway,
And horrid Perſecution ſcout for Piey ;
Their native Soil and youthful Scenes they fled,
Where bounteous Nature all her Bleſſings ſhed,
And ſiſter Art had ranſack'd foreign Shores,
Made every Dainty croud their Britiſh Stores,
Had rais'd the ample Dome and lofty Spire,
And ſpacious Theatre, were Crouds admire
The mighty Feats perform'd in ancient Days,
That ſpring to Life, reviv'd in Engliſh Plays.
Theſe Pleaſures all, our Fathers left behind,
But bro't the Seeds of Science in their Mind,
Here planted firſt fair *Freedom* with Applauſe,
Which give the Reliſh to all other Joys :
Guard then the Plant,—this ſavage Land adorn,
This Work they left their Children then unborn.

By Nathaniel Ames.

BOSTON: Printed and Sold by
R. Draper, Edes & Gill, and T & J. Fleet.

Jewish shekel and patriotic poem on an Ames title page.

THᴇ PATRIOTIC AMERICAN FARMER.

J—N D·K-NS—N, Esǫ; Bᴀʀʀɪsᴛᴇʀ at Lᴀᴡ.

Who with Attic Eloquence, and Roman Spirit, hath af-
ſerted the Liberties of the Bʀɪᴛɪsʜ Colonies in America.

'Tis nobly done to Stem Taxations Rage,
And raiſe the Thoughts of a degenerate Age,
For Happineſs and Joy, from Freedom ſpring;
But Life in Bondage is a worthleſs Thing.

Portrait of John Dickinson, Ames's *Astronomical Diary*, 1772.

256

JOHN WILKES, Esquire.

[Engraved for *Weatherwise's* Almanack; 1769.]

1769

Hail WILKES, immortal in the List of Fame,
Thy hateful Foes shall hide their Heads in Shame,
When you the Sweets of *Liberty* restore
To *Britain's* Isle, and who can wish for more?

Portrait of John Wilkes, *Weatherwise's New England Town and
Countryman's Almanack* for 1769.

quickly degenerated into doggerel. Long before the Revolution, Nathan Bowen's almanac for 1723 carried this effusion on its title page:

> *Tyrants & Tyranny! What can be worse?*
> *(To all but Slaves) an Everlasting Curse.*
> *When his wild will constrains you to Obey,*
> *He then insults you like a Beast of Prey.*

Edes and Gill, notorious among the new North American patriots, published "A new Song" in their almanac for 1770. One stanza encouraged sentiments that would have made Rudyard Kipling blush. One may wonder what Thomas Jefferson would have thought of them:

> *Some future day shall crown us the Masters of the Main,*
> *And giving laws and Freedom to subject France and*
> *   Spain;*
> *When all the isles o'er ocean spread shall tremble*
> *   and obey*
> *Their lords, their lords, their lords, the lords of*
> *   brave America.*

West's *New-England Almanack* for 1775 included patriotic verse tinged with nationalism:

> *Americans! for Freedom firmly join,*
> *Unite your Councils, and your Force combine,*
> *Disarm Oppression—prune Ambition's Wings,*
> *And stifle Tories, e'er they dart their Stings;*
> *And then your plunder'd Rights shall be restor'd,*
> *And Tyrants tremble when you grasp the Sword.*

A verse on the November calendar page is titled, "The Genius of America to Her Sons":

> *Are Americans born to bear*
> *The galling weight of Slav'ry's chain?*
> *A patriot's noble ardor share,*
> *And freedom's sacred cause maintain.*
> *Arise, my sons, shew your unconquer'd might*
> *A freeman best defends a freeman's right.*

The theme of *The Kentucky Almanac* for 1795 was the French Revolution. Among works that alluded to the Revolution was "A New Song, Called the GUILLOTINE," composed by Joel Barlow, one of the Connecticut Wits. Admiration of French political expediency prompted Barlow to write: "And when great *George's* poll / Shall in the basket roll / Let mercy then controul / *The Guillotine.*"

Next to the new politics, social criticism was a popular verse theme. Inevitably, in the early American almanacs, lawyers were by far the most ridiculed of men. This satire probably had the blessings of the clergy; for they, too, railed against lawyers, who would take a case for personal gain, whether the cause was right or wrong, whereas every good Puritan knew "that litigation could be settled by the Bible and common sense." [7] The almanac contained a section called "Of Courts" or "Courts," usually prefaced by verse on lawyers. Sometimes the "Courts" section would end with a poem. Satire directed against the lawyer, however, spilled over into all pages. Daniel and Titan Leeds, and Nathaniel Ames (father and son) were perhaps the most prolific writers of this special verse. The Ameses had personal reasons; the Leedses probably just wanted to sell almanacs. Daniel Leeds's verse for 1706 was evidently so well received that he repeated it in 1707 and 1708:

> *Lo, here's a Trade surpasseth all the rest,*
> *No Change annoys the Lawyers Interest:*
> *His Tongue buys Land, builds Houses without toil:*
> *The Pen's his Plough, the Parchment is his Soil.*
> *Him Storms disturb not, nor militia Bands.*
> *The tree roots best that in the weather stands.*

In other words, the word is mightier than the sword.

When Titan took over his father's almanac, he inherited his father's prejudice. To preface "Courts" for 1714, he wrote:

> *Who Neighbours Sue for every Trifle,*
> *The Lawyers will their Pockets Rifle.*

This same courts section ended:

> *Pens and Tongues are Lawyers Swords,*
> *Whetted sharpe with Wry-mouth'd Words,*
> *With which they cut their clyents Purse,*
> *And thereby make their Cases worse.*

Titan Leeds published the following verse signed "J. T.," in the 1720 almanac:

> *The Law hangs Thieves for their unlawful Stealing,*

> *The Law doth Punish Rogues for Roguish Dealing;*
> *But yet, I Muse from whence this Law is grown,*
> *Whores must not steal, nor yet must use their own.*

A different poem on lawyers for Leeds's almanac the next year was signed "Jo. Taylor," probably the same "J. T."

Nathan Bowen's February calendar page for 1723 carried a perennial favorite about two opposing lawyers who shook hands as friends when the case was over. The client asks, "Can you be Friends, who were such Foes but now?" The reply:

> *You Fools, says One, We Lawyers tho' so Keen,*
> *Like Shears n'er Cut our Selves, but what's between.*

Dr. Ames rarely dignified his remarks about lawyers by assigning them a special section in his almanac. Usually his comments appeared on the calendar pages with his weather prophecies. In 1738 he was big enough to include his own profession:

> *Nor Lawyers, Priests nor Doctors ne'er had been*
> *If Man had stood against th' Assault of Sin.*
> *But oh, He fell! and so accurs'd we be*
> *The World is now oblig'd to use all Three.*

And he might have added, obliged to use almanac-makers also.

There was nothing too trivial to be twisted into verse—for the almanac-makers, at least—though it was, by and large, an irritating habit of the time. In the middle of a six-line stanza for March 1708, Daniel Leeds recollected an inaccuracy in a rival's meteorology:

> *But once in five times scarce to hit's a failure*
> *Committed last year frequently by Taylor:*
> *Nay, more, his Rain was fair, his fair was Rain.*

The writers seemed well aware of the amateurishness of their efforts, yet gaily persisted. Leeds again, 1712:

> *The Author ne'er was Learned to attain,*
> *Neither to Arts nor a Poetick strain.*

John Jerman in 1721 began to play rhyme-tricks:

> *If this with Acceptance find,*
> *It may yet put me in a Mind,*
> *Next Year to publish this same Kind,*
> *Where you may find Additions.*

He addressed his "little Book" in 1723 with four quatrains of this low caliber:

> *Now little Book, when Printed*
> *Thou must thy Journey take*
> *Among all Sorts of Readers*
> *Thy Present for to make.*

An unusual explanation, partly in verse, of a copperplate engraving in Weatherwise's *Town and Country Almanack* for 1781 likened the fate of the navigators of an air balloon to all those whose aspirations cause them to soar too high:

> The AIR BALLOON represented in the plate, was the construction of three young gentlemen in the south of England, who being proud of their performance, ventured in it and were carried about fifty miles in three hours, but by some unforeseen accident, the Balloon caught fire, and the three unhappy men fell from the clouds. The spectators who beheld the sight were very much surprised; as by a moderate calculation it was supposed to be twelve miles high when the accident happened.

> *READERS behold a plate design'd*
> *To lend a moral to Mankind,*
> *Survey the tow'ring AIR BALLOON,*
> *Just on the verge of Wilkin's Moon—*
> *Which ALL IN FLAMES is tumbling down*
> *Its NAVIGATORS on the Town!!*
> *Whilst sore affright, and wild dismay,*
> *Concludes the woeful dismal day!!*
> *So 'tis my friends, with all who ride*
> *On Fortune's car, at Frenzy's side—*
> *They soon or late will meet a fall,*
> *And sad confusion seize on all;*
> *Who mount so high, they cannot sit,*
> *But lose their Money and their Wit.*

> *The Courtier is an Air Balloon—*
> *His hopes aspire beyond the Moon.*
> *The greedy Merchant makes another—*
> *The grasping Lawyer loves his Brother—*
> *Whilst proud Divines who talk of Heaven,*
> *Build for themselves, and not their Brethren—*
> *Are little else but silk and gauze,*
> *Prunella, puff, and bursting Noise.*

Some verse fables apparently concealed a two-faced moral lesson. One is unsure just what was Ellicott's intention when in 1792 he (or the printer) included a fable about a nightingale and a hawk. The nightingale is singing when a hawk catches her. She struggles to save herself. The hawk speaks:

> "Charmer," said he, "I wait too long,
> Hawks require food more than a song."

The hawk kills the nightingale and the author weakly concludes:

> How many virgins fall a prey
> To some base murderer in the dark.

But whose side was Ellicott on? As a virtuous yet realistic Quaker, he undoubtedly could support both viewpoints—the virgin's and the hawk's.

Daniel Leeds, however, was not ambivalent about his ideal woman in 1712:

> She is a tender thing, refin'd and pure,
> And harsh Rough handling cannot well endure;
> For like a Venice Glass, she breaks asunder,
> When boistrous Men will strive to keep her under.

Rittenhouse's *Virginia Almanack* for 1775 succinctly presented "The Qualities to be desired in a Wife":

> HELEN's cheeks, but not her heart,
>   Cleopatra's majesty,
> Atalanta's better part,
>   Sad Lucretia's modesty.[8]

In *Thomas's Massachusetts, New Hampshire . . . Almanack* (by Ezra Gleason) for 1781 were a maid's description of the man she would like to marry, and the man's requirements of a wife. The man's:

> Let her have complexion fair,
> Sparkling eyes, and auburn hair;
> Skin as White as neck of swan,
> Smooth as down that grows thereon,
>
> . . . .
>
> Let her frank and pleasant be,
> To my friends as well as me,
> And with wit and beauty's charms,
> Glad my heart and bless my arms.
> Be the produce of our joys,
> Little girls and little boys.

Not all men's views of the ideal female were as superficial as this. Low's almanac for 1777 included "The Neglected Maid's Lamentation," a long poem in which Cloe laments that, try as she may, she cannot win a husband. The author proposed the following "ANSWER":

> Poor Cloe! you own it has been your whole study,
> To dress, to trim up, to embellish your body;
> When once you've as richly adorned your mind,
> I doubt not but quickly a husband you'll find.

Freebetter's New-England Almanack for 1791 included a warning "To the LADIES":

> Dress up a man, that's tall and fair,
>   Like any pretty miss,
> Which of your sex would first declare,
>   She long'd that man to kiss.
> Just so when women dress like boys,
>   The attractive power is gone;
> Their sex forgot and all its joys,
>   When once our clothes are on.
> Those who would take the marriage vow
>   This lesson sore it teaches,
> That girls in coats and waistcoats now
>   Will one day wear the breeches.
> From nature and from beauty's line,
>   Your sex have strangely err'd;
> That dress which is not feminine
>   Must always be absurd.

David Rittenhouse's verses on women in his almanac for 1775 began with September and concluded with the following quatrain four months later:

> Each noisy scold, who uncontroul'd,
>   By reason can't be civil,
> But din mankind, I leave consign'd
>   To bedlam or the d——l.

Sterns's *Universal Almanac* for 1791 ridiculed "FASHION":

> A Bosom rais'd up to the chin—
> A perfect balloon puff within—
> A bishop in the rear to suit ye—
> These form the crooked line of beauty.

Women as wives were satirized in *Daboll's New-England Alma-nack* for 1775:

> Horses (thou sayst) and Asses, Men may try,
> And ring suspected Vessels e'er they buy;
> But Wives, a random Choice, untry'd they take.
> They dream in Courtship, but in Wedlock wake:
> Then, nor till then, the Veil's remov'd away,
> And all the Woman glares in open Day.

The same almanac playfully attacked widows:

> *The Wife of* Bath, *who was engaged to a fifth Husband before her fourth Husband's Death*
>
> —It pleas'd the Lord to take my spouse at last,
> I tore my gown, I soil'd my locks with dust,
> And beat my breasts, as wretched widows—must.
> Before my face, my handkerchief I spread,
> To hide the floods of tears I did————not shed.

The Kentucky Almanac for 1797 contained:

> Women are books and men their readers be—
> In whom oft times, they great errata see.
> Here sometimes we blot—there we espy
> A leaf misplac'd—at least a line awry:
> If they are books, I wish that my wife were
> An Almanac, to change her ev'ry year.

Titan Leeds in 1720 seemed well aware of the need to please some of his readers more than others:

> Some Write so humerous Dogmaticall,
> To Please great Sir and Madam What de call.

In 1742 Dr. Ames experimented with a satirical political dialogue and dialect in the same piece: "Ralph, a Freshman at college," undertakes to tutor "his Brother Will, an ignorant Rustick" in "State Affairs":

> Will. The Weathers Cold for Conversashon,
> Leds zettle the imbril'd Nashion,
> Come, here's zound Zyder, a good Fier,
> Then gradify my just dezier.[9]

Ralph tries to explain the British Parliament to his ignorant brother, who understands well enough to comment that "This Barlemend's a dreadful Thing." Ralph obviously seems to have made his point, which included political prejudice in its precepts:

> *For if the Parliament had said,*
> *That in each Banker's proper head*
> *A Pair of mighty Horns should grow,*
> *'Tis Law, Ergo, It must be so.*

Next to lawyers and politicians, the deceived husband was a favorite figure of fun. As early as 1670, John Richardson included, in a long poem called "The Countrymans *Apocrypha*," the following lines, ostensibly on astrology:

> *The Moon is habitable, some averre:*
> *And that some Creatures have their Dwelling there:*
> *Judge what you please; but yet 'tis very true,*
> *This year the Moon a Pair of Horns will shew.*

Low's almanac for 1777 alluded (more directly) in a short rhymed jest to the same subject:

> *Says Collin, in Rage, contradicting his Wife*
> *"You never yet told me one Truth in your life."*
> *Vex'd Fanny, no way could this Thesis allow,*
> *"You're a Cuckold," says she, "Do I tell the truth now?"*

Marriage is the subject of the following stanza from the March page of T. Leeds's almanac for 1729, published by Keimer in Philadelphia:

> *Nick slighted Women, Marriage he decry'd;*
> *To which his friend Tom waggishly reply'd,*
> *In Marriage are two happy Days allow'd,*
> *A Wife in Wedding-Sheets and in a Shroud,*
> *How can the Marriage State then be accurs'd,*
> *Since the last Day's as happy as the First?*

Lines three and four were repeated verbatim in Ezra Gleason's *Bickerstaff's Boston Almanack* for 1777. Low's almanac for 1770 contained a three-couplet stanza called "The Man's Choice, Whether he would be hanged or married.":

> *Wedding and Hanging, Destinies Dispatch,*
> *But Hanging seems by far the better Match.*

In his almanac for 1759, Hutchins bewailed the decadence of a once sacred institution. "Wedlock, Ancient and Modern" concludes:

> Love Vows are now all lost and Jargon;
> And Wedlock's grown a Smithfield Bargain.

Poor Job (James Franklin, Jr.) jibed both marriage and the marriers in this "Epigram" of 1750:

> Cries Celia to a Rev'rend D——ne.
> What Reason can be giv'n,
> Since Marriage is an holy Thing,
> That there are none in Heav'n?
> There are no Women, he reply'd:
> She quick returns the Jest,
> Women there are, but I'm afraid
> They cannot find a Priest.

Almost certainly of London origin, the following forerunner of the nineteenth-century limerick appeared in T. Leeds's almanac for 1729:

> 'Tis said, Mother Sparges
> Kept two Gravesend Barges;
> Yet she, as I'm told,
> Being stingey and old,
> So adored her Gold,
> That she dy'd to save Charges.

The Maryland almanac for 1764 contained a bawdy satire on women and the Romish confessional that extended through all twelve calendar pages. "The Mad-Dog. A TALE" introduces the heroine:

> A PRUDE, at Morn and Evening Prayer,
> Had worn her Velvet Cushion bare;
> Upwards she taught her Eyes to roll,
> As if she watch'd her soaring Soul.

She counts her beads, to "set all Things even" every week at confession, where she "blubbers forth her sins":

> Who could that tempting Man resist?
> My Virtue languish'd, as he kiss'd;
> I strove,—till I could strive no longer;
> How can the Weak subdue the Stronger?
> The Father ask'd her where and when?

> *How many? and what Sort of Men?*
> *By what Degrees her Blood was heated?*
> *How oft' the Frailty was repeated?*
> *Thus have I seen a pregnant Wench*
> *All flush'd with Guilt before the Bench,*
> *The Judges (wak'd by wanton Thought)*
> *Dive to the Bottom of her Fault.*

The priest assigns her penance, and she hurries away to keep an appointment—where she sins again. When she returns to confession, the priest speaks:

> *Madam, I grant there's something in it,*
> *That Virtue has the unguarded Minute;*
> *But pray now tell me what are Whores,*
> *But Women of unguarded Hours?*
> *Then you must sure have lost all Shame,*
> *What ev'ry Day and still the same,*
> *And no Fault else! 'tis strange to find*
> *A Woman to one Sin confin'd!*

She explains that she was chaste until her favorite lapdog went mad and bit her on the lip as she fondled him. This "set her youthful Blood fermenting." The Priest says there are cures: doctors can treat "these Distempers of the Mind":

> *They send you to the Ocean's Shore,*
> *And plunge the Patient o'er and o'er.*

But female cunning had the answer to this drastic treatment, in the guise of modesty, of course:

> *The Dame reply'd; alas! in vain*
> *My kindred forc'd me to the Main;*
> *Naked and in the Face of Day:*
> *Look not, ye Fisherman, this Way!*
> *What Virgin had not done as I did?*
> *My modest Hand, by Nature guided,*
> *Debarr'd at once from human Eyes*
> *The Seat where Female Honour lies,*
> *And though thrice Dipt from Top to Toe,*
> *I still secur'd the Post below,*
> *And guarded it with Grasp so fast*
> *Not one Drop through my Fingers Past;*
> *Thus owe I to my bashful Care*
> *That all the Rage is settled there.*

267

The author then philosophizes that all are mad ("save you and me"). Everybody has been "bit" and, when "dipt," they kept some part dry: the thieves, their hands; courtiers, their ears; etc. The December verse ends with the thought that woman's most deadly weapon is between her lips:

> All Women dread a watry Death:
> They shut their Lips to hold their Breath,
> And though you Duck them ne'er so long,
> Not one salt Drop e'er wets their Tongue;
> 'Tis hence they Scandal have at Will,
> And that this Member n'er lies still.

Poor Robin started at a gallop in his very first almanac for 1728. The poem on his last page is presented in the form of a Renaissance argument, including the conventional catalog, and a slightly less conventional punch line:

> Have you e'er seen the raging stormy Main,
> Toss a Ship up, then cast her down again?
>
> Sometimes she seems to touch the very Skies,
> And then again upon the Sand she lies.
>
> Or have you seen a Bull when he is jealous,
> How he does tear the Ground, and roars & bellows?
>
> Or have you seen the pretty Turtle Dove,
> When she laments the Absence of her Love?
>
> Or have you seen the Fairies, when they sing,
> And dance with Mirth together in a Ring?
>
> Or have you seen our Gallants make a Pudder
> With Fair & Grace, and Grace & Fair Ann Scrudder?
>
> Or have you seen the Daughters of Apollo
> Pour down their rhymming Liquors in a hollow
> Cane?_____
> In spungy Brain congealing into Verse;
> If you have seen all this, then kiss mine ——.[10]

The twentieth-century "common man" would doubtless consider some of the early almanac literary content difficult reading. Pope and Dryden were to readers of that day as Yeats and Eliot are to today's. How many of today's farmers would relish "The Swans of Coole" or "Prufrock," reading them almost daily for a year at a time? Yet the pages of the colonial almanacs were filled with verse from Pope, Dryden, Milton, Shakespeare, Young, and others. In publishing verse, men such as Ames and Low were as sincere in their day as are the programmers of educational television in ours, and possibly not less effective.

Conclusion

From its outset, the colonial almanac was more than practical. Ostensibly utilitarian, the earliest almanacs nevertheless contained verse, personalized prefaces, and essays of sometimes commendable quality. Though the formal essay did not attain great popularity in England until the early eighteenth century (with Addison and Steele), American almanackers were writing popular scientific explanations of comets and the solar system in clear and precise prose by the mid-seventeenth century. In these essays, in some of the prefaces, and in a few of the narratives, one observes the beginnings of a colonial literature. In fact, the early American almanac gave the common man, decades before the advent of colonial newspapers, his only exposure to secular writings, whether quotations from British authors or original verse and prose.

Wherever a printing press was established in the colonies, one of its first publications was an almanac. The printer himself was often the author or co-maker, and, in the case of John Foster, also the engraver. Furthermore, the frequent by-play between the author and printer, together with the feuds between almanackers, contributed uniquely to the history of American humor.

The colonial almanac, being popular literature, both mirrored and influenced its times. For over half a century, the colonial almanac had no competition as secular reading matter for the common man. Its influence on the thinking of the average New Englander during the seventeenth century cannot be overestimated.

270

And, long after the introduction of newspapers, it remained the most popular of secular literary media throughout the American colonies.

The Cambridge press published excellent astronomical almanacs and laid the foundation for the more versatile and comprehensive productions of the eighteenth century. Harvard tutors and graduates presented in their almanacs the Copernican astronomy that Harvard taught. Since almost every literate colonial in New England read the almanacs, they became an influential factor in converting this literate public to a less primitive theory of the universe. From the Copernican theory, the physics of Galileo and Newton was but a step removed.

While the seventeenth-century almanac popularized Copernican astronomy, the eighteenth-century almanac publicized Newtonian science, with its emphasis on the celestial mechanics of the solar system, and of God as the Great Clockmaker. However, the theological implications of Copernican astronomy and Newtonian physics were carefully avoided by the Harvard Puritans who created the colonial almanac, and by their successors. When astronomy, toward the close of the seventeenth century, began to give way to husbandry and trade as prime almanac matter, the increasingly practical tone of almanacs did not necessarily represent the embrace of skepticism or even deism, so far as the typical colonial was concerned.

By the mid-eighteenth century, a decline in Puritanism had resulted in deism on the one hand and evangelicism on the other, neither of which would have found favor with the Harvard philomaths. Despite the almanac's influence, the deistic tinge in the most widely read almanacs of the eighteenth century (those of the Ames and Franklin families) did not deter many readers from participating in the religious enthusiasm of the Great Awakening (1740–45) * and frontier revivalism—events generally ignored by the almanackers. A rare, and oblique, reference to the evangelical

---

* In 1740 the Rev. George Whitefield's second visit to America prompted wild, enthusiastic evangelicism that caused widespread hysteria and great controversy.

movement occurred in the 1744 almanac of Nathaniel Ames, II, who quoted an essay from *The Spectator* "Concerning mistaken Devotion." Ames reminded the reader that "Devotion, when it does not lie under the check of Reason, is very apt to degenerate into Enthusiasm." Perhaps the almanackers of that time wisely refrained from risking their reputations and sales by commenting on so controversial a theme, which could make and unmake both churches and ministers.

The mounting multiplicity of dissenting sects throughout the entire colonial period, and the migration of settlers from colony to colony, promoted a practical sort of toleration, despite governmental intolerance. Ezra Gleason's almanac for 1774 contains, for instance, "The Unbeliever's Creed." Its sardonic presentation of atheistic, rationalistic, and heretical stances, though heavy-footed, is intended as satiric humor. Such stances, to the Mathers a century earlier, would have been sufficient cause for exile—as heretical as Mrs. Hutchinson's Antinomian emotionalism:

> I believe that there is no God, but that matter is God, and God is matter; and that it is no matter whether there is any God or no. I believe, that the world was not made, that the world made itself; that it had no beginning, that it will last forever, world without end. I believe that Man is a beast; that the soul is the body, and the body the soul; that after death is neither body nor soul. I believe that there is no religion; that natural religion is the only religion; and that all religion is unnatural. I believe not in Moses; I believe in the First Philosophy; I believe not in the Evangelists; I believe in Chubb, Collins, Toland, Tindal, Morgan, Mandeville, Woolston, Hobbes, Shaftesbury; I believe in Lord Bolingbroke, I believe not in St. Paul. I believe not Revelation, I believe in Tradition; I believe in the Talmud; I believe in the Al-Koran; I believe not in the Bible; I believe in Socrates; I believe in Confucious; I believe in Sanchomiathon; I believe in Mahomet; I believe not in Christ. Lastly, I believe in all Unbelief.

The spirit of dissent in religion attended, and partly inspired, the growing preoccupation with rights and liberty during the second half of the eighteenth century. Although almanacs generally ignored the Great Awakening and the religious enthusiasms that followed in its wake, notions of self-government—and particularly resentment over taxation with or without representation—increasingly became topics for discussion in certain widely published almanacs from the middle decades of the century, notably almanacs by West, Ames, Franklin, Low, Edes and Gill, and Edmund Freebetter (pseud.).

On the other hand, various almanacs not only ignored the political scene but continued to publish as if the War for Independence were not happening, either out of Loyalist sympathies or as a hedge against the rebellion's failure. For whatever reason, the Crown and its agents did not trouble to suppress the almanacs, possibly because these, even when libertarian, espoused general principles on an annual basis, in contrast to the suppressed newspapers, which had been reporting specific clashes as they happened, with presumedly inflammatory consequences. Certain almanackers, then, can be said to have participated—together with such noted pamphleteers as Thomas Paine and Alexander Hamilton—in encouraging the freedom movement throughout the War for Independence, perhaps considerably raising the morale of freedom fighters.

As the absolute power of the pulpit declined, the almanac became increasingly an adjunct of the pulpit in helping to inculcate moral and social standards. Proverbs, jingles, and homiletic prose encouraged fairness in business dealings, hard work and frugality, and the avoidance of wrongdoing. These admonitions were, of course, in the Puritan tradition of "pious industry," but the emphasis was progressively less on piety.

Although all almanacs aimed at a more-or-less provincial readership with common utilitarian concerns, almanacs tended to reflect differences in culture and attitudes between larger geographical regions. The Southern almanacs contained more literature, particularly more narratives. *The Virginia Almanack*, for example, included up to twenty-four pages of literature within a single issue. The content of Southern almanacs was generally (but not always) less pious than the Northern in theme and diction. Southern almanacs also contained more articles on planting crops and gardening. In fact, the term "garden" is emphatically present

273

A PICTURESQUE VIEW of

EXPL

I The Commerce of Great Britain represent
in the figure of a Milch Cow.

II The American Congress sawing off her hor
which are her natural strength and defence: tho
one being already gone, the other just a going.

III The jolly plump Dutchman milking the poor
tame Cow with great glee.

IV & V The French and Spaniard each catchi
at their respective shares of the produce, and rur
ning away with bowls brimming full, laughing to
one another at their success.

VI A distant view of Clinton and Arnold, in New Yo
concerting measures for the fruitless scheme of en
ving America — Arnold sensible of his guil

Cartoon Frontispiece from *Weatherwise's New*

NEW YORK

ATION
ops his head and weeps.
I The British Lion lying on the ground fast asleep
that a pug-dog tramples upon him; as on a life-
s log, he seems to see nothing hear nothing
d feel nothing.
II. A free Englishman in mourning standing by
, wringing his hands, casting up his Eyes in de
ndency and despair, but unable to rouse the Lion
correct all these invaders of his Royal Prero-
tive and his subjects property

England Town & Countryman's Almanack for 1781.

275

in Southern almanacs, notably *The Kentucky Almanack,* and the *Palladium of Knowledge,* a South Carolina and Georgia almanac. There was more about horses, even to Tobler's defense, in 1774, of horseracing as a sport in South Carolina and Georgia. And in a plantation society, the Southern writer could safely refer to the rustic as a "clod." Such Cavalier treatment of the son of the soil would have been unwise, to say the least, in New England. In effect, Southern almanacs differed from New England almanacs in reflecting a more worldly society and a more secular literary culture.

By the end of the eighteenth century, women printers, Blacks, and foreigners had added their efforts to those of philomaths, physicians, other printers, and businessmen, to make the eighteenth-century almanac the most outstanding in the history of American almanacs. The almanac's most eminent editors and publishers were active during this century: the Leeds family, the Ames family, the Franklin family, Christopher Sauer, Nathanael Low, Benjamin West, Isaiah Thomas, and Robert B. Thomas. Their almanacs attained full development as literary form, and surpassed those of the seventeenth century in variety of content and richness of humor. Their tone was less severe, their subjects more diversified, and their humor more subtle. Verse, anecdotes, and stories received more space; and articles were increasingly directed to the ladies. Belles lettres appeared: verse from Dryden and Pope, and essays from Bacon, as well as earnest literary attempts by the colonials.

Ironically, the most attractive and original contribution to colonial letters is the preface, a part of the almanac not likely to have been regarded by some of its creators as literature. It was in the prefaces that the editor-author-publisher-printer gave himself full sway, and the result is often the inimitable mix of vehemence and humor that typifies what is most pleasant in the colonial American temperament.

Some almanac-makers excelled in one literary form; some in another. As essayists, the early Cambridge men were not equalled until Ames, a half-century later. Benjamin Franklin's fortes were prefaces and proverbs; Nathaniel Ames's, essays and verse. The

THE

SOUTH-CAROLINA and GEORGIA

ALMANACK,

FOR THE YEAR OF OUR LORD
1764.

(Being BISSEXTILE or LEAP-YEAR.)

Fitted to the Meridian of 33 Degrees North Latitude, which renders it ferviceable to the Provinces of NORTH and SOUTH-CAROLINA, GEORGIA, FLORIDA, and LOUISIANA.

CONTAINING

The GARDENER'S KALENDAR, PROFIT and LOSS in the LATE WARS and many other useful Things.

By JOHN TOBLER, Efq;

Here, Reader, fee, in Youth, in Age, or Prime,
The ftealing Steps of never-ftanding Time,
With Wifdom mark the Moment as it flies,
Think what a Moment is—to him that dies,

GEORGIA:
SAVANNAH, Printed by JAMES JOHNSTON.

Tobler's almanac issued especially for South Carolina and Georgia, Georgia's first almanac.

277

best almanacs contained a variety of literary forms that were composed with skill, taste, and a judicious infusion of humor, wit, and satire. But this can scarcely be said of colonial almanacs as a whole. The almanacs of Benjamin Franklin, Nathaniel Ames, and Benjamin West display to greatest advantage the happy union of useful information and light, entertaining reading of a literary nature. And some "poets" who published their works exclusively in almanacs were as good as or better than many of those included in typical anthologies of early American writings. Max Savelle, in discussing the beginnings of American poetry, mentions poets such as the Connecticut Wits, who wrote for the educated reader. He adds:

> But there was another stream of verse—one dares not call it poetry—that was largely anonymous and that sprang from a group of writers who were obviously closer to the people and to the American soil. These, the people's poets, were the writers in the almanacs and the newspapers.[1]

Even so, Joel Barlow, Connecticut Wit, appeared in almanacs, and so did other wits—usually British, though occasionally French. Philip Morin Freneau (the "Father of American Poetry") prepared *The Monmouth Almanac, for the Year, M,DCC,XCV* and published it himself.

Verse, indifferent, bad, and sometimes good, was perennial in the American almanac. The seventeenth and eighteenth centuries were, of course, the ages *par excellence* of versifying—everybody was doing it. The colonies were no exception, whenever there was leisure from the daily grind. But poetry and song had existed for aeons previously. Why this sudden popular explosion of interest?

The primary reason may have been technological—a reflection of the printer's influence on the literary form of the almanac. Before paper and print grew cheap, verse and song were largely passed from mouth to ear. They were heard rather than seen. They were usually sonorous. But the printer introduced a new factor, necessarily neglected by the parchment scribe, and this was the look of regular meter on the printed page. Visual satisfaction was added to auditory and sometimes, in the case of bad verse, over-ruled the latter. Finally, mere versification in print became an end in itself, and a decadent literary fashion.

There may have been contributory motivations. Not least among these was surely the ban imposed by the extreme left of the Reformation on all popular and aristocratic entertainment, save the writing of verses—on serious, moral, and religious themes. The metrical psalms were a peculiarly Protestant production. Of course, the Puritan versifier soon broadened his subject matter. It may not be too fanciful to believe that, in their versifications, Puritan men and women danced—without the malediction of their sternest sects.

There was also a prevailing educational and instructional motive, a desire by a few to leaven the mass, and what better means than on the wings of poesy? No matter if sometimes the feathers flew off. Witness Ames in 1754:

> I have this Year collected the Poetry for the Almanack from several Authors . . . I don't pretend to direct the Learned—The Rich and Voluptuous will scorn my Direction, and sneer or rail at any that would reclaim them, but since this Sheet enters the solitary Dwellings of the Poor & Illiterate, where the studied Ingenuity of the Learned Writer never comes, if these brief Hints do good, it will rejoice the Heart of
>
> your humble Servant,
Nath. Ames.

And Low in his almanac for 1762:

> I did not design it [almanack] to inform or direct the Learned, but for the Entertainment of those few Poor and Illiterate (that are not so biassed against the Art as the Multitude are) where the studied Ingeny, and elegant Cadence of the learned Genius never comes. . . .

A few strange survivals of the colonial era linger on today. In the *Old Farmer's Almanac* for December 1971:

> *The solstice's a kind of grin and bear it season,*
> *We can stand all this cold and dark we reason*
> *If only for the promise we hope will come true*
> *That spring is ahead, all pink and green and blue.*

279

In the same almanac for August 1974:

> *The blackberry vine bends with its weight*
> *Of fruit down in the lane,*
> *And adds its testimony, too,*
> *That August's here again.*

And for September 1974:

> *Now the celestial balance weights the light,*
> *Giving an equal length to day and night;*
> *And the clear air keeps a divided seat,*
> *Affording sometimes cold, and sometimes heat.*

Evidently eighteenth-century colonial America still lives—in twentieth-century almanac verse.

There are two almanac-makers who contend for the honor of setting a standard of excellence for the entire genre: Nathaniel Ames and Benjamin Franklin. Several historians concur that Ames was a better almanac-maker than Benjamin Franklin.[2] Some formed their own judgments, and others were probably influenced more by Moses Coit Tyler than by the almanacs themselves. Tyler seems to have been the first to claim that the Ames almanac was superior as literature to the folksy, pragmatic *Poor Richard*. Tyler's praise of Ames is euphoric:

> Nathaniel Ames made his almanac a sort of annual cyclopaedia of information and amusement,—a vehicle for the conveyance to the public of all sorts of knowledge and nonsense, in prose and verse, from literature, history and his own mind, all presented with brevity, variety, and infallible tact. He had the instinct of a journalist; and, under a guise that was half-frolicsome, the sincerity and benignant passion of a public educator. He carried into the furthest wildernesses of New England some of the best English literature; pronouncing there, perhaps for the first time, the names of Addison, Thomson, Pope, Dryden, Butler, Milton; and repeating there choice fragments of what they had written. Thus, eight years before Benjamin Franklin had started his almanac, Nathaniel Ames was publishing one that had all of its best qualities,—fact and frolic, the

wisdom of the preacher without his solemnity, terse sayings, shrewdness, wit, homely wisdom, all sparkling in piquant phrase.[3]

Franklin, too, has his supporters. One of the most recent is J. A. Leo Lemay, who simply states that Franklin's almanac is the best in the world; [4] and Bruce Granger:

> No other American philomath created and developed within his pages such original types as Richard and Bridget Saunders; in subtlety no other equaled Franklin's hoax on Titan Leeds. Although Moses Coit Tyler has called Nathaniel Ames's *Astronomical Diary and Almanack* (1726-1764) "in most respects better than Franklin's," the best that can be said for it is that it had a much larger subscription. Certainly Ames's sayings fall short of Franklin's in respect to perspicuity, elegance, and cadence.[5]

The reader has been presented with enough samplings from both almanacs to judge for himself, depending upon his personal tastes. If he ranks essays and verse over prefaces and proverbs, he may indeed prefer Ames's almanacs; but Franklin's literary superiority can scarcely be challenged in vivacity and "piquant phrase."

The seventeenth-century reader had very little choice of reading material: the almanac and the Bible. In the eighteenth century, the almanac admirably held its popularity despite the availability of a relatively large amount of other printed matter. John Hayes, printer of Ellicott's almanac for 1791, succinctly summed up the almanac's status then:

> Among the numerous publications of the present age, an almanac also annually claims the attention of the community. Its usefulness is acknowledged, and when properly selected, its subject-matter may convey, to readers of every class, both instruction and pleasure.

In its heyday the almanac had no substitute. From its pages the farmer and his family could learn when to plant, when and how to tend the sick, and how to care for their stock. For the man of affairs, it was an indispensable aid, a protection, a measure of security, a helpmeet, a crutch, a veritable companion. It was his clock and his calendar and, later in its development, it was an anthology of literary material—his *Reader's Digest*. In short, the almanac was the literary form that met his most pressing daily needs. As one early almanac-maker said, "A person without an almanac is somewhat like a ship without a compass; he never knows what to do, nor when to do it."

Woodcut arms of the United States,
in Wheeler's *North American Calendar
& Rhode Island Almanack* for 1789.

Notes

INTRODUCTION

1. Charles Nichols, "Notes on the Almanacs of Massachusetts," *Proc. of the American Antiquarian Society* (AAS), NS 22 (April 10, 1912), p. 27; Samuel Briggs, *Essays, Humor, and Poems of Nathaniel Ames, Father and Son* (Cleveland, Ohio: Short & Fortman, 1891), p. 20.
2. Israel Sweet, "Prose Literature of the Colonial Almanacs (1763–1767)" Thesis, Columbia University, 1946, p. 38.
3. Albert Carlos Bates, "Checklist of Connecticut Almanacs 1709–1850," *Proc. of the AAS*, NS 24 (April 1914), p. 108.
4. Richard Hixson, *Isaac Collins* (New Brunswick, N.J.: Rutgers University Press, 1968), p. 30.
5. The Van Leuwenhoek material was first published in the 1743 *Mercurius Nov-Angelicanus, or, An Almanack* by William Nadir, pseudonym for William Douglass. Dr. Douglass, noted Boston physician, botanist, and essayist, was a Scot, trained in medicine at Edinburgh, Leyden, and Paris.
6. The following almanacs were published in 1732 (for the year 1733) by Andrew Bradford: William Birkett, *An Almanack;* John Jerman, *The American Almanack;* Jacob Taylor, *The Pennsylvania Almanack;* Titan Leeds, *The American Almanack;* Thomas Godfrey, *The Pennsylvania Almanack;* and *Der TEUTSCHE Pilgrim: Mitbringende Einen Sitten-Calender.* Four other almanacs, probably available to Philadelphians, were published in Boston and prepared by Nathaniel Ames, Nathaniel Whittemore, John Partridge (pseudonym), and Nathan Bowen. Two other almanacs may also have been distributed in Philadelphia: one, by Theophilus Grew, printed in Annapolis, Maryland, and another, by James Franklin, Jr., printed in Newport, Rhode Island.

CHAPTER 1

1. Samuel Briggs, "The Origin and Development of the Almanack," a paper read before the Western Reserve and Northern Ohio Historical Society, Jan. 12, 1887, *Tracts,* 2 (Cleveland, Ohio: Western Reserve Historical Society, 1888), No. 69, 440. Matthew Stickney, "Almanacs and Their Authors," *Essex Institute Historical Collections,* 8 (1866), p. 32.
2. James Orchard Halliwell mentions the *al-mon-aght* theory seriously, adding simply, "an eastern origin would appear to me more probable" ("Early Almanacs," in *The Companion to the British Almanac of the Society for the Diffusion of Useful Knowledge* [London, 1839], Article V, p. 53.

3. Ainsworth R. Spofford, "A Brief History of Almanacs," *An American Almanac . . . for 1878* (New York: The American News Company, 1878), p. 21.

4. Briggs, "Origin and Development," p. 441; George Emery Littlefield, "Notes on the Calendar and the Almanac," *Proc. of the AAS*, NS 24 (1914), p. 52.

5. Quoted in Briggs, "Origin and Development," p. 441.

6. There are four existing calendars generally attributed to Gutenberg: the *Almanach auf das Jahr, 1448*, the so-called Astronomical Calendar (Mainz, 1448); *Eyn manung der cristenheit widder die durken*, the so-called Turkish Calendar (1455); *Coniunctiones et opposiciones solis et lune . . . nec non dies pro medicinis laxativis sumendis . . .* , the so-called Medical or Bloodletting Calendar (Mainz, ca. 1456); and the *Cisianus*, a medieval feast calendar in verse (Mainz, ca. 1457). (cf. *Gesamtkatalog die Wiegendrucke* [Leipzig: 1925–40] 1285; Karl Löffler and Joachim Kirchner, *Lexicon d. gesamten buchwerens* [Leipzig: 1935–37] II, 307; *Gesamtkatalog*, 1286; Ibid., 7054.)

7. This almanac is claimed as France's first by Charles Nisard, *Histoire des livres populaires*, 2nd ed. (1854; rpt. New York: Burt Franklin, 1965), I, 2. Littlefield ("Notes," p. 59) says it was adapted from Jehan de Brie's 1379 (*Vrai régime du gouvernement des bergers*. Thomas Wright in "The History of Almanacs" (*Macmillan's Magazine*, 7 [Jan. 1863], 176) says that the *Kalendrier des Bergers* was translated into English in 1480. If Wright's *Kalendrier* and Littlefield's *Grand Compost des Bergers* (translated in 1493) are the same French almanac, the difference in dates of the *first* English translation is thirteen years.

8. Briggs, "Origin and Development," p. 443.

9. Ibid., p. 459. Samuel Butler satirized Lilly in *Hudibras* as Sidrophel:

> *Do not our great reformers use*
> *This Sidrophel to forebode news?*
> *To write of victories next year,*
> *And castles taken yet i' the air?*

10. Wright, "History of Almanacs," p. 178.

11. Spofford, "Brief History," pp. 22–23.

12. Bernard Faÿ, *Franklin, the Apostle of Modern Times* (Boston: Little, Brown and Company, 1924), pp. 156–157. The *Protestant Almanack* series was published intermittently between 1680 and 1699 by "Philoprotest, a Well-willer to the Mathematicks."

CHAPTER 2

1. Donald Crawford McMurtrie gives February 13, 1741, as the date of Bradford's *American Magazine*, and February 16, 1741, for Franklin's *General Magazine*, in *A History of Printing in the United States* (1936; rpt. New York: Burt Franklin, 1969), II, 38–39. Historical beginnings of the newspaper and the magazine are given in Lawrence C. Wroth, *The Colonial Printer* (Portland, Me.: The Southworth-Anthoensen Press, 1938), pp. 19, 237.

2. Letter to the author from D.S. Neill, Assistant Librarian, Bodleian Library, 15 June 1972.

3. "Letters of John Tulley," *Massachusetts Historical Society Proceedings*, 3d Ser., 30 (Nov. 1916), p. 76.

4. Richard Hixson, *Isaac Collins*, p. 45.

5. John Bach McMaster, *Benjamin Franklin as a Man of Letters* (Boston: Houghton Mifflin Company, 1887), p. 101.

6. A. S. Rosenbach, *A Book Hunter's*

Holiday (Freeport, N.Y.: Books for Libraries Press, 1968), p. 180; Robb Sagendorph, *America and Her Almanacs* (Dublin, N.H.: Yankee, Inc., and Boston: Little, Brown and Company, 1970), p. 44.

7. Arthur B. Tourtellot, *The Charles,* American River Series (New York: J. J. Little and Ives Company, 1941), p. 102.
8. Briggs, "Origin and Development," p. 464.
9. Moses Coit Tyler, *A History of American Literature During the Colonial Time,* rev. ed. (1878; rpt. 2 vols in 1, New York: G. P. Putnam's Sons, 1902), II, 121.
10. Littlefield, "Notes," p. 54.
11. Nisard, *Histoire,* p. 100.
12. Compare an earlier British version in Edward Pond's almanac for 1633:

> *Should I but dare t' omit the Anatomie,*
> *Which long enough hath gul'd my country friend,*
> *He with contempt would straight refuse to buy*
> *This book, and 't is no* Almanack *contend.*
> *Ask him its use, he'le say he cannot tell;*
> *No more can I: yet since he loves 't so well,*
> *I'le let it stand, because my book should sell.*

(Quoted in Briggs, "Origin and Development," p. 451.)
13. Sagendorph, *America and Her Almanacs,* p. 19.
14. McMaster, *Benjamin Franklin,* pp. 97–98.
15. *Diary of Cotton Mather,* American Classics Edition (New York: Frederick Ungar Publishing Co., 1957), I, 276. Since they are neither few nor pungent, I have not quoted the lines. Mather was a prolific and undiscriminating author.
16. There were two editions this year: one in Boston and one in New York.

This verse appears in both.
17. Nichols, "Notes," p. 27.
18. Isaiah Thomas, *The History of Printing in America,* 2 vols. (rev. ed. 1874; rpt. New York: Burt Franklin, 1972), I, 231.
19. Anna J. De Armond, *Andrew Bradford, Colonial Journalist* (Newark: University of Delaware Press, 1949), p. 212.
20. Samuel Briggs, *Essays, Humor, and Poems of Nathaniel Ames, Father and Son, of Dedham, Massachusetts, from their Almanacks 1726–1775* (Cleveland, Ohio: Short & Forman, 1891), p. 33.
21. Clyde Augustus Duniway, *Development of Freedom of the Press in Massachusetts* (1906; rpt. New York: Burt Franklin, 1969), pp. 74–75.
22. Thomas, *History,* I, 84.
23. Leonard W. Levy, *Legacy of Suppression: Freedom of Speech and Press in Early American History* (Cambridge: The Belknap Press of Harvard University Press, 1960), p. 62.
24. Levy, *Legacy of Suppression,* p. 65, n.
25. John T. Winterich, *Early American Books & Printing* (Boston & New York: Houghton Mifflin Company, 1935), pp. 54–55.
26. Levy, *Legacy of Suppression,* p. 50.
27. Ibid., p. 36.
28. Briggs, "Origin and Development," p. 469.
29. From Franklin's "An Apology for Printers" (*Pennsylvania Gazette* for June 10, 1731) and quoted in Faÿ, *Franklin,* p. 166. Cf. Milton: "Let Truth and Falsehood grapple; who ever knew Truth put to the worse in a free and open encounter" (*Areopagitica,* 1644).
30. Faÿ, *Franklin,* p. 160.
31. Elizabeth Anthony Dexter, *Colonial Women of Affairs* (1924; rpt. Cambridge, Mass.: The Riverside Press, 1931), p. 166.

CHAPTER 3

1. *Winthrop's Journal*, ed. by James Kendall Hosmer (New York: Charles Scribner's Sons, 1908), I, 293.
2. Sagendorph's reference, in *America and Her Almanacs* (p. 31), to a copy in the John Carter Brown Library in Providence, Rhode Island, is mistaken.
3. "The Early American Almanac," *The Bookman*, 2 (1895–96), 283.
4. *Winthrop's Journal*, I, 260.
5. George Emery Littlefield, *The Early Massachusetts Press, 1638–1711* (1907; rpt, 2 vols. in 1, New York: Burt Franklin, 1969), I, 52. Samuel Eliot Morison does not agree with Littlefield and other historians that Glover first came to Boston about 1634 and returned to England to solicit funds for the college (*The Founding of Harvard University* [Cambridge: Harvard University Press, 1935], pp. 225–226, n.).
6. Littlefield, *Early Massachusetts Press*, pp. 99 ff.
7. George Parker Winship, *The Cambridge Press, 1638–1692* (Philadelphia: University of Pennsylvania Press, 1945), pp. 140–142.
8. Ibid., pp. 75–76.
9. Littlefield ("Notes," p. 61) says that two leaves—the first and last—are missing; Winship (*Cambridge Press*, p. 76) says that three—the first two and the last—are missing. Winship is probably correct. There are only ten pages: two memorandum pages (which do not count), and calendar pages for May through February.
10. Nichols, "Notes," pp. 25–26. The almanac for 1657 is also attributed to Samuel Bradstreet by Samuel Eliot Morison, in *Harvard College in the Seventeenth Century* (Cambridge: Harvard University Press, 1936), I, 135.
11. Winship, *Cambridge Press*, p. 80; John L. Sibley, *Biographical Sketches of Graduates of Harvard College* (Boston: Massachusetts Historical Society, 1873), I, 61.
12. Samuel A. Green, *John Foster* (Boston: Massachusetts Historical Society, 1909), p. 79; Annie R. Marble, "Early New England Almanacs," *New England Magazine*, 19 (Jan. 1899), 552; Charles Evans, *American Bibliography*, 14 vols., Vols. I-XII ed. by Charles Evans, Vol. XIII ed. by Clifford K. Shipton, Vol. XIV (*Index*) ed. by Roger Pattrell Bristol (Publishers and dates vary, 1941–1959).
13. Briggs, *Essays*, p. 28, n.
14. Charles Angoff, *Literary History of the American People* (New York: A. A. Knopf, 1931), I, 241. There is no apparent explanation for the reference by Briggs to a 1695 Gatchell almanac, nor for the decision by Angoff (who had read Briggs) to select 1695 as the date for the Gatchell almanac. Evans does not list the alleged 1695 almanac in *American Bibliography*. Milton Drake, however, in *Almanacs of the United States* (New York: Scarecrow Press, 1962), lists the 1695 almanac (I, 277) and the 1715 (I, 284), citing as his source for the 1695: Emily Foster Happer, "Seventeenth Century American Almanacs," *Literary Collector*, 9, no. 2 (1905). Happer (pp. 47–48) says: "From 1697 to '99 almanacs have been found by W. Williams, 1687 . . . Increase Gatchell, 1695. . . ." The 1695 entry in Drake reads: "An Almanack for 1695. Cambridge: Samuel Green." Samuel Green was the Cambridge printer from 1649 through 1692, the year the college suspended printing operations. Several copies of Gatchell's 1715 almanac exist.
15. J. H. Swasey says that John Anderson's almanac for 1774 was "the earliest almanack to have any attempt at decoration on the first page" ("Rhode Island Almanacs of Long Ago," *Newport Historical Society Bulletin*, No. 92 [1939], p. 6). This estimate is

wrong by 127 years—perhaps by more, for the Danforth 1646 extant copy lacks the first page, which (for all we know) may also have been decorated.

16. Anne Hutchinson was excommunicated and banished from the Bay Colony for her Antinomian heresies. One of her chief adversaries was the Reverend Thomas Shepard (1605–1649), a founder of Harvard College and Pastor of the Church at Cambridge—not to be confused with his son, the almanac-maker and minister of the same name.

17. Morison, *Harvard College*, 1, 216. Vincent Wing, Brigden's authority, was an English almanac-maker (1658) and the first author in English of a work that explained Copernicus, Galileo, and Kepler.

18. Perry Miller, *The New England Mind: From Colony to Province* (Cambridge: Harvard University Press, 1962), p. 47.

19. Clarence S. Brigham, "An Account of American Almanacs and their Value for Historical Study," Reprinted from the *Proc. of the AAS*, October 1925 (Worcester, Mass.: The Society, 1925), p. 210.

20. Littlefield, *Early Massachusetts Press*, II, 3.

21. Information regarding the first engraver is contradictory. On p. 37 of *America and Her Almanacs,* Sagendorph says, "This man was not only Boston's first printer but also America's earliest known wood engraver." He prints a copy of Foster's familiar woodcut of Richard Mather. On p. 177, Sagendorph writes of Alexander Anderson: "Eventually, Anderson abandoned his medical career and, greatly influenced by the work of England's Thomas Bewick, became not only America's first wood engraver but, in the opinion of many, her greatest." Anderson lived a century later than Foster. Anderson is also referred to as America's first wood engraver in Frederick M. Burr, *The Life and Works of Alexander Anderson, M.D.* (New York: Burr Brothers, 1893), p. 17.

22. Sagendorph erroneously states that John Tulley (almanac series, 1687–1702) introduced the Man of Signs to American almanacs (*America and Her Almanacs,* p. 46).

23. Samuel Eliot Morison and Samuel A. Green disagree as to the author of "Observations of a Comet seen this last Winter 1680" in Foster's 1681 almanac. Morison believes that the unsigned essay was a copy of Thomas Brattle's report to the Royal Society of London (the observations used by Newton), but Green attributes the essay to Foster, pointing out that the following quotation alludes to "Heaven's Alarm to the World" by Increase Mather: "*But of these things we have lately heard in Public by a Reverend Divine among us, in a Sermon occasioned by this Ominous Appearance,*" showing that such occurrences are "Presages of great Calamityes." (Morison, *Harvard College,* I, 220–221, n.; Green, *John Foster,* p. 47.) Dr. Donald K. Yeomans compared Brattle's original observations (*Royal Greenwich Observatory manuscript volumes, Flamsteed papers,* xli, 22) with the essay in Foster's almanac, finding differences in the values for the ecliptic latitude and longitude. Foster's almanac was printed early in 1681; Brattle's letter to Flamsteed, Director of the Royal Greenwich Observatory, is dated 4 June 1681. Furthermore, Increase Mather's *Kometographia* states that the comet of 1680 was "followed by John Foster, the late Printer in Boston." Mather ignores Thomas Brattle. Dr. Yeomans, an astronomer, concludes that Brattle could have combined his own observations with Foster's, and that Newton's "observer in New England" (mentioned

in his *Principia*) could have been both Brattle and Foster ("The Origin of American Astronomy—Seventeenth Century," an unpublished paper by Donald K. Yeomans, Computer Sciences Corporation, Silver Spring, Maryland).

24. The similarity between the two epitaphs is noted by Green (*John Foster*, p. 35) and by Thomas Goddard Wright, *Literary Culture in Early New England, 1620–1730* (New Haven, Conn.: Yale University Press, 1920), p. 163. Wright pushes the origin of the idea back to Benjamin Woodbridge's elegy on John Cotton in 1652, which compares Cotton to a "living, breathing Bible." Woodbridge had pursued the metaphor:

> O, what a monument of glorious worth,
> When, in a new edition, he comes forth,
> Without erratas, may we think he'll be
> In leaves and covers of eternity!

25. Spofford, "Brief History," p. 24.
26. Confusion about Bradford and "1687" resulted in the 1910 *Encyclopaedia Britannica's* error that Bradford's press printed the first U.S. almanac in 1687. (Eric Sloane's facts in the 1969, and subsequent, editions of the *Britannica* are correct.) D. T. Lutes writes that *Poor Richard*, "probably the earliest of the almanacs published in this country," was published in 1687 ("One Book—the Almanac," in *America is West*, ed. by John T. Flanagan [Minneapolis: The University of Minnesota Press, 1945], pp. 314–315). *Poor Richard* was published forty-six years after 1687, and neither *Poor Richard* nor the year 1687 has anything to do with the first almanac published in America.
27. Spofford ("Brief History," p. 24), Sagendorph (*America and Her Almanacs*, p. 103), and Littlefield ("Notes," p. 62) contend that the first New York almanac was prepared by John Clapp and published by William Bradford for the year 1697. Here, the confusion over whether Leeds or Clapp is first in New York may be because Daniel Leeds was a Philadelphian, but that should hardly make a difference. However, Littlefield says: "The first *genuine* [italics mine] New York almanac is 'An Almanac for 1697. By John Clapp.'" Littlefield does not explain "genuine."

Agnes M. Lathe overlooks Pennsylvania completely in her chronology: "For seventy-two years Massachusetts was the only colony to publish an almanac. Then in 1697 New York entered the lists" ("A Rummage among Colonial Almanacs," *The Chautauquan* [Mar. 1894], p. 724). But Atkins' *Kalendarium Pennsilvaniense* was published in 1685—almost ten years before New York "entered the lists."

28. For example, Nichols, "Notes," p. 25.
29. Briggs, *Essays*, p. 19.
30. Regarding seventeenth-century American almanacs, Lathe says: "In all these almanacs the year began with March . . . it was not until 1694 that the reckoning was changed to our present system. The number for that year 1694, introduced another improvement in the form of blank leaves between the months" ("A Rummage among Colonial Almanacs," p. 723). A 1694 almanac introduced neither the "present system" nor the blank leaves. Andrews errs by an even wider margin: "In all Almanacs up to the year 1752, the old style of reckoning was observed, the year beginning on Lady's Day, March 25th" ("The Early American Almanac," p. 285).
31. Sagendorph lists "An Almanac by John Tulley, 1693. First U.S. weather forecasts" (*America and Her Alma-*

nacs, p. 283). But Benjamin Harris' almanac for 1692 had weather predictions (for example, for May 23rd, "pretty Hot") and Tulley himself had them as early as 1687.

32. Tourtellot, *The Charles,* p. 106.

33. Tulley, "Letters," p. 76.

34. The theory that the earth is suffering from gas pains when it quakes was also expressed by Shakespeare:

> *Diseased nature oftentimes breaks forth*
> *In strange eruptions; oft the teeming earth*
> *Is with a kind of colic pinched and vexed*
> *By the imprisoning of unruly wind*
> *Within her womb, which for enlargement striving*
> *Shakes the old beldam earth and topples down*
> *Steeples and moss-grown towers.*
> Henry IV, *III, i, 27–31*

35. There is no record of the Hannah Swarton account in the Evans *Bibliography.* Although Evans examined newspapers for advertisements of publications to be included in his listings, he and his successors apparently omitted the almanacs as possible sources.

36. Sagendorph states that Tulley's 1702 almanac "led, for example, to the publication of America's earliest book advertisements. One of these was an 'Antidote against all Manner of Gripings, called Aqua-Antiorminalis' [book?]" (*America and Her Almanacs,* p. 48). The earliest book advertisement in an American almanac appeared thirty-three years before, in Joseph Browne's 1669 edition. In Leeds's 1694 almanac, William Bradford listed several books for sale at his printshop. Tulley's own almanac carried book ads as early as 1692.

37. Tourtellot, *The Charles,* p. 101.

38. Nichols, "Notes," p. 30.

CHAPTER 4

1. Sagendorph, *America and Her Almanacs,* p. 121.

2. This story is best told by Briggs (*Essays,* pp. 24–25), who acquired his information from Erastus Worthington's *History of Dedham* (Boston, Mass.: Dutton and Wentworth, Printers, 1827). The original sketch of the sign, found in Dr. Ames's papers and dated August 18, 1749, is reproduced in Briggs between pages 24 and 25. Briggs, an authority on the Ameses, had access to the Ames papers and thoroughly researched the history of Dedham, Massachusetts, where they worked. From Briggs comes the most accurate information about the Ameses.

3. Briggs, *Essays,* p. 33. Sagendorph (*America and Her Almanacs,* p. 24) attributes this quotation to "old Nathanael Ames" in 1765. It was, however, the younger Dr. Ames who noted this in his diary; his father had died the previous year.

4. Tourtellot, *The Charles,* p. 111.

5. Wright, "History," p. 184.

6. Howard M. Chapin, "Ann Franklin," in *Bibliographical Essays* (Cambridge: Harvard University Press, 1924), p. 339.

7. Howard M. Chapin, "James Franklin, Jr.," *The Americana Collector,* 2 (June 1926), 325.

8. Chapin, "James Franklin, Jr.," p. 326.

9. Howard M. Chapin, "Check List of Rhode Island Almanacs 1643–1850," *Proc. of the AAS,* NS 25 (1915), p. 23. George Whitefield, British evangelist, had created quite a stir in America in 1740. Faÿ points out that Benjamin Franklin had supported Whitefield with his paper, *The Pennsylvania Gazette,* and with his money (*Franklin,* p. 190).

10. Frederic Hudson says that Ann took over the press again because "James

Franklin the second suddenly left Newport and never returned" (*A History of Journalism from 1690 to 1872* [New York: Harper & Brothers, Publishers, 1873], p. 110). A euphemism for "James died"?

11. Faÿ, *Franklin*, p. 159. Rosenbach says that in 1728 Franklin and his partner Meredith issued a single-leaf almanac (*A Book Hunter's Holiday*, p. 186). Winterich says that the printing firm was that of Franklin and Meredith and that Thomas Godfrey was commissioned to prepare the almanacs from 1730 to 1732, at which time Godfrey began working for Andrew Bradford (*Early American Books*, p. 84).

12. Benjamin Franklin, *The Autobiography of Benjamin Franklin*, with an introduction by Henry Steele Commager (New York: Random House, The Illustrated Modern Library, 1944), pp. 108–109.

13. The 1929 *Britannica* (and subsequent editions) has corrected the 1910 edition's error: that *Poor Richard* "may have been suggested by a somewhat similar publication by Thomas, of Dedham, Mass." (I, 712). Dedham was the home of Nathaniel Ames. The Isaiah Thomas almanac series began in 1775; the Robert B. Thomas series, in 1793.

14. Faÿ, *Franklin*, p. 167.

15. Rosenbach's (*A Book Hunter's Holiday*, p. 192) failure to examine carefully these almanacs resulted in his statement that

> The success of "Poor Richard" naturally attracted many imitators, poor in fancy and "poor" in name, such as Poor Will, Poor Ned, Poor Roger, Poor Thomas, Poor Job, and one, more audacious, Poor Richard Improved!

16. Franklin, *Autobiography*, p. 108.

17. Ainsworth R. Spofford, ed., *Benjamin Franklin, Autobiography. Poor Richard. Letters* (New York: D. Appleton and Company, 1904), p. 102.

18. John Clyde Oswald, *Benjamin Franklin, Printer* (Garden City, N.Y.: Doubleday, Page & Company, 1917), p. 128.

19. Carl L. Becker in *Dictionary of American Biography*, VI, 587.

20. Sagendorph says, "West is best remembered today for the fact that in his *Boston Bickerstaff's* appear the first Calendar page illustrations to be seen in any of the American almanacs" (*America and Her Almanacs*, pp. 112–113). He gives examples from the 1784 edition. However, on each of the right-hand calendar pages (two pages for each month) in Franklin's *Poor Richard* for 1749 calendar page illustrations appear.

Sagendorph may have simply misread Nichols, who says that the Boston Bickerstaff series was "the first to be illustrated in Massachusetts" ("Notes," p. 35). Nichols is probably not referring to such illustrations as the Man of Signs and the sometimes elaborate diagrams that had been used a century earlier in American almanacs, but rather to cartoons, portraits, dramatic scenes, and the like.

21. Chapin, "Check List," p. 25.

22. Dates of West's almanac series in this section are derived from Nichols, "Notes," p. 35.

23. Nichols, "Notes," pp. 33–34.

24. Clifford K. Shipton, *Isaiah Thomas: Printer, Patriot and Philanthropist 1749–1831* (Rochester, N.Y.: The Printing House of Leo Hart, 1948), pp. 31–32.

25. Ibid., pp. 3–4.

26. *The Diary of Isaiah Thomas*, ed. by Benjamin T. Hill, *Transactions and Collections of the AAS*, Vols. 9 and 10 (Worcester, Mass.: American Antiquarian Society, 1909), II, xiii.

27. James H. Fitts, "The Thomas Almanacs," *Essex Institute Historical Collections*, 12 (1874), 252.

28. Henry Morton Robinson, "The Almanac," *The Bookman,* 75 (June-July, 1932), 219.

29. Nichols, "Notes," p. 33.

30. Silvio A. Bedini, *The Life of Benjamin Banneker* (New York: Charles Scribner's Sons, 1972), p. 211.

31. Andrew Ellicott, George's cousin, also calculated almanacs, sometimes with his own name in the title (1786, 1787, 1790–93) and sometimes furnishing the calculations only, as for *Poor Robin's Almanack* for 1788, printed by Matthias Bartgis. The Ellicott almanacs, published by Mary Katharine Goddard and, later, by John Hayes, are of superior quality.

32. Bedini, *Life,* pp. 165–172, *passim.*

33. Ibid., p. 170.

34. Ibid., p. 148.

35. Ibid., p. 149.

36. Ibid., p. 171.

37. Ibid., p. 186. This is the same Dr. Rush who has been called the "Father of American Psychiatry."

38. Ibid., p. 198.

39. Ibid.

40. Benjamin Brawley, *Early Negro American Writers* (Chapel Hill: The University of North Carolina Press, 1935), p. 77.

41. Two articles by Martha E. Tyson appear to be accurate ("A Sketch of the Life of Benjamin Banneker; From Notes Taken in 1836," read by J. Saurin Norris before the Maryland Historical Society, October 1854 [Baltimore: John D. Toy, n.d.] and *Banneker, The Afric-American Astronomer. From the Posthumous Papers of Martha E. Tyson. Edited by Her Daughter* [Philadelphia: Friends' Book Association, 1884]). But John H. B. Latrobe claimed that Banneker was of pure African descent ("Memoir of Benjamin Banneker, Read before the Historical Society of Maryland," *Maryland Colonization Journal,* NS 2, No. 23 [May 1845], 353–364). Similar errors were made by M. D. Conway ("Benjamin Banneker, Negro Astronomer," *The Atlantic Monthly,* 11 [January 1863], 80), and Pearl Strachan ("Leap Year Almanac of 1796," *The Christian Science Monitor Magazine* [March 11, 1944], 6). Saul K. Padover confuses statements made in Banneker's private papers with those in his almanacs ("Benjamin Banneker. Unschooled Wizard," *The New Republic,* 118 [February 2, 1948], 23–25). Strachan quotes several pieces of almanac ephemera (not by Banneker) to prove Banneker's writing ability. Many authors have attributed Dr. Benjamin Rush's Peace Plan from the 1793 almanac to Banneker.

42. Bedini, *Life.*

43. Ibid., pp. 330–335.

44. Paul Leicester Ford, *The Journals of Hugh Gaine, Printer* (New York: Dodd, Mead & Company, 1902), II, 135.

45. An important exception is Edes & Gill's *North-American Almanack, and Massachusetts Register for 1770.* It contains an essay, "Extract from the Life of Publius Clodius Britano Americanus," which was continued in the following issue, and was politically oriented, but of a literary nature in that an invented character speaks the mind of the partiot.

46. Mary Katharine Goddard, the Baltimore printer, is listed as postmaster in this almanac and in several others during this period.

47. Nichols, "Notes," pp. 35–36, *passim.* Although Nichols says that this woodcut refers to Montgolfier's experiments in France a year before the 1785 issue was printed, the "Explanation of the PLATE" describes a burning balloon in "the south of England."

48. Sagendorph's statement that "The name Abraham Weatherwise was also used by Christopher Sower, a German of Philadelphia as early as 1739"

(*America and Her Almanacs,* p. 116), is in error.

49. C. G. Frantz, "The Religious Teachings of the German Almanacs," Diss. Temple University, 1955, p. 3; Spofford, "A Brief History," p. 26.

50. Frantz, "The Religious Teachings of the German Almanacs," p. 142.

51. Translations of mottoes are from Edward W. Hocker, *The Sower Printing House of Colonial Times* (Norristown: The Pennsylvania German Society, 1948), p. 21.

52. Abraham H. Cassell, "The German Almanacs of Christopher Sower," *Pennsylvania Magazine of History and Biography,* 6 (1882), 63–64.

53. Ibid., pp. 67–68.

54. Hocker, *Sower Printing House,* pp. 21–25, *passim.*

55. Thomas, *History of Printing,* I, 195.

56. Chapin, "Ann Franklin," p. 344.

57. Dexter, *Colonial Women,* p. 170.

58. Thomas, *History,* II, 100.

59. Dexter, *Colonial Women,* p. 175.

60. Ibid., p. 176.

61. Thomas, *History,* I, 203.

62. Joseph Towne Wheeler, *The Maryland Press* (Baltimore: The Maryland Historical Society, 1938), p. 12.

63. Quoted from *Maryland Journal* (Nov. 14, 1786) in Wheeler, *The Maryland Press,* p. 18.

64. Wheeler, *Maryland Press,* p. 14.

65. Ibid., p. 16.

PART TWO INTRODUCTION

1. J. A. Leo Lemay, *A Calendar of American Poetry in the Colonial Newspapers and Magazines and in the Major English Magazines Through 1765* (Worcester, Mass.: American Antiquarian Society, 1972), pp. xi, xii.

2. Elizabeth Christine Cook, *Literary Influences in Colonial Newspapers, 1704–1750* (New York: Columbia University Press, 1912), p. 6.

CHAPTER 5

1. Although the title page is missing from the extant copy, the Evans' *Bibliography* attributes the work to Bradford in Philadelphia. The Bradfords had the opportunity to enjoy the almanackers' feuds first, for they printed simultaneously (for example, for 1746) the almanacs of William Ball (by William Bradford), Titan Leeds (by Cornelia Bradford), John Jerman (Cornelia), Jacob Taylor (William), and William Birkett (Cornelia).

2. Cf. Thomas Hardy's "The Man He Killed":

Yes, quaint and curious war is!
You shoot a fellow down
You'd treat if met where any
*   bar is,*
Or help to half-a-crown.

3. Max Savelle, *Seeds of Liberty: the Genesis of the American Mind* (Seattle: University of Washington Press, 1948), p. 427.

CHAPTER 6

1. In 1914, Littlefield wrote, "Astrology, however, is still in vogue among the more ignorant classes" ("Notes," p. 60). And Kittredge in 1924 wrote "The false science of the stars is so nearly obsolete nowadays among intelligent people that one finds it hard to realize what a hold it had upon the popular mind in the eighteenth century" (George Lyman Kittredge, *The Old Farmer and His Almanack* [Cambridge: Harvard University Press, 1924], p. 39).

2. Frantz, "The Religious Teachings of the German Almanacs," pp. 95–97, *passim.*

3. Alice Morse Earle says that "In nothing is more contrast shown between our present day and colonial times than in the habits of liquor

drinking" (*Home Life in Colonial Days* [1898; rpt. New York: Grosset & Dunlap, Publishers, 1909], p. 164). Earlier, she mentions that, although President John Adams earnestly advocated temperance reform, "to the end of his life he drank a tankard of hard cider every morning when he first got up" (p. 161).

4. Lawrence Wroth, in *The Colonial Printer,* refers to "a recent investigation" that shows the power of "these little books of domestic utility," through political essays that prove the almanac to have "greater importance among American writings than they have formerly been credited with," (p. 229). The "investigation" is Chester Noyes Greenough's "New England Almanacs 1766–1775, and the American Revolution." (*Proc. of the AAS,* 45 [1935] pp. 288–316.) Greenough is extremely selective. He does not divulge how many almanacs he examined, but the ones he used as representative of each year preceding the Revolution are primarily from Nathaniel Ames and Nathanael Low, both avowed patriots. Hugh Gaine, prominent printer and prolific almanac-maker of this period, was a Tory.

5. Greenough says that the allegory refers to the governor ("New England Almanacs," p. 300).

CHAPTER 7

1. Darrel Abel says that the almanac's "practical counsel" included "recommendations of the best dates for planting crops or catching fish" (*American Literature* [Woodbury, N.Y.: Barron's Educational Series, Inc., 1965], I, 157). Specific dates were not mentioned, but month-by-month suggestions, based on the moon's phases, were sometimes given for the care of farm plants and animals. There is no evidence of dates for "catching fish." From information about the tides and the moon, the fisherman drew his own conclusions. The familiar little black fish symbol (half-fish, blank fish, etc.) opposite calendar dates did not occur during the colonial period. Fishing was serious business; fishing for fun would have been incompatible with Puritan theology.

2. Savelle, *Seeds of Liberty,* p. 131.

3. Americans had an almanac tradition, derived from England, of mixing astrology and medicine. In 1589 a British almanac by Gabriel Frende suggests:

In May thou may'st with safety
Both Bath and take Purgation;
Use Vomit and Phlebotomy,
And Eyke evacuation.

Briggs quotes this quatrain in "The Origin and Development," p. 446. He also discusses, on page 442, an almanac for 1634 by John Woodhouse, which decribes when to bathe, to let blood, and sweat, according to the planets and depending on the humours. For example, advice varies "for the Sanguine, the Moone being in Cancer or Pisces" and "for the Melancholicke in Libra or Aquarius."

CHAPTER 9

1. J. A. Leo Lemay, "Benjamin Franklin," in *Major Writers of Early American Literature,* ed. by Everett Emerson (Madison: The University of Wisconsin Press, 1972), pp. 213–214.

CHAPTER 10

1. Samuel Eliot Morison, *Harvard College,* I, 133.

2. Quoted in Kittredge, *Old Farmer,* p. 40.

3. This idea is not original with Ames. The British *Poor Robin* for 1675 had included the following couplet on the January calendar page:

And although we hate sects and their vile partakers,
Yet those who want fires must now turn Quakers.

(Quoted in Briggs, "Origin and Development," p. 461).

4. Lemay found this anonymous poem printed in the *New Hampshire Gazette*, No. 129, March 23, 1759 (*Calendar of American Poetry*, p. 217).

5. Jacob Taylor, in his almanac for 1741, followed the same format as Josiah Flint. He dispensed with the "old Heathen furniture" and used the names of apostles, evangelists, and martyrs in his calendar verse. His 1743 almanac contained a series of versified Biblical stories.

6. Cf. Milton's *Paradise Lost*, Book III, 236–240.

. . . me for him, life for life,
I offer; on me let thine anger fall;
Account me man; I for his sake will leave
Thy bosom, and this glory next to thee
Freely put off, and for him lastly die.

A wiser Ames might have chosen a theme that had not been so incomparably realized.

7. Miller, *The New England Mind*, p. 35.

8. Cf. William Blake:

In a wife I would desire
What in whores is always found
The lineaments of gratified desire.

9. Ralph and Will clearly had a family background in "Zummerzett,"

England, judging by their hard "Zyder" and harder *z*'s. Dialect was rarely used as almanac verse. Rind's *Virginia Almanack* for 1774 had a story and song about a Scottish lad whose lass eloped with someone else. The lad laments, "Thou'rt gone awa, thou're gone awa, / Thou'rt gone awa, fra me, Mary. . . ." This verse is doubtless borrowed, whereas Dr. Ames's is probably original.

10. This poem also appears in the *New England Courant*, No. 140, April 6, 1724. The title is "To all curious CRITICKS, and Admirers of Verse and Prose," and the author "Janus" was probably James Franklin himself (Lemay, *Calendar of American Poetry*, p. 10).

CONCLUSION

1. Savelle, *Seeds of Liberty*, p. 417.
2. For example: Tyler, *A History of American Literature*, I, 123; Matthew Stickney, "Almanacs and Their Authors," 14 (1877), 82; Briggs, "Origin and Development," p. 471; Angoff, *Literary History*, I, 242; N. W. Lovely, "Notes on New England Almanacs," *New England Quarterly*, 8 (1935), 265; and David D. Denker, "American Almanacs in the Eighteenth Century," *Journal of the Rutgers University Library*, 17 (1954), 13.
3. Tyler, *History of American Literature*, I, 123.
4. Lemay, "Benjamin Franklin," p. 215.
5. Bruce Ingham Granger, *Benjamin Franklin: An American Man of Letters* (Ithaca, N.Y.: Cornell University Press, 1964), p. 75.

Bibliographical Essay

DOCUMENTATION

My examination of at least 500 seventeenth- and eighteenth-century almanacs represents a study of approximately three-fourths of those that are available. Reading the almanacs listed in Milton Drake's checklist, *Almanacs of the United States,* is not quite so formidable a task as it appears. Many of the almanacs listed are not extant: some are "assumed from sequence," or "assumed from advertisements" in newspapers, while copies of others have simply not been found. To estimate the number of extant almanacs available for research, I counted the almanacs listed for Maryland. From 1729 (the year of the first Maryland almanac) to 1800, Drake lists 130 almanacs; 50 of these, or more than 38 percent, do not exist. This count seems to be typical of extant almanacs from the other colonies.

References to almanacs in the text are made so as to enable the reader to identify each one more thoroughly through the use of the bibliography, where they are listed alphabetically by author or, if the author is unknown, by title. Occasional textual references to publishers occur when more than one almanac by the same name was published for the same year. This method of reference eliminates hundreds of cumbersome reference notes. Page numbers for quoted matter are included when available. Dates of almanacs refer to the year of use rather than of publication.

Quotations from the almanacs are usually given in their original form. The early spelling and punctuation have been retained, except in rare cases where punctuation would have made interpretation difficult. To avoid confusion, printing errors in almanac titles have been corrected. Where excerpted verse quotations have terminated with internal punctuation (or, in some cases, with no punctuation), I have substituted a period. Original capitalization has also been copied wherever practicable. Some of the type fonts are impossible to reproduce. They often varied widely within a single publication. Almanacs were not easy to print, requiring, in fact, all the printer's skill. Sometimes they seem to display the entire equipment of the printing shop —all the symbols and type fonts. The printer's flamboyant use of various type styles and sizes may well be taken as an affirmation of his unique role as co-maker of the almanac. Reproduction of arbitrary upper-case spellings, particularly in titles, can at times be disconcerting if used in textual references. Besides, the "upper case" was frequently a large type font rather than genuine capital letters. And even the genuine capital letters were printed in various sizes. Illustrations of almanac pages show the impracticality of attempting to duplicate this early material as printed.

The letter *s* has been used rather than the letter almost identical with *f*, reproduction of which is of real significance only to the student of orthography. Almost all *s*'s were printed as *f*'s until after the first half of the eighteenth century, at which time we find a combination of *s*'s and *f*'s—often within the same line (for example, in "A story of Craeffas" in Benjamin West's almanac for 1763). By the end of the eighteenth century, the general practice was the *s* rather than *f*. Also, by this time, the *k* was being dropped from the word *almanack*, although *almanack* persisted as late as 1850. *Sic* has not been used in this study unless it was used in the source quoted.

PREVIOUS SCHOLARSHIP ON THE ALMANAC

Despite the considerable material available on almanacs, a comprehensive scholarly study has not been made previously. The literary historians, except for Tyler, have generally ignored the almanac. The social historians, except for Savelle, have done little more. The best material on almanacs is submerged in journals, the periodical publications of historical societies, the *Proceedings of the American Antiquarian Society* (AAS), and histories (socioeconomic, literary, printing). A few monographs have been written on almanac-makers—as printers.

Very few books have been published about almanacs. The earliest is Samuel Briggs's *Essays, Humor, and Poems of Nathaniel Ames, Father and Son* (1891). Briggs's book is an excellent edition of the literary contents (omitting the calendars, courts, etc.) of the Ames almanacs, with perceptive editorial notes. The Doubleday edition (1928) of *Poor Richard's Almanack* consists of a small selection of facsimiles, and comments by Phillips Russell. Paul Leicester Ford culled the almanacs to produce *Benjamin Franklin, Prefaces, Proverbs, and Poems* (1889). Professor George Lyman Kittredge's *The Old Farmer and His Almanac* (1924) is an interesting collection of miscellany. He uses Robert B. Thomas' *Old Farmer's Almanac* as a point of departure for a potpourri of historical events—including a chapter on witchcraft. Edward A. Fry's *Almanacks for Students of English History* (1915) contains an arrangement of tables from a set of thirty-five almanacs, enabling students of history to determine dates accurately and easily. *America and Her Almanacs* (1970), by Robb Sagendorph (editor of the *Old Farmer's Almanac* from 1939 to 1970), is the only book consistently dealing with almanacs that is not an anthology. His book is written for the general reader or browser and is copiously illustrated with charming woodcuts. While entertaining, it is not sufficient for the scholar. Sagendorph has also edited *The Old Farmer's Almanac Sampler* (1957), a collection of some of the best of the Robert B. Thomas almanacs.

Checklists published in periodicals have been superseded by Milton Drake's two-volume *Almanacs of the United States* (1962), an impressive and indispensable reference work. The earlier checklists, however, are still valuable for comments and sidelights not contained in Drake. A few historians affiliated with historical societies have published excellent in-depth studies of the origin and development of the almanac, notably in *Proc. of the AAS* and *Essex Institute Historical Collections.* One of the very best essays, "The Origin and Development of the Almanack," was a paper presented by Samuel Briggs as early as 1887. The most valuable source of chronology (for almanacs and printers) for the present study has been the Charles Evans' *American Bibliography,* whose listing of all works printed in early America permits some comparative judgments and statistical relevancies.

In many studies of early American history, the almanac has been entirely ignored. Of the intellectual historians who have used the almanac as evidence, Professor Max Savelle, *Seeds of Liberty* (1948), has given it the most emphasis as a reflection of colonial life and as a chronicler of the development of early American philosophical concepts. He discusses the almanac in relation to religion, science, philosophy, economic thought, literature, art and painting, and patriotism.

Comments by literary historians and critics have generally been confined to an offhand judgment in passing that the almanac is a neglected—but important—literary genre. Moses Coit Tyler (1878), first literary historian of American literature, treated the almanac far more adequately than his successors have done. Perry Miller and Thomas H. Johnson in *The Puritans* (1938) include "Two Almanac Poems" and refer to the almanac casually in regard to the "new science" (I, 631-35, 732). Darrel Abel's *American Literature* (1963) mentions the Ames almanacs in a line and gives a few paragraphs to *Poor Richard* (I, 157-70, *passim*). Robert E. Spiller's *Literary History of the United States* (1963, 3rd edition) dismisses the entire subject of almanacs in one line (p. 63). The critics and historians have generally disregarded almanacs in their evaluation of early American literature, almost as if publication of native literary efforts in almanacs automatically precluded consideration as bona fide literature. Excerpts from almanacs have rarely been anthologized, except for selections from Franklin's *Poor Richard*. Kenneth B. Murdock collected Samuel Danforth's poems in *Handkerchiefs from Paul* (1927), and George F. Horner and Robert A. Bain have printed in *Colonial and Federalist American Writing* (1966), under a special heading "Almanacs," some verse and sayings from the Ames almanacs (pp. 355-58).

Within the canon of published scholarship, there exists wide divergence of opinion about such basic matters as: the identity of the first almanac printed in America, the date of the first Pennsylvania almanac, whether the first "book" printed in America was an almanac or the *Bay Psalm Book*, whether the almanac is even a book, how many years Franklin actually prepared *Poor Richard* and whether *Poor Richard Improved* was a continuation of Franklin's *Poor Richard*, the identity of the first to be circulated beyond the limits of the colony in which it was published, at what time March ceased to be the first month in the calendar, the first appearance of illustrations, and at what time wit and humor appeared in the almanac. There is confusion about the Ameses (father, son, and grandson) and about dates in general, and occasional difficulty in relating people to their proper geographical locations. These errors sometimes result from lack of material, from not having the opportunity to review the *Early American Imprints* Microprint collection (keyed to Evans' *Bibliography* and available since 1959), from quoting sources without checking, and from substituting imaginative speculation for homework. It is interesting to note that the best scholarship—by the librarians of various historical societies and by Moses Coit Tyler—was performed long before the almanacs were available on Microprint.

Bibliography

PRIMARY SOURCES

The almanacs listed correspond to the numbered items in Charles Evans' *American Bibliography, 1639–[1800]*, so that the identification is made ordinarily simply by giving the almanac-maker's name, the year for which the almanac was printed, and the Evans' number with an initial E. If the year is not determinate, as when the same maker issued more than one almanac in the same year, the reference includes either the printer or a title arbitrarily shortened. Occasionally, a complete title is given, for reasons which will be obvious to the reader.

Ames, Nathaniel, II. 1726; E2601. 1727; E2725. 1728; E2838. 1729; E2984. 1730; E3128. 1731; E3248. 1733; E3499. 1734; E3622. 1735; E3743. 1736; E3866. 1737; E3982. 1738; E4109. 1739; E4217. 1740; E4335. 1741; E4469. 1742; E4667. 1743; E4878. 1744; E5116. 1745; E5330. 1746; E5531. 1747; E5731. 1748; E5899. 1749; E6089. 1750; E6276. 1752; E6628. 1754; E6953. 1758; E7830. 1759; E8072. 1762; E8786. 1763; E9053. 1764; E9324.

Ames, Nathaniel, III. 1765; E9570. 1767; E10227. 1768; E10540. 1769; E10815. 1771; E11547. 1772; E11961. 1773; E12304. 1774; E12643. 1775; E13112.

Ames, N. Philomath (pseudonym). 1791; E22313.

Atkins, Samuel. 1686; E382.

Anderson, John (pseudonym). 1773; E12310. 1774; E12647.

Andrews, George. 1761; E8533.

Andrews, William. 1774; E12649.

Astrologist, Adam (pseudonym). 1795; E26536.

B., J. See Browne, Joseph.

B., S. 1657; E44.

Banneker, Benjamin. 1792; E23148. 1793; E24071. 1794; E25140. 1795; E26608. 1796; E28231. 1797; E30019.

Bickerstaff. See West, Benjamin.

Birkett, William. 1746; E5543.

Bowen, Nathan. 1722; E2205. 1723; E2322. 1724; E2415. 1725; E2506. 1728; E2845. 1733; E3508.

Bradford, William. See Leeds, Titan (pseudonym). See also Atkins for 1686.

Bra[c]kenbury, Samuel. 1667; E113.

Brattle, Thomas. 1678; *E245*.

Brattle, William. 1682; *E314*. 1694; *E687*.

Brigden, Zechariah. 1659; *E54*.

Briggs, Isaac. 1798; *E31867*.

Browne, Joseph. 1669; *E135*.

Calendrier pour l'année 1781; E17110.

Chauncy, Israel. 1663; *E76*. 1664; *E87*.

Chauncy, Nathaniel. 1662; *E69*.

Cheever, Samuel. 1660; *E57*. 1661; *E66*.

Clapp, John. 1697; *E779*.

Clough, Samuel. 1701; *E906*. 1702; *E970*. 1703; *E1041*. 1704; *E1104*. 1706; *E1203*. 1707; *E1243*.

The Columbian Almanack. 1799; *E33539*.

Copernicus (pseudonym). See Rivington.

Daboll, Nathan. 1773; *E12371*. 1774; *E12743–44*. 1775; *E13235*. 1776; *E14001*. 1777; *E14724–25*. 1778; *E15280–81*. 1779; *E15777*. 1780; *E16250*. 1781; *E16755*. 1782; *E17131*. 1783; *E17507*. 1784; *E17902*. 1785; *E18432–33*. 1786; *E18982, E19596*. 1787; *E19595*. 1788; *E20313*. 1789; *E21038–39*. 1790; *E21779–80*. 1791; *E22439–40*. 1792; *E23305–306*. 1793; *E24240–41*. *E24366*. 1794; *E25368, E25564*. 1795; *E26841–42, E27066*. 1796; *E28523–24*. 1797; *E30308–309*. 1798; *E32012–13*. 1799; *E33595–96*. 1800; *E35368–69*.

Danforth, Samuel. "An Astronomical Description of the late Comet or Blazing Star." *E99*.

Danforth, Samuel (1666–1727). 1686; *E403*.

Dudley, Joseph. 1668; *E121*.

Edes, Benjamin. 1796; *E28615* (*A Sheet Almanack*).

Edes and Gill. 1769; *E11078*. 1770; *E11479*. 1771; *E11870* (see Stearns).

Ellicott, Andrew. 1781; *E16770*. 1782; *E17145*. 1783; *E17527*. 1785; *E18457*. 1786; *E18999*. 1787; *E19619*. 1789; *E21071*. 1790; *E21808*. 1791; *E22482*. 1792; *E23347*. 1793; *E24295*.

Ellsworth, Samuel. 1785; *E44527*. 1786; *E19000*.

Essex Almanack. 1771; *E11675*.

Father Abraham's Almanack. See Weatherwise, Abraham.

Father Tammany (pseudonym). See Workman, Benjamin.

Fleet, Thomas. 1720; *E2023*.

Flint, Josiah. 1666; *E107*.

Foster, John. 1675; *E198*. 1676; *E212*. 1677; *E229*. 1678; *E247*. 1679; *E268*. 1680; *E283–84*. 1681; *E300*.

Franklin, Ann. See *The Rhode-Island Almanack*.

Franklin, Benjamin. 1733; *E3541*. 1734; *E3657*. 1735; *E3786*. 1736; *E3903*. 1737; *E4017*. 1738; *E4141*. 1739; *E4247*. 1740; *E4364*. 1742; *E4719*. 1748; *E5952*. 1749; *E6139*. 1752; *E6670*. 1753; *E6845*. 1754; *E7003*. 1755; *E7196*. 1756; *E7420*. 1757; *E7668*. 1758; *E7899*.

Franklin, James, Sr. See *The Rhode-Island Almanack*.

Franklin, James, Jr. See Shepherd, Job.

Freebetter, Edmund. See Daboll, Nathan.

Freeman, Frank (pesudonym). 1767; *E10305*.

Frenau, Philip Morin. 1795; *E27018*.

Gaine's New York Pocket Almanack. See Moore, Thomas (pseudonym).

Gaine, Hugh. 1775; *E13290.* 1778; *E15303.* 1779; *E15803.* 1780; *E16281.* 1782; *E17168.*

Gatchell, Increase. 1715; *E1741.*

George, Daniel. 1776; *E14062.* 1778; *E15306.* 1781; *E16785.*

Gillam, Benjamin. 1684; *E359.*

Gleason, Ezra. *Bickerstaff's Boston Almanack.* 1777; *E14776.* 1780; *E16287.* See also West, Benjamin.

———. *The Massachusetts Calendar.* 1774; *E12791.*

———. *The Massachusetts, New-Hampshire, and Connecticut Almanack.* 1779; *E15813.* 1780; *E16288.* 1781; *E16786.* See Stearns for 1789.

———. *Thomas's Massachusetts, Connecticut, Rhode-Island, New-Hampshire and Vermont Almanack.* 1782; *E17174.* 1795; *E27052.* 1797; *E31291.*

———. 1775; *E13299.* Thomas's New-England Almanack; or, The Massachusetts Calendar, for the Year of Our Lord Christ, 1775; Being the Third after Bissextile or Leap-Year. From the Creation of the World, According to the best of Prophane History, 5724 But By the Account of Holy Scriptures, 5737; Julian Period, 6488; From Noah's Flood, 4069; From the Destruction of Sodom, 3677; From the Building of Rome, 2926; From the Building of London, 2882; From the Destruction of Troy, 2657; Higaria, or the Flight of Mahomet, 1184; New-England First Planted, 166; Planting the Massachusetts-Bay, 147; Building of Boston, the Capital of N.E., 145; Founding of Harvard College, 136; Of King George the III's Reign, 15; Containing Every Thing Necessary and Useful in an Almanack. To Which Is Added, The Life and Adventures of a Female Soldier. Massachusetts-Bay: Boston. Printed and Sold by Isaiah Thomas, at his Printing-Office, the South-corner of Marshall's-Lane, near the Mill-Bridge. [1774.]

Goddard, Mary K. See *The Maryland and Virginia Almanack.* See also Ellicott, Andrew.

Goddard, Sarah. See West, Benjamin. *The New-England Almanack for 1768.*

Goddard, William. See Ellicott, Andrew.

Harris, Benjamin(?) 1692; *E595.*

Hobart, Nehemiah. 1673; *E175.*

Hutchins, John Nathan. 1753; *E6857.* 1759; *E8153.* 1766; *E10023.* 1767; *E10341.* 1768; *E10656.* 1769; *E10931.*

Jerman, John. 1721; *E2125.* 1723; *E2344.* 1740; *E4372.*

The Kentucky Almanac. 1794; *E25688.* 1795; *E27184.* 1797; *E30658.* 1800; *E35684.*

The Lady's Almanack. By a Female. Being her First Public Production of the Nature. 1786; *E19748.*

The Lady's Astronomical Diary. 1792; *E23485.*

Leeds, Daniel. 1687; *E408.* An Almanack for the Year of Christian Account 1687. Particularly respecting the meridian and latitude of Burlington, but may indifferently serve all places adjacent, By Daniel Leeds, Student in Agriculture. Printed and sold by William Bradford, near Pennsylvania, pro Anno 1687.

———. 1688; *E430.* An Almanack for the Year of Christian Account 1688. . . . [Philadelphia: Printed by William Bradford. 1687.] Condemned by the judgment of the Friends of the Philadelphia quarterly meeting for its light and airy views and the Printer ordered to surrender all that he hath, and call in all that were sent away.

———. 1693; *E646*. 1694; *E692*. 1695; *E716*. 1698; *E821*. 1704; *E1112*. 1705; *E1164*. 1706; *E1208*. 1707; *E1247*. 1708; *E1297*. 1709; *E1356*. 1710; *E1393*. 1711; *E1457*. 1712; *E1501*. 1713; *E1548*. 1714; *E1612*. For 1714, see also Leeds, Titan.

Leeds, Felix. 1728; *E2891*. 1730; *E3175*.

Leeds, Titan. 1714; *E1684*. 1715; *E1747*. 1716; *E1748*. 1717; *E1814*. 1718; *E1889*. 1719; *E1962*. 1720; *E2028*. 1721; *E2126*. 1722; *E2227*. 1723; *E2345*. 1724; *E2439*. 1725; *E2543*. 1726; *E2647*. 1727; *E2756*. 1728; *E2892*. 1729; *E3047*. 1730; *E3177* (printed by D. Harry in Philadelphia). 1730; *E3176* (printed by Nearegress & Arnot in Rhode Island). 1731; *E3294*. 1733; *E3558*. 1734; *E3674*. 1735; *E3786*. 1736; *E3919*. 1738; *E4150* (printed by Andrew Bradford in Philadelphia). 1738; *E4151* (printed by William Bradford in New York).

Leeds, Titan (pseudonym). 1739; *E4259* (printed by Andrew Bradford in Philadelphia). 1739; *E4260* (printed by William Bradford in New York). 1740; *E4374*. 1742; *E4736*. 1743; *E4985*. 1744; *E5222*. 1746; *E5618*.

———. *The Dead Man's Almanack*. 1744; *E5223*. 1745; *E5423*.

Lodowick, Christian. 1695; *E717*.

Low, Nathanael. 1762; *E8906*. 1763; *E9164*. 1764; *E9422*. 1765; *E9714*. 1767; *E10358*. 1769; *E10951*. 1770; *E11317*. 1771; *E11704*. 1772; *E12100*. 1773; *E12438*. 1774; *E12837*. 1775; *E13384*. 1776; *E14168*. 1777; *E14829*.

Mary K. Goddard's Pennsylvania, Delaware, Maryland, and Virginia Almanack. 1779; *E43487*. 1785; *E44532*.

The Maryland Almanack. 1764; *E9426*. 1768; *E10672*.

The Maryland and Virginia Almanack. 1782; *E43991*.

Mather, Cotton. 1683; *E351*.

Mather, Nathaniel. 1685; *E395*.

Maxwell, Samuel. 1731; *E3320*.

Moore, Thomas (pseudonym). 1775; *E13448*. 1788; *E20533*.

More, Roger (pseudonym). 1765; *E9742*. 1768; *E10396*.

More, Thomas (pseudonym). 1750; *E6370*. 1754; *E7064*. 1768; *E10696*.

Nadir, William (pseudonym for William Douglass). 1743; *E4935* and *E5763*.

The New-England Almanack for 1768. See West, Benjamin.

The New Jersey Almanack. See Weather-Guesser, Copernicus.

The New Pennsylvania Almanac. 1792; *E46237*.

Newman, H. 1690; *E544*. 1691; *E574*.

Nowell, Alexander. 1665; *E104*.

Oakes, Urian. 1650; *E32*.

Poor Job. See Shepherd, Job (pseudonym for James Franklin, Jr.).

Poor Richard's Almanack and *Poor Richard Improved* (1733–1758). See Franklin, Benjamin.

Poor Richard (pseudonym; authors vary). 1765; *E9827*. 1768; *E10765*. 1774; *E12997*. 1789; *E21400*.

Poor Robin. See *The Rhode-Island Almanack*.

Poor Robin's Almanack (printed by Bradford in Philadelphia). 1742; *E4789*. 1744; *E5276*.

Poor Roger. See More, Roger.

Poor Thomas. See More, Thomas.

Poor Will's Almanack. 1796; *E29335*. 1798; *E32699*. See also Andrews, William and Birkett, William.

Poulson's Town and Country Almanac. 1797; *E31189.*

The Rhode-Island Almanack for the Year 1728 *[E2952]* Carefully Fitted, and Exactly Calculated to the Meridian of Newport, on Rhode-Island. Being the first ever published for that meridian. By Poor Robin. Newport: Printed by J. Franklin at his Printing House on Tillinghast's Wharf, near the Union Flag Tavern.

The Rhode-Island Almanack. 1729; *E3099.* 1730; *E3211.* 1732; *E3472.* 1733; *E3501.* 1734; *E3720.* 1735; *E3957.* 1737; *E4073.* 1738; *E4192.* 1739; *E4307.* 1740; *E4416.* 1741; *E4592.*

Richardson, John. 1670; *E154.*

Rittenhouse, David. 1775; *E13578.* 1776; *E14434.* 1777; *E15067.* 1778; *E15581.* 1779; *E16056.* 1780; *E16506* and *E16507.*

———. *Weatherwise's Town and Country Almanack.* 1781; *E16979.* 1782; *E17354.* 1785; *E18764.*

Rivington. 1774; *E12737.*

Russell, Daniel. 1671; *E164.*

Russell, Noadiah. 1684; *E376.*

S., J. See Sherman, John.

S., T. 1656; *E43.*

Sauer, Christopher. 1740; *E4370.* 1741; *E4528.* 1743; *E4972.* 1754; *E7022.* 1757; *E7682.* (In German. For translation, see Frantz, Clair Gordon *[Secondary Sources].*)

Saunders, Richard. See Franklin, Benjamin (Poor Richard, 1733–1758).

Sharp, Anthony (pseudonym). 1782; *E17348.* 1785; *E18759.*

Shepard, Jeremiah. 1672; *E172.*

Shepard, Thomas. See S., T.

Shepherd, Job (pseudonym). 1750; *E6414.* 1751; *E6606.* 1752; *E6780.* 1753; *E6929.* 1754; *E7117.* 1755; *E7313.* 1758; *E8037.*

Sherman, John. 1674; *E196.* 1676; *E223.* 1677; *E241.*

Sherman, Roger. 1750; *E6415.*

The South Carolina and Georgia Almanack. See Tobler, John.

Stafford, Joseph. See *The Rhode-Island Almanacks* for 1737 and 1738.

Stearns, Samuel. 1771; *E11870* (Edes and Gill). 1772; *E12235.* 1773; *E12566.* 1776; *E14473.* 1788; *E20725.* 1791; *E22917.*

[Stearns, Samuel]. 1789; *E21115.*

Taylor, Jacob. 1705; *E1196.* An Almanack for the Year 1705. . . . To which is added by C.[aleb] P.[usey], some remarks on D. L[eed]'s abuses to the Quakers in his this years two Almanacks. Printed at Philadelphia by Tiberius Johnson. [1704.]

———. 1706; *E1236.* 1707; *E1281.* 1708; *E1333.* 1709; *E1373.* 1710; *E1434.* 1711; *E1488.*

Taylor, Jacob (pseudonym?). 1726; *E2708.* 1741; *E4608.* 1743; *E5069.*

Thomas, Isaiah. See Gleason, Ezra and [Stearns, Samuel].

Thomas, Robert Bailey. 1793; *E24847.* 1794; *E26254.*

Thomas's New-England Almanack. See Gleason, Ezra.

Thornton, Elisha. 1791; *E22932.* 1792; *E23820.*

Tobler, John. 1756; *E40804.* 1758; *E8047.* 1763; *E9284.* 1767; *E10509.* 1768; *E10785.* 1769; *E11092.* 1770; *E11502.* 1773; *E12581.*

Travis, Daniel. 1709; *E1377.* 1710; *E1435.* 1711; *E1490.*

Tully, John. 1687; *E435.* 1688; *E454.* 1689; *E499.* 1690; *E548.* 1691; *E578.* 1692;

E630. 1693; *E682.* 1694; *E710.* 1695; *E740.* 1696; *E776.* 1697; *E815.* 1698; *E854.* 1699; *E897.* 1700; *E955.* 1701; *E1028.* 1702; *E1097.*

The Virginia Almanack. 1770; *E11488* (Purdie & Dixon). 1770; *E11514* (Rind). 1771; *E11913* (Purdie & Dixon). 1771; *E11912* (Rind). 1774; *E13059.* 1774; *E12981* (Rind). See also Rittenhouse, David (for 1775–1780).

Weather-Guesser, Copernicus (pseudonym). 1768; *E10798* and *E11109.*

Weatherwise, Abraham (pseudonym). See also Rittenhouse, David.

———. *Boston Weatherwise.* 1759; *E8280* and *E8282.*

———. *Father Abraham's Almanack.* 1767; *E10520.* 1769; *E11110.* 1774; *E13069.* 1781; *E16976* (by David Rittenhouse). 1782; *E17350.*

West, Benjamin. *An Astronomical Diary, Kalender, or Almanack.* By Isaac Bicker-staff. 1789; *E21590.*

———. *Bickerstaff's Boston Almanack.* 1768; *E10801.* 1769; *E11112.* 1770; *E11526.* 1772; *E12281.* 1774; *E13074.* 1784; *E18304.* 1786; *E19372.* 1789; *E21592.*

———. *Bickerstaff's New-York Almanack.* 1778; *E15706.*

———. *The New-England Almanack.* 1763; *E9303.* 1766; *E10205.* 1767; *E10521.* 1768; *E10802.* 1769; *E11113.* 1772; *E12282.* 1774; *E13075.* 1775; *E13764.* 1781; *E17067* and *E17068* (*Bickerstaff's New-England Diary*). 1789; *E21594.*

Wheeler, Bennett. *Wheeler's North-American Calendar* (by Benjamin West). 1789; *E21597.*

Whitefield, Nathaniel (pseudonym?). 1760; *E41092.*

Whittemore, Nathaniel. 1714; *E1724* and *E39606.* 1719; *E2008.* 1724; *E2494.*

Williams, William. 1685; *E400.* 1687; *E436.*

Workman, Benjamin. 1793; *E25059.*

Wreg, Theophilus (pseudonym for Theophilus Grew). 1758; *E7908.*

SECONDARY SOURCES

Books

Abbott, Charles Conrad. *Outings at Odd Times.* New York: D. Appleton and Company, 1890.

Abel, Darrel. *American Literature.* 4 vols. Woodbury, N. Y.: Barron's Educational Series, Inc., 1963. 1

Adams, James Truslow. *The Founding of New England.* Boston: Little, Brown and Company, 1930.

Angoff, Charles. *Literary History of the American People.* 2 vols. New York: A. A. Knopf, 1931.

Aswell, James R., ed. *Native American Humor.* New York and London: Harper & Brothers, 1947.

Bedini, Silvio A. *The Life of Benjamin Banneker.* New York: Charles Scribner's Sons, 1972.

Boorstin, Daniel. *The Americans: The Colonial Experience.* New York: Random House, 1958.

Brawley, Benjamin. *Early Negro American Writers.* Chapel Hill: The University of North Carolina Press, 1935.

Briggs, Samuel. *Essays, Humor, and Poems of Nathaniel Ames, Father and Son, of Dedham, Massachusetts, from their Almanacks 1726–1775.* Cleveland, Ohio: Short & Forman, 1891.

Buckingham, Joseph T. *Personal Memoirs and Recollections of Editorial Life.* 2 vols. Boston: Ticknor, Reed, and Fields, 1852.

Burr, Frederick M. *The Life and Works of Alexander Anderson, M.D.* New York: Burr Brothers, 1893.

Byington, Ezra Hoyt. *The Puritan as a Colonist and Reformer.* Boston: Little, Brown and Company, 1899.

Cook, Elizabeth Christine. *Literary Influences in Colonial Newspapers, 1704–1750.* New York: Columbia University Press, 1912.

Curti, Merle. *The Growth of American Thought.* New York: Harper & Brothers Publishers, 1943.

De Armond, Anna Janney. *Andrew Bradford, Colonial Journalist.* Newark, Dela.: University of Delaware Press, 1949.

Dexter, Elizabeth Anthony. *Colonial Women of Affairs.* 1924; rpt. Cambridge, Mass.: The Riverside Press, 1931.

Dictionary of American Biography, ed. by Dumas Malone. New York: C. Scribner's Sons, 1928–1958.

Dow, George Francis. *Every Day Life in the Massachusetts Bay Colony.* Boston: The Society for the Preservation of New England Antiquities, 1935.

Duniway, Clyde Augustus. *Development of Freedom of the Press in Massachusetts.* 1906; rpt. New York: Burt Franklin, 1969.

Earle, Alice Morse. *Child Life in Colonial Days.* 1899; rpt. New York: The Macmillan Company, 1957.

———. *Customs and Fashions in Old New England.* New York: Charles Scribner's Sons, 1894.

———. *Home Life in Colonial Days.* 1898; rpt. New York: Grosset & Dunlap, Publishers, 1909.

Edelstein, David. *Joel Munsell: Printer and Antiquarian.* New York: Columbia University Press, 1950.

Emerson, Everett, ed. *Major Writers of Early American Literature.* Madison: The University of Wisconsin Press, 1972.

The Encyclopedia Americana. International ed. New York: Americana Corporation, 1969.

Encyclopaedia Britannica. Encyclopaedia Britannica, Inc. Vols. I, 1910, 1929, 1955, 1969.

Farmers' Almanac for the year of our Lord 1974, ed. by Ray Geiger, Philom. Vol. 154. Lewiston, Me.: Almanac Publishing Co., 1973.

Faÿ, Bernard. *Franklin, the Apostle of Modern Times.* Boston: Little, Brown and Company, 1924.

Fisher, Samuel Herbert. *The Publications of Thomas Collier, Printer, 1784–1808.* Litchfield, Conn.: The Litchfield Historical Society, 1933.

Fisher, Sydney Geo[rge]. *Men, Women, and Manners in Colonial Times.* 2 vols. Philadelphia: J. B. Lippincott Company, 1898. I.

Flanders, Louis W. *Simeon Ide: Yeoman, Freeman, Pioneer Printer.* Rutland, Vt.: The Tuttle Company, 1931.

Ford, Paul Leicester. *The Journals of Hugh Gaine, Printer.* 2 vols. New York: Dodd, Mead & Company, 1902. II.

———, ed. *The Works of Thomas Jefferson.* 12 vols. New York: G. P. Putnam's Sons, 1904. XI.

Forster, T. *Perennial Calendar.* London: Printed for Harding, Mavor, and Lepard by J. Moyes, Greville Street, 1824.

Franklin, Benjamin. *The Autobiography of Benjamin Franklin*, with an Introduction by Henry Steele Commager. New York: Random House, Inc., The Illustrated Modern Library, 1944.

——. *Poor Richard's Almanack*. Preface by publishers, foreword by Phillips Russell. Garden City, N. Y.: Doubleday, Doran and Company, Inc., 1928.

——. "The sayings of Poor Richard;" the prefaces, proverbs and poems of Benjamin Franklin, originally printed in Poor Richard's almanacs for 1733–1758, collected and edited by Paul Leicester Ford. Brooklyn, N.Y., 1890 (rpt. New York: Burt Franklin, 1974).

Freneau, Philip Morin. *Poems*. Monmouth, N. J.: n.p., 1795.

Fry, Edward Alexander. *Almanacks for Students of English History*. London: Phillimore & Co., Ltd., 1915.

Granger, Bruce Ingham. *Benjamin Franklin: An American Man of Letters*. Ithaca, N. Y.: Cornell University Press, 1964.

Green, Samuel Abbott. *John Foster: The Earliest American Engraver and the First Boston Printer*. Boston: Massachusetts Historical Society, 1909.

Greene, Lorenzo Johnston. *The Negro in Colonial New England: 1620–1776*. New York: Columbia University Press, 1942.

Greenough, Chester Noyes. *Collected Studies*. Cambridge, Mass.: Merrymount Press, 1940.

Grier's Almanac 1974. Atlanta, Ga.: Grier's Almanac Publishing Co., 1974.

Hixson, Richard. *Isaac Collins: A Quaker Printer in 18th Century America*. New Brunswick, N. J.: Rutgers University Press, 1968.

Hocker, Edward W. *The Sower Printing House of Colonial Times*. Norristown, Pa.: The Pennsylvania German Society, 1948.

Hornberger, Theodore. *Scientific Thought in the American Colleges, 1638–1800*. Austin, Texas: The University of Texas Press, 1945.

Horner, George F., and Robert A. Bain. *Colonial and Federalist American Writing*. New York: The Odyssey Press, Inc., 1966.

Hudson, Frederic. *A History of Journalism from 1690 to 1872*. New York: Harper & Brothers, Publishers, 1873.

Jackson, Mason. *The Pictorial Press, its Origin and Progress*. 1885; rpt. New York: Burt Franklin, 1968.

Johnston, Sir Harry H. *The Negro in the New World*. 1910; rpt. New York: Johnson Reprint Corporation, 1969.

Kittredge, George Lyman. *The Old Farmer and His Almanack*. Cambridge, Mass.: Harvard University Press, 1924.

Kuhn, Thomas S. *The Copernican Revolution*. New York: Random House, 1959.

The Ladies Birthday Almanac for the year 1974. Chattanooga, Tenn.: The Chattanooga Medicine Co., 1973.

Lemay, J. A. Leo. "Benjamin Franklin" in *Major Writers of Early American Literature*. Ed. by Everett Emerson. Madison, Wisc.: The University of Wisconsin Press, 1972.

Lemay, J. A. Leo. *A Calendar of American Poetry in the Colonial Newspapers and Magazines and in the Major English Magazines Through 1765*. Worcester, Mass.: American Antiquarian Society, 1972.

Levy, Leonard W. *Legacy of Suppression: Freedom of Speech and Press in Early American History*. Cambridge, Mass.: The Belknap Press of Harvard University Press, 1960.

Littlefield, George Emery. *Early Boston Booksellers 1642–1711*. 1900; rpt. New York: Burt Franklin, 1969.

——. *The Early Massachusetts Press, 1638–1711*. 1907; rpt. 2 vols. in 1. New York: Burt Franklin, 1969.

Loggins, Vernon. *The Negro Author: His Development in America*. New York: Columbia University Press, 1931.

Marble, Annie Russell. *From Prentice to Patron: The Life Story of Isaiah Thomas*. New York: D. Appleton-Century Company, 1935.

——. *Builders and Books: The Romance of American History and Literature*. New York: D. Appleton and Company, 1931.

——. *Heralds of American Literature*. Chicago: The University of Chicago Press, 1907.

Mather, Cotton. *The Diary of.* . . . 2 vols. American Classics Edition. New York: Frederick Ungar Publishing Co., 1957.

McMaster, John Bach. *Benjamin Franklin as a Man of Letters*. Boston: Houghton, Mifflin and Company, 1887.

McMurtrie, Donald Crawford. *A History of Printing in the United States*. 1936; rpt. New York: Burt Franklin, 1969.

Miller, Perry. *The New England Mind: From Colony to Province*. Cambridge, Mass.: Harvard University Press, 1962.

Miller, Perry and Thomas H. Johnson. *The Puritans*. 2 vols. 1938; rpt. New York: Harper & Row, 1963.

Morais, Herbert M. *Deism in Eighteenth Century America*. New York: Russell & Russell, 1960.

Morison, Samuel Eliot. *Builders of the Bay Colony*. Boston and New York: Houghton, Mifflin Company; Cambridge, Mass.: The Riverside Press, 1930.

——. *Harvard College in the Seventeenth Century*. 2 vols. Cambridge, Mass.: Harvard University Press, 1936. I.

——. *The Founding of Harvard University*. Cambridge: Harvard University Press, 1935.

——. *The Intellectual Life of Colonial New England*. 2nd. ed. Ithaca, N. Y.: Cornell University Press, 1965.

——. *Three Centuries of Harvard: 1636–1936*. Cambridge, Mass.: Harvard University Press, 1936.

Morley, Henry, ed. *Character Writings of the Seventeenth Century*. New York: George Routledge and Sons, Limited, 1891.

Mott, Mrs. A[bigail (Field)]. *Biographical Sketches and Interesting Anecdotes of Persons of Colour to which is added a Selection of Pieces in Poetry*. New York: Printed by order of the trustees of the residuary estate of Lindley Murray. M. Day, Printer, 1839.

Murdock, Kenneth Ballard. *Handkerchiefs from Paul, being Pious and Consolatory Verses of Puritan Massachuetts*. Cambridge, Mass.: Harvard University Press, 1927.

——. *Literature and Theology in Colonial New England*. Cambridge, Mass.: Harvard University Press, 1949.

Nisard, Charles. *Histoire des Livres Populaires*. 2nd ed. 2 vols. 1854; rpt. New York: Burt Franklin, 1965.

The Old Farmer's Almanac Calculated on a New and Improved Plan for the Year of Our Lord 1974 by Robert B. Thomas [Ed. by Robb Trowbridge]. Dublin, N. H.: Yankee, Inc., 1974.

Orcutt, William Dana. *From My Library Walls: A Kaleidoscope of Memories.* New York: Longmans, Green and Co., Inc., 1945.

Oswald, John Clyde. *Benjamin Franklin, Printer.* Garden City, N. Y.: Doubleday, Page & Company, 1917.

———. *Printing in the Americas.* New York: The Gregg Publishing Company, 1937.

The Oxford English Dictionary, ed. by Sir James Augustus Henry Murray. Oxford: At the Clarendon Press, 1933. I, III.

Patterson, Lyman Ray. *Copyright in Historical Perspective.* Nashville, Tenn.: Vanderbilt University Press, 1968.

Perrin, Porter G. *Thomas Green Fessenden.* University of Maine Studies, 2nd ser., No. 4. Orono, Me.: University Press, 1925.

Pierce, Frederich Clifton. *Pierce Genealogy, No. IV.* Albany, N. Y.: J[oel] Munsell's Sons, 1889.

Rosenbach, A[braham] S[imon] W[olf]. *A Book Hunter's Holiday: Adventures With Books and Manuscripts.* 1936; rpt. Freeport, N. Y.: Books for Libraries Press, 1968.

Sagendorph, Robb. *America and Her Almanacs: Wit, Wisdom & Weather 1639–1970.* Dublin, N. H.: Yankee Inc., and Boston: Little, Brown and Company, 1970.

———, ed. *The Old Farmer's Almanac Sampler.* New York: Ives Washburn, Inc., 1957.

Savelle, Max. *Seeds of Liberty: the Genesis of the American Mind.* Seattle: University of Washington Press, 1948.

Shipton, Clifford K. *Isaiah Thomas: Printer, Patriot and Philanthropist 1749–1831.* Rochester, N. Y.: The Printing House of Leo Hart, 1948.

Sibley, John Langdon. *Biographical Sketches of Graduates of Harvard College.* 3 vols. Boston: Massachusetts Historical Society, 1873.

Spiller, Robert E., *et al. Literary History of the United States.* 3rd ed., rev. New York: The Macmillan Company, 1963.

Spofford, Ainsworth R., ed. *Benjamin Franklin: Autobiography. Poor Richard. Letters.* New York: D. Appleton and Company, 1904.

Tapley, Harriet Silvester. *Salem Imprints 1768–1825: A History of the First Fifty Years of Printing in Salem, Massachusetts.* Salem: The Essex Institute, 1927.

Thomas, Isaiah. *The Diary of . . . ,* ed. by Benjamin Thomas Hill. 2 vols. *Transactions and Collections of the American Antiquarian Society.* Vols. IV and V. Worcester, Mass.: American Antiquarian Society, 1909.

———. *The History of Printing in America.* 2 vols. 2nd rev. ed. 1874; rpt. New York: Burt Franklin, 1972.

Tourtellot, Arthur Bernon. *The Charles.* American River Series. New York: J. J. Little and Ives Company, 1941.

Trent, William Peterfield. *A History of American Literature, 1607–1865.* New York: D. Appleton and Company, 1903.

Tyler, Moses Coit. *A History of American Literature During the Colonial Time.* rev. ed. 1878; rpt. 2 vols. in 1. New York: G. P. Putnam's Sons, 1902.

Van Doren, Carl. *Benjamin Franklin.* New York: The Viking Press, 1938.

Weeden, William B. *Economic and Social History of New England 1620–1789.* 2 vols. New York: Hillary House Publishers Ltd., 1963.

Wheeler, Joseph Towne. *The Maryland Press.* Baltimore: The Maryland Historical Society, 1938.

310

Winship, George Parker. *The Cambridge Press, 1638–1692.* Philadelphia: University of Pennsylvania Press, 1945.

Winterich, John T. *Early American Books & Printing.* Boston: Houghton Mifflin Company, 1935.

Winthrop, Gov. John. *Winthrop's Journal,* ed. by James Kendall Hosmer. 2 vols. New York: Charles Scribner's Sons, 1908.

Wish, Harvey. *Society and Thought in Early America.* New York: Longmans, Green and Co., 1950.

The Wretched Mess Calendar for 1971 incorporating Poor Wretched's Almanac . . . by Poor Wretched. West Yellowstone, Montana: The Wretched Mess News, Inc., 1970.

Wright, Richardson. *Hawkers and Walkers in Early America.* Philadelphia: J. B. Lippincott Company, 1927.

Wright, Thomas Goddard. *Literary Culture in Early New England, 1620–1730.* New Haven, Conn.: Yale University Press, 1920.

Wroth, Lawrence C. *The Colonial Printer.* Portland, Me.: The Southworth-Anthoensen Press, 1938.

———. *A History of Printing in Colonial Maryland.* Published by the Typothetae of Baltimore, 1922.

Articles

"Almanac of Samuel Danforth, 1649." *Massachusetts Historical Proceedings,* 10 (Aug. 1868), 325–329.

Andrews, W. L. "The Early American Almanac" *The Bookman,* 2 (1895–6), 283–286.

Beecher, Henry Ward. "The Death of our Almanac," in *Star Papers.* New York: J. C. Derby; Boston: Phillips, Sampson, 1855.

"Benjamin Banneker, Negro Astronomer." *The Atlantic Monthly,* 11 (January 1863), 79–80.

Blagden, Cyprian. "Thomas Carnan and the Almanack Monopoly," a paper read before the Bibliographical Society in London, Nov. 17, 1959. *Studies in Bibliography,* 14, 23–43.

Brasch, Frederick E. "The Newtonian Epoch in the American Colonies." *Proceedings of the American Antiquarian Society,* NS 64 (1939), 314–332.

Briggs, Sam[uel]. "The Origin and Development of the Almanack," a paper read before the Western Reserve and Northern Ohio Historical Society, Jan. 12, 1887. *Tracts,* 2, No. 69 (1888), 435–477.

Brigham, Clarence S. "An Account of American Almanacs and Their Value for Historical Study." Reprinted from *Proceedings of the American Antiquarian Society* for Oct. 1925. Worcester, Mass.: The Society, 1925, pp. 195–226.

Cassell, Abraham H. "The German Almanacs of Christopher Sower." *Pennsylvania Magazine of History and Biography,* 6 (1882), 58–68.

Chapin, Howard Millar. "James Franklin, Jr., Newport Printer." *The Americana Collector,* 2 (June 1926), 325–329.

———. "Ann Franklin of Newport, Printer, 1736–1765," in *Bibliographical Essays: A Tribute to Wilberforce Eames.* Cambridge, Mass.: Harvard University Press, 1924, pp. 337–344; rpt. New York: Burt Franklin, 1968.

Denker, David D. "American Almanacs in the Eighteenth Century." *Journal of the Rutgers University Library,* 17 (1954), 12–25.

Fitts, James H. "The Thomas Almanacs." *Essex Institute Historical Collections,* 12 (1874), 243–270.

Green, Samuel A. "Early History of Printing in New England." *Massachusetts Historical Society Proceedings,* 2nd ser., 11 (1896–1897), 240–253.

Greenough, Chester Noyes. "New England Almanac 1766–1775 and the American Revolution." *Proceedings of the American Antiquarian Society,* NS 45 (1935), 288–316.

Halliwell, James Orchard. "Early Almanacs." *The Companion to the British Almanac of the Society for the Diffusion of Useful Knowledge,* 1839, pp. 52–57.

Happer, Emily Foster. "Seventeenth Century American Almanacs." *Literary Collector,* 9, no. 2 (1905).

Huddleston, Sisley. "The Almanac," in *Articles de Paris, a Book of Essays.* New York: The Macmillan Company, 1928, pp. 19–23.

Jorgenson, Chester E. "The New Science in the Almanacs of Ames and Franklin." *New England Quarterly,* 8 (1935), 555–561.

Latrobe, John H. B. "Memoir of Benjamin Banneker, Read Before the Historical Society of Maryland." *Maryland Colonization Journal,* NS 2 (May 1845), 353–364.

Lathe, Agnes M. "A Rummage among Colonial Almanacs." *The Chautauquan,* 18 (Mar. 1894), 722–726.

"Letters of John Tulley." *Massachusetts Historical Society Proceedings,* 3rd ser., 30 (Nov. 1916), 74–77.

Littlefield, George Emery. "Notes on the Calendar and the Almanac." *Proceedings of the American Antiquarian Society,* NS 24 (1914), 11–64.

Lovely, N. W. "Notes on New England Almanacs." *New England Quarterly,* 8 (1935), 264–277.

Lutes, D. T. "One Book—the Almanac," in *America is West,* ed. by John Theodore Flanagan. Minneapolis: The University of Minnesota Press, 1945.

Marble, Annie Russell. "Early New England Almanacs." *New England Magazine,* 19 (Jan. 1899), 548–557.

Morison, Samuel Eliot. "The Commerce of Boston on the Eve of the Revolution." *Proceedings of the American Antiquarian Society,* NS 32 (1922), 24–51.

——. "The Harvard School of Astronomy in the Seventeenth Century." *New England Quarterly,* 9 (1934).

Newcomb, Robert. "Poor Richard's Debt to Lord Halifax." *PMLA,* 70 (1955), 535–539.

Nichols, Charles L. "Notes on the Almanacs of Massachusetts." *Proceedings of the American Antiquarian Society,* NS 22 (April 10, 1912), 15–40.

Padover, Saul K. "Benjamin Banneker: Unschooled Wizard." *The New Republic,* 118 (Feb. 2, 1948), 22–25.

Paltsits, Victor Hugo. "The Almanacs of Roger Sherman 1750–1761." *Proceedings of the American Antiquarian Society,* NS 18 (1907), 213–258.

Perry, Amos. "Some New England Almanacs with special mention of the Almanacs of Rhode Island." *Narragansett Historical Register,* 4 (July 1885), 27–39.

Robinson, Henry Morton. "The Almanac." *The Bookman,* 75 (June-July 1932), 218–224.

Spofford, Ainsworth R. "A Brief History of Almanacs," in *An American Almanac and Treasury of Facts, Statistical, Financial, and Political, for the Year 1878.*

New York and Washington: The American News Company, 1878, pp. 21–27.

Strachan, Pearl. "Leap Year Almanac of 1796." *The Christian Science Monitor Magazine* (March 11, 1944), p. 6.

Stickney, Matthew A. "Almanacs and Their Authors." *Essex Institute Historical Collections,* 8 (1866), 29–32, 101–104, 158–164, 193–205; 14 (1877) 81–93, 212–232, 242–248.

Tyson, Martha E. *Banneker, the Afric-American Astronomer. From the Posthumous Papers of Martha E. Tyson. Edited by Her Daughter.* Philadelphia: Friends' Book Association, 1884. 72 pp.

[Martha E. Tyson]. "A Sketch of the Life of Benjamin Banneker; From Notes Taken in 1836." Read by J. Saurin Norris, Before the Maryland Historical Society, October 1854. Baltimore: John D. Toy [N.D.] 20 pp.

Swasey, J. H. "Rhode Island Almanacs of Long Ago." *Newport Historical Society Bulletin,* No. 92 (1939).

Vail, R. W. G. "The New England Almanac," in *Dictionary of American History.* New York: Charles Scribner's Sons, 1940.

Wright, Thomas. "The History of Almanacs." *Macmillan's Magazine,* 7 (Jan. 1863), 173–185.

Checklists and Bibliographies

Bates, Albert Carlos. "Checklist of Connecticut Almanacs 1709–1850." *Proceedings of the American Antiquarian Society,* NS 24 (April 1914), 93–215.

Beer, William. "Checklist of American Periodicals." *Proceedings of the American Antiquarian Society,* NS 32 (Oct. 1922), 330–335.

Bristol, Roger Pattrell, comp. Secretary's News Sheet, No. 52, August 1966. *Bibliographical Society.* Charlottesville: University Press of Virginia, 1970.

———. *Supplement to Charles Evans' American Bibliography.* Charlottesville: University Press of Virginia, 1970.

Chapin, Howard M. "Check List of Rhode Island Almanacs 1643–1850." *Proceedings of the American Antiquarian Society,* NS 25 (1915), 19–54.

Drake, Milton. *Almanacs of the United States.* 2 vols. New York: Scarecrow Press, 1962.

Evans, Charles. *American Bibliography.* 14 vols. Vols. I-XIII ed. by Clifford K. Shipton, Vol. XIV ed. by Roger Pattrell Bristol. Publishers and dates vary, 1941–1959.

McMurtrie, Douglas C[rawford]. "A Check-List of Kentucky Almanacs 1789–1830." Extract from the Register of the Kentucky State Historical Society for July 1932, pp. 237–259.

Morrison, Hugh [Alexander]. *Preliminary Checklist of American Almanacs, 1639–1800.* Washington: Government Printing Office, 1902.

National Index of American Imprints Through 1800: The Short-Title Evans. 2 vols. Ed. by Clifford K. Shipton and James E. Mooney. Worcester, Mass.: American Antiquarian Society, Barre Publishers, 1969.

Theses and Dissertations

Frantz, Clair Gordon. "The Religious Teachings of the German Almanacs Published by the Sauers in Colonial Pennsylvania." Diss. Temple University, 1955.

313

Lyman, Susan Elizabeth. "Colonial Life and Learning as Reflected in American Almanacs 1639–1776." Thesis Columbia, 1933.

Sidwell, Robert T. "The Colonial American Almanacs: A Study in Non-Institutional Education." Diss. Rutgers, 1965.

Sweet, Israel. "Prose Literature of the Colonial Almanacs (1763–1767)." Thesis Columbia, 1946.

Microprint

Early American Imprints, ed. by Clifford K. Shipton. Worcester, Mass.: American Antiquarian Society, 1959.

Appendix A

MAJOR ALMANAC SERIES IN AMERICA BEFORE 1800

The following list includes most of the major almanac series that began in America before 1800. All information is compiled from a study of entries in Evans' *American Bibliography*. A source (Nichols, "Notes") has been cited in the Benjamin West section of the text, where dates differ from those in Evans. Nichols is also referenced in the I. Thomas section, where names of calculators differ from Evans'.

Aguecheek, Andrew, pseud. *The Universal American Almanack.* 1760 through 1771. Printed in Philadelphia, usually by Andrew Steuart.

Ames, Nathaniel, II (the elder Dr. Ames). *An Astronomical Diary.* 1726 through 1764. Printed primarily in Boston by Bartholomew Green and later by John Draper. Printed also in Portsmouth, N. H., by Daniel Fowle.

Ames, Nathaniel, III (the younger Dr. Ames). *An Astronomical Diary* (continuation of original Ames series). 1765 through 1775. Published in Boston; Newport, R. I.; Portsmouth, N. H.; New Haven, Hartford, and New London, Conn.

Andrews, William. *Poor Will's Pocket Almanack.* 1770 through 1786.

———. *Poor Will's Almanack.* 1771 through 1786. Both series were printed in Philadelphia by Joseph Crukshank.

The American Almanack. See Jerman, John; Leeds, Daniel; and Leeds, Titan.

The American Country Almanack. See More, Roger (pseud.); More, Thomas (pseud.).

An Astronomical Diary. See Ames, Nathaniel (II and III); Low, Nathanael; Sewall, Daniel; Sherman, Roger; Strong, Nehemiah; West, Benjamin.

The Balloon Almanack. 1786 through 1791. Also for 1795 and 1796. Printed first in Philadelphia, later in Lancaster.

Banneker, Benjamin. *Benjamin Banneker's Pennsylvania, Delaware, Maryland and Virginia Almanack.* 1792 through 1797. Titles vary, depending on printer. These almanacs were printed in Baltimore, Philadelphia, and Alexandria.

Bickerstaff, Isaac, pseud. See West, Benjamin.

Birkett, William. *An Almanack.* 1729 through 1738.

———. *Poor Will's Almanack.* 1739 through 1752. Printed primarily by the Bradfords (Andrew and Cornelia) in Philadelphia.

Bowen, Nathan. *An Almanack.* 1721.

————. *The New-England Diary.* 1722 through 1738. Printed by B. Green in Boston.

The Burlington Almanack. See Trueman, Timothy, pseud.

The Cambridge Almanack. 1639 through 1692. Extant almanacs begin with 1646, although 1651 through 1655 are missing. Titles and authors changed often. Printed by the Cambridge Press at Harvard College.

Clough, Samuel. *The New-England Almanack.* 1700 through 1708. Printed in Boston by B. Green. The title during 1705–07 was *Kalendarium Nov-Anglicanum;* the 1708 issue was *Clough's Farewell.*

The Columbian Almanac(k). 1790 through 1801. Printed in Wilmington, Philadelphia, New York, and Lancaster, Penn.

Daboll, Nathan. *Freebetter's New-England Almanack.* 1773 through 1792. From 1777 through 1792 the title was *The New-England Almanack,* by Edmund Freebetter, pseud. Almanacs with both titles appeared in 1777. *Freebetter's* was printed in Hartford by Nathaniel Patten, *The New-England Almanack* by Timothy Green in New London.

————. *The New-England Almanack.* 1793 until after 1800. Daboll did not use the Freebetter pseudonym in his series, which was continued to the late nineteenth century by members of the Daboll family.

————. *Green's Register.* 1786 through 1795 (except 1787 and 1788). From 1777 the Daboll almanacs were usually printed by the Greens in New London.

Der Hoch-Deutsch Americanische Calender. See Sauer, Christopher.

Edes & Gill's North-American Almanack. See Stearns, Samuel.

Ellicott, Andrew. 1781 through 1792. Titles vary. *The Maryland, Delaware, Pennsylvania, Virginia, and North-Carolina Almanack,* 1781. *The Pennsylvania, Delaware, Maryland, and Virginia Almanack,* 1782 through 1784. William Goddard's name was added to the 1785 title. *Ellicott's Maryland and Virginia Almanack,* 1787 through 1792. Printed primarily by William Goddard or Mary K. Goddard in Baltimore. The Goddard almanacs actually began in 1775 with Mary K. Goddard's *Pennsylvania, Delaware, Maryland, and Virginia Almanack* and continued through 1792.

The Farmer's Almanac. See Thomas, Robert B.

Father Abraham's Almanack. See Weatherwise, Abraham, pseud.

Father Tammany's Almanack, by Benjamin Workman. 1786 through 1799 (except 1790, 1794–1796). Printed in Philadelphia.

Foster, John. *An Almanack.* 1675 through 1681. The 1675 almanac was printed in Cambridge, the others in Boston by Foster.

Fox, Thomas. *The Wilmington Almanack.* 1762 through 1794. Printed in Wilmington, Delaware, usually by James Adams.

Franklin, Benjamin. *Poor Richard's Almanack.* 1733 through 1766. In 1748 the title became *Poor Richard Improved.* Franklin's direct association with the almanac ended in 1758, but the firm of Franklin and Hall in Philadelphia printed the series until 1766. Other publishers used the title during the remainder of the century.

Franklin, James, Sr. *The Rhode Island Almanack,* by "Poor Robin." 1728 through 1735. Printed in Newport, R. I., by James Franklin. Series was continued irregularly by Ann Franklin and Joseph Stafford though 1741.

Franklin, James, Jr. *Poor Job,* by Job Shepherd, pseud. 1750 through 1758 (except 1756 and 1757). Printed by James Franklin, Jr., in Newport, R. I.

Freebetter's New-England Almanack. See Daboll, Nathan.

Gaine, Hugh. *New-York Royal Sheet Almanack.* 1759 through 1767.

———. *Gaine's New-York Pocket Almanack,* by Thomas Moore, pseud. 1760 and 1761, 1769 through 1805.

———. *The New-York Pocket Almanack,* by Richard Moore, pseud. 1762 through 1768.

———. *Universal Sheet Almanack.* 1775 through 1790 (irregularly).

———. *Gaine's Universal Register.* 1775 through 1793 (almost every year). All series were printed by Hugh Gaine in New York.

George, Daniel. 1776 through 1787. Titles vary. *George's Cambridge Almanack,* 1776. *An Almanack,* 1777 through 1787. Printed primarily in Newburyport, Mass., by John Mycall and in Boston by Edward Draper.

Green's Register. See Daboll, Nathan.

Hutchins, John Nathan. 1753 through 1801. Titles vary. *An Almanack,* 1753 and 1754. *Hutchins,* 1755 through 1759. *Hutchins Improved,* 1760 through 1801. Printed by Hugh Gaine in New York.

Jerman, John. *An Almanack.* 1723 through 1730. Jerman's first almanac was *An Ephemeris* for 1721. No issue for 1722.

———. *The American Almanack.* 1731 through 1762 (except 1733 and 1761). The two series were published in Philadelphia by the Bradfords, Benjamin Franklin, and others.

The Kentucky Almanac. 1790 through 1810. Printed in Lexington by John and Fielding Bradford and by Daniel Bradford. Scattered almanacs by this title were published after 1810.

Leeds, Daniel. *An Almanack.* 1687 through 1700.

———. *The American Almanack.* 1701 through 1714. Both series were printed by the Bradfords in Philadelphia and New York.

Leeds, Titan. *The American Almanack.* 1715 through 1746 (continuation of Daniel Leeds's almanac series). Printed in Philadelphia and New York by the Bradfords, and by other Philadelphia printers. Series was continued after Leeds's death by the Bradfords through 1746.

Low, Nathanael. *An Astronomical Diary.* 1762 through 1807. Published primarily in Boston by John and Daniel Kneeland and later by Thomas and John Fleet. In 1776, printed by Isaiah Thomas in Worcester.

The Maryland Almanack. 1751 through 1776. Printed by the Green family in Annapolis. Few copies exist; most are assumed by Evans from sequence or from advertisements in the *Maryland Gazette.*

The Maryland and Virginia Almanack, by Benjamin Workman. 1788 through 1791. Printed by William Goddard in Baltimore. See Ellicott, Andrew.

The Massachusetts Calendar. See Thomas, Isaiah.

Mein and Fleeming's Massachusetts Register. 1767 through 1769. Printed in Boston by Mein and Fleeming.

More, Roger, pseud. *De Americaanse Almanak,* by "Poor Roger." 1756 through 1771 (except 1760, 1765–1767). See More, Thomas, pseud.

———. *Poor Roger.* 1751 through 1773 (except 1753–1755). Titles vary. *Poor Roger [date]. The American Country Almanack,* 1756 through 1773. *Poor Roger* was the title in 1751 and 1752, *The American Almanack* in 1773. See More, Thomas, pseud., for some of the missing issues in this series.

———. *Poor Roger's Universal Pocket Almanack.* 1757 through 1769 (except 1758). Printed in New York by James Parker and John Holt and by Parker and William Weyman; also other publishers. See More, Thomas, pseud.

More, Thomas, pseud. *De Americaanse Almanak*, by "Poor Thomas." 1752, 1753, 1766, 1767.

------. *The American Country Almanack*, by "Poor Thomas." 1746 through 1755. These two series were published by the same printers that printed the "Poor Roger" almanacs, which were apparently continuations of "Poor Thomas." See More, Roger, pseud.

------. *Poor Thomas Improved.* 1760 through 1768. Scattered imitations of Poor Thomas almanacs occurred during the remainder of the eighteenth century.

------. *The Pocket Almanac*, by "Poor Thomas," 1754 and 1755. *The Universal Pocket Almanack*, 1756 and 1760. *The New Universal Pocket Almanack*, 1764. Printed by William Weyman in New York. See More, Roger, pseud.

The New-England Almanack. See Clough, Samuel; West, Benjamin.

The New-England Diary. See Bowen, Nathan.

The New-Jersey Almanack. See Trueman, Timothy, pseud.

New-York Royal Sheet Almanack. See Gaine, Hugh.

The North-American Almanack. See Stearns, Samuel.

The North-American Calendar. See West, Benjamin.

The Pennsylvania Town and Country-man's Almanack. See Tobler, John.

A Pocket Almanack. 1779 through 1796 (almost every year). Printed by Thomas and John Fleet in Boston.

Poor Richard's Almanack, by Richard Saunders, pseud. See Franklin, Benjamin.

Poor Robin's Almanack (not to be confused with James Franklin's *The Rhode-Island Almanack* by "Poor Robin"). 1742 through 1758. The title for 1749, 1751, 1755, and 1758 was *Poor Robin's Spare Hours.* Printed by Andrew Bradford in Philadelphia. The title was used subsequently by other printers during the eighteenth century, but no sustained series is evident. See Franklin, James, Sr.

Poor Roger. See More, Roger, pseud.

Poor Thomas. See More, Thomas, pseud.

Poor Will's Almanack. See Andrews, William; Birkett, William.

Poulson's Town and Country Almanac. 1793 until approximately 1810. William Waring prepared Poulson's almanacs in 1793 and 1794, Abraham Shoemaker from 1795. Printed in Philadelphia by Zachariah Poulson.

Rittenhouse, David. See Weatherwise, Abraham, pseud.

Sauer, Christopher. *Der Hoch-Deutsch Americanische Calender.* 1739 through 1835. Printed in Germantown, Penn., by Christopher Sauer through 1758. Series was continued and printed by Christopher Sauer, Jr., to 1778, by John Dunlap in Philadelphia from 1779 through 1784, and by other printers through 1835.

Sewall, Daniel. *An Astronomical Diary.* 1781 until after 1800. Printed usually in Portsmouth, N. H.

Sherman, Roger. *An Almanack.* 1750 through 1761.

------. *An Astronomical Diary.* 1750 through 1760. Both series were printed in Boston, New York, and New London, and New Haven.

The South-Carolina and Georgia Almanack. See Tobler, John.

Stafford, Hosea, pseud. See Strong, Nehemiah.

Stearns, Samuel. *Edes & Gill's North-American Almanack.* 1769 through 1775 (sometimes without Edes & Gill in title). Printed by Benjamin Edes and John Gill in Boston. (I. Thomas in Worcester printed *The North-American Almanack* in 1776 and 1777.)

———. *The Universal Kalendar.* 1783. Title changed to *The Universal Kalendar, and the North-American Almanack,* 1784 through 1792 (except 1785 and 1786). Publishers vary.

Strong, Nehemiah ("Professor of Mathematics at Yale"). 1776 through 1807. Titles vary. *An Astronomical Ephemeris,* 1776 through 1787. *An Astronomical Diary,* 1787 through 1807. (Almanacs by both titles were printed in 1787.) *An Astronomical Diary* was printed in Hartford and in New Haven. Strong's pseudonym, Hosea Stafford, was used on the New Haven editions.

———. *Stafford's Almanack,* by Hosea Stafford, pseud. 1778 through 1798 (irregularly).

———. *The Connecticut Almanack.* 1778 through 1781.

———. *Sheet Almanack.* 1792 through 1800. These last three series were usually printed in New Haven by the Greens.

Taylor, Jacob. 1700 through 1746. Titles vary. From 1731 through 1746 the title was *Pennsylvania,* followed by the date. Many of these almanacs are assumed by Evans from sequence. Printed primarily by Andrew Bradford in Philadelphia.

Thomas, Isaiah. *The Massachusetts Calendar.* 1722 through 1774. Printed in Boston by Isaiah Thomas.

———. *Thomas's Massachusetts, Connecticut, Rhode-Island, New-Hampshire & Vermont Almanack.* 1775 through 1803. Printed in Worcester, Mass., by Isaiah Thomas. These almanacs were calculated by Ezra Gleason, except for 1785 and 1786, which were prepared by Benjamin West; and 1789, by Samuel Stearns. The series was continued after 1803 by Isaiah Thomas, Jr.

Thomas, Robert B. *The Farmer's Almanac.* 1793 through 1831. In 1832 the title became *Old Farmer's Almanac* and continued until 1911. Published today in Dublin, N. H., by Robb Trowbridge of Yankee, Inc. The original Robert B. Thomas almanacs were printed in Boston, usually by Belknap and Hall and later by Manning and Loring.

Tobler, John. *The Pennsylvania Town and Country-man's Almanack.* 1754 through 1777. Usually printed in Wilmington.

———. *The South-Carolina Almanack.* 1755 through 1759. Title changed to *The South-Carolina and Georgia Almanack,* 1760, 1764 through 1792 (except 1775, 1783, and 1788). The 1764 issue was printed in Savannah, Ga.; the others, in Charleston, S. C.

———. *The Georgia Almanack,* 1771. *The Georgia and South-Carolina Almanack,* 1774 and 1775. *The Carolina and Georgia Almanack,* 1783 and 1784. The Georgia and South Carolina almanacs can perhaps be grouped as one series, beginning with 1755 and ending in 1792, although titles changed. Tobler was therefore responsible for two main almanac series: the almanac for Pennsylvania and the almanac for South Carolina and Georgia.

Travis, Daniel. *An Almanack.* 1707 through 1723 (except 1708). Printed in Boston, usually by B. Green.

Trueman, Timothy, pseud. 1771 through 1787. Titles vary. *The Burlington Almanack,* 1771. *New-Jersey. The Burlington Almanack,* 1772 through 1778. *The New-Jersey Almanack,* 1779 through 1787. Published in Burlington by Isaac Collins through 1778 and by Isaac Collins in Trenton from 1779 through 1787.

Tulley, John. *An Almanack.* 1687 through 1702. Printed by B. Green in Boston, except for 1791 and 1792, which were printed in Cambridge by Samuel

Green. The 1693 and 1695 almanacs were printed by Benjamin Harris in Boston.

The Universal Kalendar. See Stearns, Samuel.

Universal Sheet Almanack. See Gaine, Hugh.

The Virginia Almanack. 1741 until after 1800 (almost every year). From 1741 through 1751 no calculator is credited. Printed in Williamsburg by William Hunter. Same printer and same title, calculated by Theophilus Wreg, pseudonym for Theophilus Grew. from 1752 through 1759. From 1768 through 1775, printed by John Dixon and William Hunter in Williamsburg, and by Purdie and Dixon in Alexandria. Also printed by William Rind in Williamsburg. From 1776 through 1780, calculated by David Rittenhouse and printed by John Dixon and William Hunter, and by Dixon and Nicholson in Williamsburg. From 1781 through 1787, calculated by Robert Andrews and printed by Dixon and Holt in Richmond. *The Virginia Almanack* was continued until after 1800 by various printers.

Weatherwise, Abraham, pseud. *Father Abraham's Pocket Almanack.* 1771 through 1785. Printed by John Dunlap in Philadelphia and calculated by David Rittenhouse.

——. *Weatherwise's Town and Country Almanack.* 1781 through 1792 (sometimes without "Weatherwise" in title). Many almanacs in this series were calculated by David Rittenhouse. Various Boston printers.

——. *Father Abraham's Almanack.* 1759 through 1784. Usually printed in Philadelphia by William Dunlap and later by John Dunlap. David Rittenhouse calculated this series from 1777 through 1784.

West, Benjamin. *The New-England Almanack.* 1763 through 1801 (and perhaps later). Sometimes "or Lady's and Gentleman's Diary" appended to title. From 1782 through 1801 "by Isaac Bickerstaff" was added. Printed by William Goddard and by John Carter in Providence.

——. *Bickerstaff's Boston Almanack.* 1768 through 1793 (almost every year). Titled *Bickerstaff's Genuine Boston Almanack* in 1786, 1791–1793. Both titles appeared in 1791. Printed in Boston.

——. *Bickerstaff's New-England Almanack.* 1777 through 1796.

——. *Wheeler's North-American Calendar.* 1781 through 1788. Title in 1781 through 1788 was *The North-American Calendar; or, the Rhode Island Almanack.* Printed by Bennett Wheeler in Providence.

——. *An Astronomical Diary,* by Isaac Bickerstaff. 1785 through 1797 (almost every year). Printed in Hartford and in Boston.

——. *Town and Country Almanack,* by Isaac Bickerstaff. 1795 through 1799. Printed in Norwich, Conn.

West's almanac series are particularly difficult to delineate. He participated in the preparation of approximately 200 almanacs, and many bearing his name were plagiarized. He calculated Thomas's almanacs from 1785 through 1787 and many others not included in the six series mentioned.

The Wilmington Almanack. See Fox, Thomas.

Workman, Benjamin. See *Father Tammany's Almanack.* See also *The Maryland and Virginia Almanack.*

Whittemore, Nathaniel. 1705 through 1750. Titles vary. *An Almanack,* 1705 through 1739 (irregularly). *Whittemore Continued,* 1740. A 1741 issue is assumed by Evans from sequence. In 1714 title was *The Farmer's Almanack.* Printed in Boston, primarily by Thomas Fleet from 1713.

Appendix B

CHRONOLOGY

Sherman, John	1613–1685	Fleet, Thomas	1685–1758
Danforth, Samuel	1626–1674	Leeds, Felix	1687–1744
Oakes, Urian	1631–1681	Taylor, Jacob	d. 1746
Shepard, Thomas	1635–1677	Maxwell, Samuel	1688–1778
Tulley, John	1638–1701	Sauer, Christopher	1693–1758
Brigden, Zechariah	1639–1662	Grew, Theophilus	d. 1759
Cheever, Samuel	1639–1724	Franklin, James, Sr.	1697–1735
Chauncy, Nathaniel	1639–1685	Bowen, Nathan	1697–1776
Russell, Daniel	1642–1679	Leeds, Titan	1699–1738
Nowell, Alexander	1645–1672	Franklin, Benjamin	1706–1790
Flint, Josiah	1645–1680	Ames, Nathaniel, II	1708–1764
Browne, Joseph	1646?–1678	Sauer, Chris., II	1721–1784
Richardson, John	1647–1696	Sherman, Roger	1721–1793
Dudley, Joseph	1647–1720	Edes, Benjamin	1723–1803
Foster, John	1648–1681	Gaine, Hugh	1726–1807
Hobart, Nehemiah	1648–1712	Strong, Nehemiah	1729–1807
Shepard, Jeremiah	1648–1720	West, Benjamin	1730–1813
Leeds, Daniel	1652–1720	Banneker, Benjamin	1731–1806
Brattle, Thomas	1658–1713	Rittenhouse, David	1732–1796
Russell, Noadiah	1659–1713	Low, Nathanael	1740–1808
Brattle, William	1662–1717	Goddard, William	1740–1817
Mather, Cotton	1663–1728	Ames, Nathaniel, III	1741–1822
Bradford, William	1663–1752	Stearns, Samuel	1747–1819
Chauncy, Israel	1664–1703	Gleason, Ezra	1748–1808?
Clough, Samuel	1665–1707	Thomas, Isaiah	1749–1831
Williams, William	1665–1741	Daboll, Nathan	1750–1818
Danforth, Samuel	1666–1727	(Edmund Freebetter, *pseud.*)	
Mather, Nathaniel	1669–1688	Freneau, Philip Morin	1752–1832
Newman, H.	1670–1743	Ellicott, Andrew	1754–1820
Harris, Benjamin	1673–1720	George, Daniel	1758–1804
Whittemore, Nathaniel	1673–1754	Briggs, Isaac	1763–1825
Jerman, John	1684–1769	Thomas, Robert Bailey	1766–1846

321

Appendix C

COLONY STATE TERRITORY	DATE	FIRST PRESS	FIRST ALMANAC
Massachusetts	1639	Cambridge: Stephen Day	An Almanack
Pennsylvania	1685	Philadelphia: William Bradford	Kalendarium Pennsilvaniense
New York	1693	New York: William Bradford	An Almanack
Connecticut	1709	New London: Thomas Short	An Almanack of Coelestial Motions and Aspects
Maryland	1726	St. Mary's City: William Parks (permanent)	An Almanack
	1685	St. Mary's City: William Nuthead (temporary)	
Rhode Island	1727	Newport: James Franklin	The Rhode-Island Almanack
Virginia	1730	Williamsburg: William Parks (permanent)	Grew's Almanack
	1682	Jamestown: William Nuthead (temporary)	
South Carolina	1731	Charleston: George Webb	The South-Carolina Almanack
North Carolina	1749	Newbern: James Davis	An Almanack
New Jersey	1754	Woodbridge: James Parker (permanent)	The American Country Almanack
	1723	Perth Amboy: William Bradford (temporary)	
	1727	Burlington: Samuel Keimer (temporary)	
New Hampshire	1756	Portsmouth: Daniel Fowle	An Astronomical Diary
Delaware	1761	Wilmington: James Adams	The Wilmington Almanack

322

First Press and
First Almanac by Region (1639–1800)

AUTHOR	DATE	PUBLISHER
William Peirce	1639	Cambridge: Stephen Day
William Atkins	1686	Philadelphia: William Bradford
Daniel Leeds	1694	New York: William Bradford
Daniel Travis °	1709	New London: [Thomas Short]
John Warner	1729	Ananpolis: William Parks (adv.)
Poor Robin	1728	Newport: James Franklin
Theophilus Grew	1735	Williamsburg: William Parks (adv.)
	1733	Charleston: Thomas Whitmarsh (adv.)
	1784	Newbern: R. Keith (adv.)
Roger More (Poor Roger)	1760	Woodbridge: James Parker
Nathaniel Ames	1757	Portsmouth: Daniel Fowle
Thomas Fox	1762	Wilmington: James Adams

COLONY STATE TERRITORY	DATE	FIRST PRESS	FIRST ALMANAC
Georgia	1762	Savannah: James Johnston	The Georgia and South Carolina Almanack
Vermont	1778	Dresden (now Hanover, N.H.): Alden Spooner	An Astronomical Diary
	1789	Westminster: Judah Spooner and Timothy Green (Wroth, pp. 25–27)	
East Florida	1783	St. Augustine: John Wells and Charles Wright	An Almanack
	1784	St. Augustine: John Wells (Evans)	
Maine	1785	Falmouth (now Portland): Benjamin Titcomb and Thomas B. Wait	Weatherwise's Almanack
Kentucky	1787	Lexington: John and Fielding Bradford	The Kentucke Almanack
Tennessee	1791	Rogersville: George Roulstone and Robert Ferguson	
Ohio	1793	Cincinnati: William Maxwell	
Louisiana	1794	New Orleans: L. Duclot	
	1764	New Orleans: Denis Braud (Wroth, pp. 50–51)	
District of Columbia	1795	Washington: Thomas Wilson	Poor Robin's Almanack, or The Maryland Ephemeris
	1789	Georgetown: Charles Fierer (first in what is now D.C.)	The Potomak Almanac or The Washington Ephemeris
Michigan	1796	Detroit: John McCall	
Mississippi	1798	Fort Hill: Andrew Marschalk (Wroth, p. 55)	
	1799	Natchez: Andrew Marschalk (Evans)	

Data on first printing presses are derived from McMurtrie's *A History of Printing in the United States*, Wroth's *The Colonial Printer*, and Evans' *American Bibliography*. References are given in some cases where dates vary.

AUTHOR	DATE	PUBLISHER
John Tobler	1764	Savannah: James Johnston
Samuel Ellsworth	1785	Bennington: Haswell and Russell
John Tobler	1783	St. Augustine: David Zubly, Jr.**
	1787	Portland: Thomas B. Wait
	1788	Lexington: John and Fielding Bradford (adv.)
	1790	Georgetown: Charles Fierer (adv.)
	1793	Georgetown: James Doyle

* All the Travis almanacs listed by Evans from 1707 through 1716 were published in Boston and New York. Evans' first Travis almanac in New London is for 1716; "America" appears on the title page as the place of publication. Thomas Short, who was succeeded by Timothy Green, printed in New London from 1709 to 1712. The AAS copy for 1709 was published in Boston by Bartholomew Green.

** This almanac is not listed in Evans. Drake cites the *National Union Catalog* as his source for the Zubly almanac.

Sources for the first almanacs are Evans' *American Bibliography* and Drake's *Almanac of the United States*.

Index

calendars, 5-7, 17; footnote I-6, 285; footnote III-30, 289; first month of, 58, 59; *See also* individual listings
Calendrier Francais, 121; illust., 120
Cambridge Almanack, 47; illust., 51, 54, 55
Cambridge press. *See* almanacs, philomath
Capen, Joseph, 54
Carnan, Thomas, 11-12
Carter, John, 88-90
censorship, 11, 32, 33-6
Chauncey, Israel, 41, 45
Chauncey, Nathaniel, 41, 45
Cheever, Samuel, 41, 44-5
Clapp, John, 58
Clough, Samuel, 22, 245
Company of Stationers, 11-12
Connecticut Almanack, The, 92
Continental Almanac, The, illust., 253
Copernican theory, 42, 44, 47, 52, 271; illust., 47; *See also* astronomy
copyright laws, 31-2
Crouch, Mary, 122
Crukshank, Joseph, 103, 104-6
currency conversions, 59

Daboll, Nathan, 92-5
Daboll's New-England Almanack, 92
Danforth, Samuel, 17, 38, 41, 43, 237-8
Danforth, Samuel (son), 52
Davenport, John, 44
Day, Matthew, 38
Day, Stephen, 38-40
Day, Stephen, Jr., 38
de Dacia, Petrus, 8, 19
de Elvendene, Walter, 8
de Lynne, Nicholas, 8
de Worde, Wynkyn, 10
Dexter, Gregory, 40
dominical letters, 4
Draper, Margaret, 123
Dudley, Joseph, 41, 45
Dunkers, 117
Dunlap, John, 121
Dunster, Henry, 40

Ellicott, George, 102, 103-4
Ellicott's Maryland and Virginia Almanack, 201-3, 206-7
Elliott, Clark, 92
Ellsworth, Samuel, 7, 165-6
ephemeris, 5
epitaphs, verse, 252-4
essays, formal, 162-82, 208
Essex Almanac, 35-6

etiquette, 178
Eyres, George, 241-2

fast days, 59
Fasti, Roman, 7-8
Farmer's Almanack, 29, 41, 99; illust., 100, 243
Father Abraham's Almanack, 114, 179; illust., 27, 178, 180, 202
feast days, 59
Federal Copyright Act, 31
feuds, 66, 81, 95, 132, 147, 156-61
fillers, 231-5
Flint, Josiah, 41, 45
format, 17-25, 36, 40; and Benjamin Banneker, 107-10; and Benjamin Franklin, 80-1; and Benjamin West, 88; and Hugh Gaine, 112-3; and humor, 64; and Mary K. Goddard, 128-9
Foster, John, 26, 47, 53-6, 61, 64, 270
Fowle, Daniel, 32
Fowle, Zechariah, 99
Fox, George, 66
Franklin, Ann, 77-8, 80, 123-4; and fillers, 234; and preface, 150
Franklin, Benjamin, 14, 26, 77, 80-5, 276-7, 280-1; and astronomy, 168; and censorship, 35; predictions of, 228; and preface, 151-2; proverbs of, 221, 223-4; and Titan Leeds, 72, 158-61
Franklin, James, Jr., 26, 30, 78-80, 152-5
Franklin, James, Sr., 17, 26, 31, 32, 34-5, 76-7; predictions of, 226-7; and preface, 148-50; verse of 240, 266
Freebetter, Edmund. *See* Clark Elliot
Freebetter's Connecticut Almanack, 92
Freebetter's New-England Almanack, 92, 93, 263
Freeman's Oath, The, 38
Freneau, Philip Morin, 278

Gadbury, John, 10
Gaine, Hugh, 111-13
Gaine's New York Pocket Almanack, 112
Gaine's Universal Register, or, American and British Kalendar for the Year 1775, 112
Gaine's Universal Sheet Almanack, 113
Gatchell, Increase, 42
General Magazine, The, 14
Genuine Leeds Almanack, The, 69-70
George, Daniel, 42
Gillam, Benjamin, 50

331

100237

ion Barber.

n almanacs ;
weekday bible